OUT OF JORDAN

OUT OF JORDAN

A SABRA IN THE PEACE CORPS
TELLS HER STORY

DALYA COHEN-MOR

Skyhorse Publishing

Leah Na'or, "Sof ze tamid hatkhala." Written in 1977; *Carousel* (Tel Aviv: Masada,
1980). This is a literal translation from Hebrew.

Skyhorse Publishing books may be purchased in bulk at special discounts for
sales promotion, corporate gifts, fund-raising, or educational purposes. Special
editions can also be created to specifications. For details, contact the Special Sales
Department, Skyhorse Publishing, 307 West 36th Street, 11th Floor, New York,
NY 10018 or info@skyhorsepublishing.com.

Skyhorse® and Skyhorse Publishing® are registered trademarks of Skyhorse
Publishing, Inc.®, a Delaware corporation.

Visit our website at www.skyhorsepublishing.com.

10 9 8 7 6 5 4 3 2 1

Library of Congress Cataloging-in-Publication Data is available on file.

Cover design by Brian Peterson

Print ISBN: 978-1-63450-425-6
Ebook ISBN: 978-1-5107-0037-6

Printed in the United States of America

AUTHOR'S NOTE

This is a work of nonfiction. All the events, encounters, and conversations described here are true and have been faithfully rendered as I have remembered them. The name of the village where I stayed, as well as the names of my two host families and their individual members, have been changed to protect their privacy and anonymity. For the same reason, the names of village school principals and faculty members at Mu'ta University have been changed. All other names of individuals and places have remained intact.

Also by the author

A Matter of Fate

Arab Women Writers: An Anthology of Short Stories

Mothers and Daughters in Arab Women's Literature:
The Family Frontier

Fathers and Sons in the Arab Middle East

In loving memory of my brother, Shimon Aviad,
and his daughter, Inbal

ת. נ. צ. ב. ה.

CONTENTS

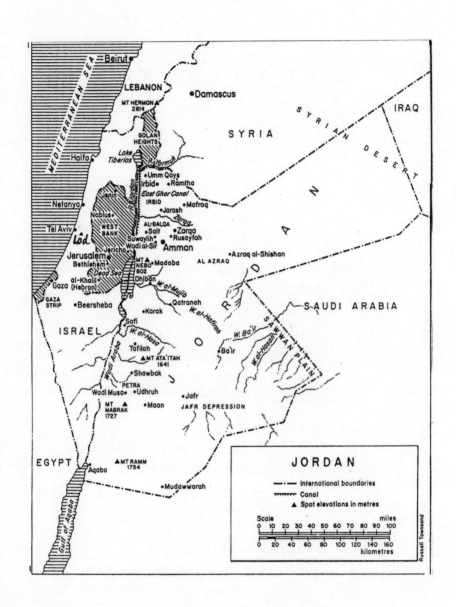

MEDITERRANEAN SEA

●Beirut

LEBANON

MT HERMON ▲
2814

●Damascus

IRAQ

SYRIA

SYRIAN DESERT

GOLANI
HEIGHTS

Lake
Tiberias

R. Yarmuk

●Haifa

●Umm Qays
Irbid● ●Ramtha

East Ghor Canal

IRBID ●Mafraq

R. Jordan

Jenin● ●Jarash

●Netanya

Nablus●

Zarqa

●Tel Aviv

WEST
BANK

AL-BALQA
●Salt ●Zarqa
Suwaylih●   ●Rusayfah
Wadi al-Sir   Amman

Lōd

Jericho●

Jerusalem●
Bethlehem●

MT ▲
NEBO ●Madaba
802

●Azraq al-Shishan

AL AZRAQ

J O R D A N

Dead Sea

al-Khalil
(Hebron)

Dhibān●

W. al-Mujib

●Gaza

●Beersheba

GAZA
STRIP

●Karak

Qatranah

W. al-Hafirah

W. Ba'ir

SAWWAN PLAIN

S·AUDI ARABIA

Safi●

ISRAEL

W. al-Hasa

●Ba'ir

W. al-Hasah

Tafilah●

Wadi Araba

▲MT ATA'ITAH
1641

●Shawbak

PETRA
Wadi Musa● ●Udhruh

●Jafr

MT ▲
MABRAK
1727

●Maan

JAFR DEPRESSION

EGYPT

▲MT RAMM
1754

Aqaba●

●Mudawwarah

Gulf of Aqaba

JORDAN

— · — · — International boundaries

〰〰〰 Canal

▲ Spot elevations in metres

Scale   miles
0 10 20 30 40 50 60 70 80 90 100

0   20   40   60   80 100 120 140 160
                              kilometres

Russell Townsend

Whatever happens to you belongs to you. Make it yours. Feed it to yourself even if it feels impossible to swallow. Let it nurture you, because it will.

Cheryl Strayed, Tiny Beautiful Things

I. PROLOGUE

IN THE EARLY MORNING OF CHRISTMAS EVE 2011, PARIS CHARLES
De Gaulle Airport was mercifully not yet crowded with travelers.
I heaved a sigh of relief as I dragged my weary body through the
empty halls of the terminal to my departure gate. The first leg of
my grueling trip from Jordan back to the United States was already
behind me. The midnight flight with Royal Jordanian from Amman
to Paris was short—only four and a half hours—but exhausting.
Packed with holidaymakers, the cabin was hot, noisy, and cramped.
I didn't sleep a wink and had a throbbing headache. I looked at the
time. It was 5:00 a.m. I had a long layover—my connecting flight to
Washington Dulles International Airport was scheduled to leave at
12:40 p.m. I wished I could lie down somewhere and close my eyes.
Two nights in a row without sleep were beyond my power of endurance. Luckily, I didn't have to change terminals or transfer my bags,
which were checked right through to my final destination.

I pulled my heavy carry-on bag behind me and followed the signs
to my departure gate. I arrived there to find a deserted lounge—there

wasn't a soul to be seen. Rows of empty metal chairs with hard seats and fixed arms met my gaze. With more than a six-hour wait ahead of me, I was desperate to crash out somewhere. I spotted a row of three armless chairs in a secluded corner of the lounge. I went over and lay across the narrow seats, hoping to grab some sleep. With my crumpled clothes, disheveled hair, and limp body squeezed into the confines of the metal chairs, I looked like a homeless person. In many ways, I *felt* like a homeless person, uprooted, forsaken, and lost.

How did I end up here, in this strange predicament, a woman of my age and stature? My head was dizzy from persistent, agonizing questions: Why? Why? Was this a blessing in disguise? Would I have been jailed or killed if I had remained in Jordan? I wanted to escape into sleep, to forget for a little while everything that had happened to me, but memories of the past few months flooded over me, throwing me into a vortex of emotions. My eyes were closed but my mind was racing through the events that had brought me here, revisiting all the scenes, incidents, and encounters, hoping against hope to make sense of it all—and find clarity.

2 . LIFE IS CALLING

IT ALL BEGAN ON THE MORNING OF APRIL 16, 2010, WHEN I attended the Employment Expo at the Marriott Conference Center in Bethesda, Maryland. The day before I had finished the final revision of my manuscript on mother–daughter relationships in Arab families and mailed it to my publisher. Now I felt free and eager to embark on a new activity, something other than writing. Writing is such a lonely occupation. I wanted a job that would take me out of my little study and give me the opportunity to meet new people and expand my horizons.

When I arrived at the Marriott Conference Center, the grand foyer was already crowded with men and women aged between forty and seventy, all job seekers. After an opening ceremony by various dignitaries who gave long and tedious speeches, we were ushered into a big ballroom to meet the employment recruiters. We roamed between rows of tables and booths staffed by representatives of dozens of companies and organizations who were collecting resumes and handing out brochures, registration forms, and business cards.

Among the prospective employers were area banks, retail stores, hotels, the Food and Drug Administration, the National Institutes of Health, public schools, and various volunteer agencies. I moved slowly from table to table, making inquiries and gathering information. Nothing that I saw was in my area of interest or training. I was either overqualified or not competitive enough for most of the jobs. Still, I continued to stop by every booth, eager to find out what was available. Suddenly, I found myself in front of the Peace Corps table. I casually picked up a brochure with the picture of an African American frolicking with a bunch of little Chinese girls on its cover. "Life is calling. How far will you go?" ran the headline. It grabbed my attention and I began to read.

> The Peace Corps mission is to promote world peace and friendship through the service of American volunteers abroad. It requires a commitment of two years. Volunteers serve in over 75 countries around the world. They integrate into another culture, learn a new language, and work in various fields, including education, health, business, information and communication technology, agriculture, and the environment. There is no upper age limit—older volunteers are valued for their life experience.

I felt a rush of excitement as I browsed through the brochure. I knew instantly that I had found what I was looking for.

It never occurred to me that I would find my calling so accidentally and yet with such clarity. As a native-born Israeli—a Sabra—who had left my country of origin and lived in the Netherlands for many years prior to settling in the United States, I had been exposed to four cultures: Israeli, Arab, Dutch, and American. I had dual training as a teacher of English (with a master's degree from the State University of Utrecht) and as a teacher of Arabic (with a doctoral degree from Georgetown University). Given my intellectual curiosity, my passion for teaching and travel, and my strong affinity for non-Western cultures, I was ideally suited for Peace Corps service. Furthermore, I was at a stage of my life where I had a unique window of opportunity to do what I wanted. Just the year before, I had walked out on my adulterous husband and extricated myself from an abusive marriage. I was now single, with no constraints, familial or otherwise, on my freedom. I could follow my passion and become part of a global family, give back to society and receive in return, and have a life-defining experience.

The Peace Corps application process, as outlined in the brochure, is extremely competitive: each year over 15,000 applications are received and about 4,000 candidates are placed. On average, the application process takes from nine to twelve months to complete. Step one in this long and challenging process is filling out an extensive application form, which includes two essays, three references, employment history, resume, community and volunteer activities, educational background, and health status review. Step two is an interview. Step three is a nomination to serve in a general work area and region of the world with an approximate departure date. Step four comprises medical and legal reviews, including a background check, to determine eligibility for service; an applicant who is medically qualified and legally cleared for service undergoes competitive and suitability evaluations. Step five is an invitation in writing to serve in a specific country, extended to selected candidates. Step six, the final one, is preparation for departure. Throughout the process, applicants can check the status and progress of their applications through "My Toolkit," an individual online account that is updated regularly.

I realized that it would be hard to get in. I needed to find ways to become a more competitive candidate. I decided to get involved in community service. The Jewish Community Center of Greater Washington was running a program called "Gateways: Services for New Americans," which provides free English classes for new immigrants in the area. The program director was looking for teachers willing to work as volunteers. I called her and offered to help. She was happy to employ me immediately as a substitute teacher and also assigned me to teach a full course in the summer. My students were mostly elderly Russian immigrants who were highly qualified professionals like chemists, biologists, physicists, dentists, and physicians, but who spoke little English. My task was to improve their communication skills and acquaint them with American values and customs. I enjoyed working with them. They were a nice group of people, enthusiastic and very diligent, and they taught me a lot about life in the former Soviet Union, especially in Russia.

After organizing my community service, I attended to the task of filling out the extensive application form. Performed online, the application does not need to be completed in one session and the applicant can save it and return to work on it later. I began working on it on April 21 and submitted it on June 9. My resume took a long time to compose. How do you summarize thirty years of work experience in a nutshell? I traveled between three continents—the Middle East, Europe, and the United States—and had a varied career as a teacher, scholar, and writer. Which of these aspects should I emphasize? This dilemma reminded me of an article I was once asked to write on the Western Wall in Jerusalem for the *Oxford Encyclopedia of the Modern World*. I was given 600 words to write about the topic. How do you tell the history of the Western Wall in 600 words? What must be mentioned? What may be omitted? It was a challenging but intellectually rewarding task. The two essays required for my application, each running between 250–500 words, also took a while to compose and I revised them several times. Finally, I had to provide the names of three people as references. After careful consideration, I named a former job supervisor, a current volunteer supervisor, and a personal friend—all trusted and supportive individuals.

Throughout the following months, I kept a close watch on my BlackBerry device. Whenever the status of my application was updated, I would get a message. I would then rush to my study to log onto my Peace Corps account and check the progress of my application. There were four evaluations on the Application Status: dental, legal, medical, and placement. Each time I completed one of these evaluations, a check mark would appear next to it. If some document was missing for any of these evaluations, I would receive a message that a hold had been placed on my application. I would then get in touch with my recruiter or the relevant desk at Peace Corps Headquarters to find out what I needed to do to clear up the hold.

I was familiar with Peace Corps Headquarters, an imposing and highly secure building on 1111 20th Street, NW, Washington, DC. I attended several information events there and listened to many personal accounts of returned volunteers. I looked at them in admiration, longing for the opportunity to travel to an unknown country, live and work with members of a new culture, and make a difference in their lives. After each information event I became even more determined to complete the application process successfully and become a Peace Corps volunteer.

Exactly two weeks after submitting my application, I received an email and a packet from Jason, the regional recruiter at the Peace Corps office, with detailed instructions on how to proceed to the next step, the interview. I had to fill two cards with my fingerprints at a local police station, sign a National Agency Check (NAC) form, obtain copies of my university degrees, certificates, and divorce decree, and make sure that the three required references had been submitted on my behalf. Once this paperwork was completed, I could call him to set up the interview.

The NAC investigation, as explained in the packet, is meant to reveal if the applicant has been arrested, charged, cited, or convicted of any offense, including driving under the influence, or if the applicant is party to any civil suits or if there are any judgments pending against him or her. In addition, it has been the Peace Corps policy since its founding in 1961 by John F. Kennedy to exclude from its service any person who has been employed by an intelligence agency or engaged in the collection, dissemination, or analysis of intelligence information. I regarded the question "Have you ever been involved in intelligence activities?" as a standard one, much like "Have you ever used drugs or been treated for substance abuse?" Both of them were irrelevant to me and were answered with a resounding no. I was a law-abiding citizen and my life was an open book.

I completed the required paperwork promptly and called Jason to set up my interview. It was scheduled for July 14 at 10:30 a.m. at the Peace Corps recruitment office in Arlington, Virginia. I had gone there once before to attend an information event. A curious incident had happened to me on that occasion. When I arrived in the lobby, a Peace Corps staff member asked me what I had come for. I replied laconically that I had been invited, meaning that I had been invited to the information event, but in Peace Corps lingo, "invited" means being formally asked, after having successfully completed all the stages in the application process, to serve as a volunteer. The staff member immediately congratulated me and inquired where I was assigned to serve. Realizing my mistake, I corrected myself and explained the reason for my arrival. Inwardly, I prayed that it would not be long before I would be "invited," in Peace Corps lingo.

I was anxious about the interview. An interview is a lot like a blind date. You worry about what to wear, what to say, and how to get the other party to talk while you take refuge in listening. To prepare myself, I spent hours browsing through the career section of a Barnes and Noble store and read several practical guides on how to interview for a job. As the interview date approached, my confidence and self-assurance grew. But on the day of the interview, I still couldn't decide what to wear. I wanted to create a youthful impression, even though age was allegedly not a factor. After trying on several outfits, I chose a denim pants suit, tied my shoulder-length hair back in a ponytail, put light makeup on my face, and wore a simple pair of pearl earrings. My slender figure and chestnut-dyed hair helped to take a few years off my age.

I took the Metro to Arlington, Virginia, got off at Rosslyn Metro Station, and started walking toward the Peace Corps recruitment office on 1525 Wilson Boulevard. It was a rainy day and despite my umbrella, my shoes got wet and my hair became frizzy from the humidity in the air. I quickened my pace, arriving breathless at my destination, and, after going through security check, asked the guard to inform Jason that I had come for my interview.

A friendly guy in his late twenties, Jason's calm demeanor immediately put me at ease. He asked many questions about my background and experiences. I told him about my exposure to four different cultures: I grew up in Israel, lived in the Netherlands for more than a decade, spent two summers in Cairo, Egypt, and had resided in Maryland for the past twenty years. I moved back and forth between Israeli, Arab, Dutch, and American cultures, speaking Hebrew, Arabic, Dutch, and English. He asked me to describe the challenges I had faced when I was in Cairo and the valuable lessons I had learned that would inform my Peace Corps service. I was happy to talk about my trips to Cairo, first in 1986 when I was a PhD candidate at Georgetown University's Arabic department, and then in 1999 when I was a CASA III research fellow. On both occasions, I had followed a special program at the Arabic Language Institute of the American University in Cairo and had lived in the university dorms, first on Falaki Street in downtown Cairo and then in the suburb of Zamalek.

During my stays in Cairo, I spent a great deal of time going to libraries and bookshops to collect material for my research projects. I walked many miles, climbed many dark staircases, waited endlessly in small and hot offices, and searched patiently through stacks of dusty books—all for the sake of locating a particular text or edition. Naturally, I had to rely on the assistance of bookshop clerks and librarians to find what I needed. They often told me to come back "tomorrow," assuring me that they would have the book I asked for. I would hasten to return the next day, only to discover that "tomorrow" is a very vague and fluid concept, ranging from a couple of days to a couple of weeks and even to a couple of months—"Middle East time," as the saying goes. I learned not to take the word "tomorrow" literally but loosely, and to be patient and flexible. You cannot live in Cairo and be under time pressure. The weather is extremely hot, the streets are extremely crowded, and the traffic is extremely slow. It's futile to set deadlines.

Every time I hailed a cab and asked the driver to take me to a certain address, he would automatically utter, "Inshallah" ("If God wills"). I would smile to myself and repeat softly, "Inshallah." Then I would chat with him about small things, from the weather to the traffic to the popular song playing on the radio. Once, I had gotten into a cab and the driver kept strangely silent and didn't utter the traditional phrase "Inshallah," so I kept silent too. Then the weirdest thing happened: he got lost on the way and a ten-minute ride turned into a forty-five minute ride. When I finally arrived at my destination, I was terribly nauseous and late to my appointment. I thought to myself: *If only we had said "Inshallah!"*

Prior to my stay in Cairo, I had never lived in a segregated society and never had to cope with limitations on my style of dress. I discovered that wearing modest attire—long sleeves, ankle-length skirts, and even a headscarf—actually protected me from the merciless rays of the sun and from mosquito bites. There was a practical and beneficial side to this dress code. I always covered my arms and legs, and the local people regarded me with approval.

On my second stay in Cairo, I resided in a huge dorm building that was divided in two: one half comprised the women's quarters and the other half the men's. There were two separate entrances and elevators, one for women and one for men. Several doormen constantly watched these entrances and elevators to prevent people of the opposite sex from wandering in the wrong direction. In the beginning, I felt extremely uncomfortable being watched by these doormen and resented them. With time I discovered that because they barred men from entering the women's quarters, we were safe. We could walk in shorts and nighties in the hallways and not have to worry that a man would pop out of nowhere and see us, attack us, or burglarize our rooms. I began to appreciate this living arrangement. I smiled at the doormen and exchanged pleasantries with them. They reciprocated with gestures of friendliness. Whenever I came with heavy grocery bags, they would help me carry them to the elevator and open and close the door for me. I felt secure and protected.

One of the most valuable lessons that I had learned from my two summers in Cairo was to approach life with a sense of humor. It is an indispensable tool for coping with obstacles, disappointments, and adversities. The simple Egyptians I had interacted with, from door-men to clerks to shopkeepers, were always laughing and cracking jokes, even though the realities of their lives were harsh. Altogether, a sense of humor, resilience, self-reliance, and resourcefulness proved to be crucial qualities in my journeys across various countries and cultures, both as an individual and as a single parent.

Jason seemed pleased with my answers. He was typing the entire interview on his computer. Right out of the blue, he asked if I was in a relationship. I was taken aback—it sounded like an intrusion into my private life. But he went on to explain that leaving a lonely boyfriend behind might interfere with a volunteer's ability to con-centrate on her work. I replied candidly that I was unattached. Then he posed the all-important question: "Where would you like to serve?" I responded that I was willing to go wherever the Peace Corps would send me. I knew from the various information events I had attended and the brochures I had read that the Peace Corps places a strong emphasis on an applicant's flexibility and willing-ness to serve anywhere he or she is assigned. Jason checked which programs were available, taking into account their estimated dates of departure. "What do you think of university English teaching in Central Asia or Asia in June 2011?" he asked. "I would love to go to Asia," I replied enthusiastically, thinking that China would be an amazing place for me to serve in, if I lucked out. Finally he said, "Do you have any questions? "Yes," I said. "Are you a former Peace Corps volunteer?" He nodded, with a twinkle in his eye. "Can you tell me where you served and what it was like?" For a while, it was Jason who talked and I listened, mesmerized.

I walked out of the Peace Corps office building with a spring in my step. It was still raining but I didn't bother to open my umbrella. I didn't care if I got wet or my hair became frizzy. I was beside myself with joy.

That same day in the early afternoon, I received my nomination. It came in an email from Jason. The email read: "I am pleased to nominate you for the following Peace Corps assignment: University English Teaching, Central Asia/Asia, Estimated Date of Departure, June 2011." The email further stated, "Please keep in mind that the program to which you were initially nominated may not be the program to which you are ultimately invited." The rest of the email contained detailed instructions about the next steps in the application process, which included the medical, legal, suitability, and competitive reviews. I immediately sent Jason a thank-you note. He replied: "I do not usually respond to thank-you emails, although I always do appreciate them. After reviewing your file I was really looking forward to your interview and it was great to hear about your experiences and your unique background. It was a learning experience and one I'll remember for sure... I hope the remainder of your application process goes smoothly and successfully." This positive reinforcement enhanced my motivation and strengthened my determination to become a Peace Corps volunteer.

I called my closest friend and confidant, Miri, a native-born Israeli like me who lived in the same community, and shared the good news. She was the only person who knew about my Peace Corps application. Early on I had decided not to tell anyone else about it. I didn't want to hear critical and disparaging remarks like, "What? Are you crazy? At your age you want to live in the jungle and pee into a hole in the ground?" I had received this kind of reaction from one of the doctors I had asked to fill out a Peace Corps health form on my behalf; she was so negative and discouraging that I never visited her clinic again. I felt relaxed knowing that no one knew what I was up to, so no one could interfere with my plans. True, no one would be there to rejoice with me if I was accepted, but at the same time no one would gloat over me if I was rejected.

A few days after my nomination, I received a package from the Peace Corps medical office outlining the requirements for physical, dental, and eye exams. As soon as I looked at it, I knew that this was the biggest hurdle that I would have to overcome to be eligible for Peace Corps service. In this respect, age is definitely a factor: older people have more health issues than their younger counterparts. I was overwhelmed by the number of medical tests that I was required to undergo: blood work; urinalysis; electrocardiogram; screening for HIV, hepatitis B, and colorectal cancer; physical exam; dental exam complete with a Panorex and four bitewing films; and eye exam complete with eye glasses prescription. I also had to provide the results of a recent pap smear, mammogram, bone density test, and a copy of my immunization history. Because I reported on my initial health status that I had experienced tinnitus (ringing in the ear) in the past, I was asked to take a new audiogram. The Peace Corps provides a small contribution toward medical expenses incurred during the medical qualification process. Any specialty evaluation, such as an audiogram, hepatology consultation, and titer tests (to determine immunity to a specific disease), were my own financial responsibility. With my high-deductible health insurance coverage, I ended up paying a substantial amount of money out of pocket for these tests. I believed that I was investing in myself and moving closer toward fulfilling my aspirations.

Meanwhile, life went on and I had other commitments and obligations to attend to. Besides my teaching activities, I was working to meet two deadlines: to prepare an index for my new book and then to proofread the typeset pages. My publisher, the much-acclaimed Brill in Leiden, the Netherlands, wanted the book to be ready for the annual meetings and book fair of the Middle East Studies Association (MESA) in San Diego in mid-November 2010. It was a very hectic period, but I felt vibrant and productive. When the Jewish High Holidays arrived, I had completed this arduous task and was ready to join in the traditional celebrations with my congregation.

As I had anticipated, I encountered problems in my medical evaluation. Titer tests do not distinguish between antibodies generated by vaccination and those generated by natural exposure to disease agents through infection. The results of the hepatitis B screening that I took showed that I was positive for hepatitis B core antibody and surface antibody. The nurse at the Peace Corps medical office insisted that I go to a specialist for further evaluation. I vaguely remembered that as a child growing up in Israel, I had received a series of vaccinations against diseases, including tuberculosis and smallpox, which were not administered in the United States or Europe, but I no longer possessed those records. I also remembered that before I had traveled to Egypt in 1986 and 1999, I had received some shots and boosters for polio, tetanus, and possibly also hepatitis, but I wasn't sure. The only thing I was sure of was that I had *never* had hepatitis. Reluctantly, I made an appointment to see a digestive disease specialist, fully aware that this was a waste of my time and money. When the specialist saw the results of my blood work, she immediately ruled out the possibility that I was infected: my liver enzymes were normal. She also discounted the possibility that I had been vaccinated against the disease in Israel, saying that in those days Israeli children didn't receive this type of vaccination. Her conclusion, as she wrote in a letter for the Peace Corps medical office, was unequivocal: "Dalya's serologic pattern is consistent with old, resolved hepatitis B infection.

She is immune to hepatitis B. I see no contraindication to her entering Peace Corps from a hepatic point of view."

Although this conclusion satisfied the Peace Corps medical office, it bothered me. I called Miri, who is a few years younger than me, and asked her, "Do you remember if we ever received a vaccination against hepatitis B during our childhood or youth in Israel?" "Of course we did," she instantly replied. "When?" I asked, flabbergasted. "When we were drafted into the army," she said. "Oh, my God," I gasped. How could I have forgotten this? It was one of the obligatory shots that every new soldier in Israel Defense Forces received upon being drafted. I had served in the I.D.F. in the late 1960s. "I'd totally forgotten about this," I said ruefully. "You can still call the Peace Corps medical office and tell them," Miri said. "It doesn't matter anymore," I told her. "The subject is now closed."

The tuberculin skin test was also a problem. I always get a severe reaction to this test and a false positive because I received the BCG vaccine as a child. When I was a university student and later a teacher in the Netherlands, I had to have chest X-rays instead of a skin test to check if I was infected. But that was decades before. Now, at my age, I worried about unnecessary exposure to X-rays. I also worried that my G6PD enzyme deficiency, which prohibits me from taking sulfa drugs and antimalarial drugs such as quinine, would interfere with my eligibility to serve. I expressed my concerns to the Peace Corps physician who had given me a comprehensive physical exam and reviewed the results of my various tests. She calmed me down, stating that I was in a good shape.

Roughly three months after I had received my medical package, I completed all the medical tests and submitted the results. I called the nurse at the Peace Corps medical office and asked her about the status of my medical review. "You're good to go," she announced cheerfully. "I'm going to give you the all clear." Twenty-four hours later, I received a message that the status of my application had been updated. When I logged onto my account, I found a check mark next to the medical evaluation entry and the words: "Complete. Peace Corps has completed your medical review. There are no medical holds on your account at this time."

I was ecstatic. Now nothing could stop me from attaining my goal. The next review, the legal one, was a piece of cake. After all, I was a law-abiding citizen with a clean slate. I just needed to wait patiently for the process to run its course. In the meantime, I was as free as a bird. Why not take a trip to Israel to visit my family? I hadn't seen them in a long time. My elderly mother was diagnosed with Alzheimer's and my brother had been battling leukemia for several years. I felt guilty for not going there sooner but I had been embroiled in an acrimonious divorce and when it was finally over, I needed to rearrange every aspect of my life anew.

I had left Israel shortly before my twentieth birthday and had lived most of my adult life abroad. Over the years, I had lost contact with my childhood friends and my ties with my family had seen many ups and downs. In 1988 my father passed away, and after the first Persian Gulf War in 1991, my younger sister emigrated to Australia. Although my lifestyle, mentality, and values had been influenced by my lengthy exposures to Dutch and American cultures, I was still a Sabra at heart and missed the country of my origin. I booked a flight leaving for Israel in mid-December 2010, and returning to the United States in the first week of January 2011. My older sister, Susan, invited me to stay with her in her apartment rather than in a hotel, and I readily accepted. I was now single and felt like being in the bosom of my family, so to speak.

As usual, the trip was grueling. There is no direct flight from Washington, DC to Tel Aviv, so I first flew to New York City, a leg that took five hours because of a long layover, and from there I continued with El Al Airline to Tel Aviv, a twelve-hour nonstop flight. By the time I reached my destination, I had been on the road for almost twenty hours. These arduous flights were the main reason that my visits to Israel were few and far between.

My sister Susan lived with her husband and adult son in Rishon Lezion. She looked after our widowed mother, who lived a short distance away in a small apartment of her own, with a Filipino maid. At the age of eighty-four, our mother was frail and her memory was fading. She knew who I was because they had prepared her for my visit and had shown her my pictures. It saddened me to see the decline in her cognitive and physical functioning. Susan called her daily to ask how she was doing, took her to the doctors, and supervised the maid. I visited our mother several times and stayed with her when the maid had a couple of days off. She had moments of clarity that appeared and disappeared like fireflies, briefly illuminating the darkness of her mind. In those rare moments, I had unforgettable snippets of conversation with her. She told me why she was afraid of the night: when she went to bed she would see her whole life pass before her eyes like a movie. She also told me why, at the age of sixteen, she had left her parents' home in Baghdad and came to Israel all by herself: she wanted to be free of paternal control and shape her own destiny. It was back in 1942, when Israel was not even established as a state yet. I knew all that—I had heard the story many times in my youth. I admired my mother for her courage and was filled with compassion for her. She had no idea that I had dedicated my new book, *Mothers and Daughters in Arab Women's Literature: The Family Frontier*, to her and that I had published it under my maiden name in honor of both of my parents.

If my mother's condition was depressing, my brother's condition was alarming. The chemotherapy treatment that he had received over the past four years had failed and he needed a bone marrow transplant. The year before, his daughter—and only child—had been diagnosed with an extremely aggressive breast cancer that had spread to her vital organs. She had been in the prime of her life and the mother of two teenage daughters. It was a terrible blow and a huge tragedy. My brother's wife was an Ashkenazi Jew and her family had a high incidence of breast cancer. Both her mother and her sister were stricken with this disease, although at a much older age. As for my brother, I believed that the radiation treatment that he had received as an adolescent to remove a keloid scar just below his neck had something to do with his leukemia. But the records pertaining to this radiation treatment, which was done in Israel in the early 1960s, no longer existed and so this potential link could not be investigated.

Despite his overwhelming problems, my brother, Shimon, took the time to meet with me twice, once in his apartment in Kiryat Uno and once in a restaurant in Caesarea. A mechanical engineer by training with a successful career behind him, he was now retired. He was a handsome man with a full head of shiny black hair and a youthful appearance, just one year my senior. Kindhearted and caring, even when he was going through his darkest moments, he still lent me an ear and offered whatever advice he could with regard to my marital crisis. Now he looked somber, with deep sadness in his eyes. He chatted with me all evening but his expression remained clouded with worry. I didn't dare ask about his daughter, Inbal. I knew that he was taking care of her and her two girls—his granddaughters—full time so that her husband could continue to work. Inbal refused to let anyone see her in the final stage of her battle with cancer. She wanted to be remembered as she once was: beautiful, vivacious, and full of the joy of life. My heart went out to my brother. Inwardly, I kept asking: Why do bad things happen to good people? As we hugged and said goodbye, I wondered if I would see him again. This frightening thought had never occurred to me before.

During my stay in Israel, I had limited access to the Internet. I checked my email account occasionally to see if there was any message from the Peace Corps. There was none. I had a lot of free time on my hands, so I decided to reconnect with some old friends. First, I called my high school friend, Varda, and arranged to meet with her. It was a pleasant meeting and we had a great time reminiscing about the past and updating each other on what had happened in our lives. She told me that her brother and both of her parents were now deceased and that her two adopted children were doing well. I told her the sordid tale of the betrayal and double life of the man I was married to for many years. She was shocked to hear that I got divorced so late in life, saying that I had a lot of courage to go it alone at my age. Deep down, I wondered if it was courage—or fear. Fear for my life, fear for my sanity, fear for my dignity. Then this friend, a clinical psychologist by profession, confided in me that she suffered from bouts of depression and that sometimes she couldn't bring herself to get out of bed. I wondered what was troubling her. She had married well to a guy who adored her and was wealthy—by local standards. Was it because she couldn't bear children? Because she wasn't a great beauty? Childbearing is overrated, and beauty is in the eye of the beholder. She was endowed with a brilliant mind and a great personality. I liked her a lot and didn't want to pry into her soul. Perhaps she would find it easier to express herself in writing. We exchanged email addresses and promised to correspond. To my astonishment, she didn't have her own email address but shared a joint one with her husband. "We have no secrets from each other," she declared, grinning widely. I wondered how her friends could write to her about personal matters, knowing that everything passed through her husband's eyes, or how she herself could write personal letters to her friends, knowing that her husband would see them. I assumed that this would lead to a sanitized and superficial correspondence that would eventually become meaningless and fizzle out. But why jump to conclusions? Time would tell. We hugged each other warmly and said goodbye.

My meeting with another longtime friend, Dalia, was equally pleasant. I shared the same first name with her, spelled slightly differently. It was a popular name for girls of our generation in Israel. When I had last visited her, she was the mother of four children; now she told me that she had become the proud grandmother of six grandchildren! She, too, was shocked to hear about my late divorce.

She said that I should consider moving back to Israel where I would not feel lonely. I thought of the famous saying "Wherever you go, there you are" of the wise philosopher Confucius. Loneliness was ingrained in my character and it followed me around like a shadow. Still, I appreciated Dalia's concern and good intentions. I knew for certain that if I called on her, she would do everything she could to help me.

I enjoyed traveling around the country and seeing its beautiful sights. I wandered about the Old City of Jerusalem, where I visited the Western Wall, the Temple Mount tunnel, the Jewish Quarter, and the Arab bazaar. I roamed the flea market of Jaffa and walked along the charming Tel Aviv promenade, which runs along the Mediterranean seashore. I was amazed by the country's phenomenal pace of development: fast highways, new shopping centers and residential areas, and new businesses and commercial districts. The signs of affluence were visible everywhere, in the cars that crowded the streets, in the shops that offered all kinds of consumer goods, and in the cafés and restaurants that were packed full with people.

At that time, a terrible fire broke out on Mount Carmel in Haifa, destroying thousands of acres of trees and claiming the lives of more than thirty police officers who were trapped on the bus that was sent to help evacuate residents from the area. There was a huge public outcry and finger pointing. As I read the daily newspapers and watched the news on television, I realized how complex Israeli society was. On the one hand, it was highly successful in developing a thriving democracy, a sophisticated technology, and a vibrant cultural life. On the other hand, it was confronted with continuous social and political problems and never-ending security problems. At age sixty-two, Israel still faced formidable challenges.

The date of my departure finally arrived. I hugged my sister and thanked her for her hospitality, aware that many expectations and assumptions that we had about each other had been irrevocably shattered on this visit. As I sat in the cab that took me to Tel

Aviv Ben Gurion International Airport, I prepared myself mentally for the grueling trip ahead. The airport was crowded with travelers, and so was the plane. I endured some twenty hours of sleep deprivation and physical discomfort until I finally landed at Ronald Reagan Washington National Airport, where I took a cab to my home in Potomac, Maryland. The cab glided silently through the traffic—or so it seemed after having traveled on Israel's noisy and bumpy buses for the last couple of weeks. When we reached my neighborhood, I noticed that many houses still had Christmas decorations on their façades and that the ground was covered with snow. I loved the open spaces of my neighborhood, nestled around the Avenel golf course; it is a peaceful area surrounded by woods, ponds, parks, and pathways for walking. I was happy to come home and resume my normal activities.

After a day's rest, I checked the status of my Peace Corps application. When I logged onto my account, I discovered that there was a hold on my legal evaluation. It must have been placed there while I was out of the country. I immediately called the Education Desk at the Peace Corps office to find out the reason for this hold and how to clear it up. I was told to get in touch with Torrey, the Peace Corps placement eligibility specialist. Torrey wanted a copy of my divorce agreement and documentation showing that I had enough funds to meet my mortgage payments during my absence. I felt that the demand to see my divorce agreement was an intrusion into my private life. What did it have to do with Peace Corps service? But Torrey insisted that I submit it along with statements of my bank account showing income and monthly deductions. Without these documents she could not grant me legal clearance and my application process would come to a halt. I reluctantly complied with her demands, worrying about the potential backlash that these documents could spark.

January 2011 was a sad time in the life of my family. First, I was informed that my brother had suffered a relapse of his disease. He was in need of a stem cell transplant, and I was asked by his hematologist to take a serology test to determine if I was a suitable donor. Immediately, I visited my primary care physician to undergo a blood test and emailed my brother to tell him that the results would be available within a few days. Then the second blow came. On January 23, I received a message from my brother, saying, "Shalom Dalya. Sorry to tell you. Inbal is not with us anymore. Love, Shimon." My niece had succumbed to her disease and had passed away at the age of forty. It was a terrible loss. My brother had only one child, this daughter—*kivsat harash.*[1] How could he be consoled? His two granddaughters, now motherless, would have to be under constant medical supervision to safeguard their health. I called my brother and sister-in-law and expressed my heartfelt condolences on their daughter's untimely passing. My brother said to me plainly, "We will never get over this loss." It pained me to hear him utter these words. He had always been a model of courage and perseverance for me. Now he sounded like he was in the depths of despair.

My communications with Torrey stretched out over six weeks. Finally, in mid-February, I received the long-awaited message that the status of my application had been updated. My Peace Corps account showed that the legal hold had been removed and that all evaluation entries had a check mark next to them. My application process was complete! It was a moment of sheer exhilaration. But I couldn't sit back and relax—there was still a lot of work to do. That same day the Peace Corps office requested that I fill out a skill addendum, focusing on my experience in teaching English as a foreign language, and mail them copies of my diplomas. Shortly afterward I was asked to describe how I had been preparing for Peace Corps service, what my expectations of Peace Corps service were, how my family and friends felt about my decision to serve, and how I felt about separating from them for twenty-seven months (three months of pre-service training and twenty-four months of service). These were all repetitive questions that I had already answered before in my application essays and at my interview. Nevertheless I answered them fully and promptly.

On March 18, a Peace Corps placement and assessment specialist named Christa informed me that the program I was originally nominated for—university English teaching in Central Asia/Asia, departing in June 2011—had closed. She was now considering me for teacher trainer placement in the North Africa/Middle East region, departing in October 2011. Would I be available for this departure date? I was quite disappointed by this news. I had looked forward to departing in June and this meant a long delay—an additional five months of waiting. Besides, I felt "saturated" with Arab culture. What more could I learn about it that I didn't already know? After all, it had been the focus of my work for more than twenty years. I was eager to learn a wholly new language and integrate into a wholly new culture. The Peace Corps was active only in one country in North Africa—Morocco—and one country in the Middle East—Jordan. I didn't speak the Moroccan dialect; it is difficult and different from the Egyptian or Levantine dialects. As for Jordan, it has a huge Palestinian population. How would they look at me, a Sabra, with a distinct Hebrew accent? But why worry? There is a peace treaty between Jordan and Israel. Had I not spent two summers in Egypt all by myself and loved it? Had I not enjoyed my trip to Morocco, visiting Fez, the Atlas Mountains, Rabat, and Casablanca? Had I not been impressed by my journey to Tunisia, where I had watched female police officers direct traffic in the streets of the capital city and heard the local people spontaneously alternate between French and Arabic in their speech? Perhaps it would be an exceptional learning experience to live for two years in an Arab country and get a "view from within" of their culture and society. Indeed, it could be the culmination of my scholarly career. Most importantly, saying yes to a placement in the North Africa/Middle East region would show *flexibility* on my part, a quality that the Peace Corps emphasizes as the key to effective service. With this thought uppermost in my mind, I answered Christa that I would be available for Peace Corps placement in the North Africa/Middle East region, departing in October 2011. A few days later, on March 22, I received her reply: "Thanks for your email. Because we work in quarters, I'm not able to move forward with sending an invitation for the program departing in October. I plan on sending an invitation to you for this particular program in April, when the fall quarter begins."

During the long waiting period, I carried on with various activities. I taught English to Russian immigrants at Gateways, took a refresher course in French at Montgomery College to prepare for the scenario that I would be placed in Morocco, and worked assiduously on the second volume of my research project into Arab family life, with a focus on fathers and sons. I had begun this work several years before, and the success of the first volume, which was devoted to Arab mothers and daughters, had given me a lot of impetus to complete it.

The year 2011 marked the Peace Corps fiftieth anniversary. In connection with its golden jubilee celebration, I was invited to an event titled "Recognizing Our Future Volunteers—A Special Evening for Applicants, Friends, and Family," to be held on April 12 at Peace Corps Headquarters in Washington, DC. I had participated in several such events before and knew what to expect: we would hear inspirational stories from former volunteers and join in the sendoff of future volunteers. Would I be one of them? That evening, I was filled with nervous anticipation. I took the Metro to downtown DC, got off at Farragut North, and walked to Peace Corps Headquarters on 20th Street. When I arrived, the social hall was already teeming with applicants and guests. I sat close to the podium and chatted with my neighbors until the program began. We watched documentaries about Peace Corps service around the world and listened to a number of speeches by dignitaries and returned volunteers. Then the moment arrived when "invitations" to serve in the Peace Corps were officially presented to those who had successfully completed the application process. It was a simple ceremony: an applicant's name was read out loud; the applicant approached the podium and received from the presiding officer a blue packet with the words "Peace Corps invites you to serve" written on it; the applicant opened it in front of the gathering and announced the name of the country of his or her assignment. When my name was called out, I leapt from my seat and rushed to the podium to receive the blue packet, my heart pounding with excitement. I opened the flap of the packet and tried to pull out the little booklet inside called "Your Assignment." Perhaps because the packet was overstuffed or perhaps because I was nervous, I couldn't pull it out. There was a moment of silence while everyone watched me in suspense. Finally, I managed to extricate the booklet out of the packet. I glanced quickly at the country's name and announced to the entire gathering, "Jordan."

I was surprised—and at the same time I wasn't surprised. I had specified the Middle East as one of my areas of interest, had enthusiastically accepted a nomination in Central Asia/Asia, and was ultimately assigned to Jordan, just across the border from Israel. What a fluke! I vaguely remembered reading in one of the booklets that the Peace Corps doesn't like to assign volunteers to or near a country where they have family. Hadn't the various Peace Corps officers and desk specialists who handled my application read in my resume that I was born and raised in Israel? Could this placement be an oversight on their part? But why worry? I told myself: "Surely the Peace Corps staff know what they are doing. They have been assigning volunteers all over the world for years. I must *trust* their judgment and accept this assignment." In fact, it would allow me to enjoy the best of both worlds: to serve in Jordan and to visit my family in Israel.

After the ceremony, we had some time to mingle with members of the Peace Corps staff, all of them strikingly young, perhaps in their mid- to late-twenties. I ran into Christa, who offered me her warm congratulations. I asked her what had happened with my original nomination to Central Asia/Asia. She replied that a lot of factors go into the picture when selecting a placement for a volunteer, among them the availability of medical facilities in the country of service in case of an emergency, and this was a consideration in my case. Her explanation sounded lame to me. First, I was in good health. Second, the Peace Corps was active in many other countries with excellent medical facilities. Suddenly her young age bothered me. I wondered if she possessed enough knowledge and understanding to assign a person of my background to Jordan. Was she familiar with the modern history of the Middle East? With the Arab-Israeli conflict? With the overwhelming percentage of Palestinians in Jordan's population?

I went home and called Miri to tell her the news. She wasn't the least bit enthused. She thought it was dangerous for me to go to Jordan because of my identity. I argued that I should trust the Peace Corps; if they assigned me to Jordan they knew what they were doing. She said, "If you want so much to live among Arabs, why don't you go to Israel and live among the Bedouins in the Negev or the Druz in the Upper Galilee?" I disagreed. "It's not the same. These Arabs live under Israeli rule. They are Israeli Arabs. I want the total Arab experience, that is, to live among Arabs in an Arab country under Arab rule." She was strongly opposed to the idea. "Why are you so worried?" I asked. "After all, I've spent two summers by myself in Egypt, and I've been to Morocco and Tunisia." She was still not swayed. "You forget that 60 percent of the population in Jordan is Palestinian. That's a big difference. And there have been terrible hotel bombings in Amman in 2005 by al-Qaeda-affiliated terrorists."

I looked up the history of the Peace Corps in Jordan. The agency began to operate there in 1997, following discussions between the late King Hussein and former President Clinton. American-born Queen Noor was instrumental in establishing this relationship. Due to security concerns, the Peace Corps suspended its program and withdrew the volunteers in November 2002. Two years later, in 2004, the Peace Corps resumed its activities in Jordan, sending English teachers (J7), followed by special education and youth development volunteers (J8), for assignments in underserved schools and

centers. In July 2005, volunteers in all three sectors arrived together
as one group (J9). I would be a member of the J15 group in the
landmark year in which the Peace Corps was celebrating its fiftieth
anniversary.

After pondering long and hard about my assignment, I came to
the conclusion that it was a matter of *trust*. If I trusted the Peace
Corps, then I should accept their assignment. If I didn't trust the
Peace Corps, then why in the world had I applied to them for volunteer work? Two days later I informed the Peace Corps Education
Desk that I accepted their assignment to serve in Jordan. Within
twenty-four hours I got a message that the status of my application
had been updated. When I logged onto my account, I found a check
mark next to the entry "Invitation" and the words: "Congratulations!
You have accepted your invitation to serve in Jordan. You will soon be
receiving additional information from your country desk, the travel
office, and the office of staging about preparing for service." I felt a
glow of satisfaction as I read those words. Here I was, nine months
after submitting my application, seeing the fruits of my labor. I had
put my heart and soul into this application and each hurdle that I had
faced on the road had pushed me to work harder and harder. I felt
that I had grown in the process and become more resilient.

But I couldn't sit back and relax. There was a constant flow
of requests coming from the Peace Corps office. I had to send an
updated resume and aspiration statement to the Peace Corps staff in
Jordan because none of my application materials was sent overseas.
I had to fill out several surveys, passport and visa related forms, and
life insurance and personal possessions insurance forms. Finally, I had
to prepare for the pre-departure orientation, referred to as "staging"
in Peace Corps lingo.

My departure date was set for October 21, six months away. From
now on I had to manage my time carefully so that all my affairs
would be in order before I left. My primary objective was to complete
the second volume of my research project into Arab family life and

send the manuscript to prospective publishers. My secondary objective was to prepare my townhouse for my long absence. I installed new smoke and gas detectors, tiled two terraces, sealed the driveway, and did some exterior painting. These were costly but much needed maintenance activities.

In late July, my brother's condition deteriorated. He was waiting for an isolation unit in the hemato-oncology division at Beilinson Hospital in Petakh Tikva to become available so that he could be admitted and receive the bone marrow transplant. Although all of us, his three sisters, were found to be suitable donors, his doctor chose my sister who lived in Australia to be the donor simply on the basis of age: at fifty, she was the youngest among us. We were all waiting anxiously for news. On August 7, my brother informed me by email that he was finally admitted to the hospital. The procedure would take thirty days; the first step would be chemotherapy treatment to suppress his immune system, and then the stem cell transplant would take place. On August 22, he wrote to me that he was six days after the transplant and that his immune system was close to zero. It would take three weeks until his system could produce new white blood cells. After that, his messages became sporadic and I communicated mostly by phone with his wife, who stayed at his bedside day and night. In mid-September, I tried to call her as usual but she didn't answer. I tried my brother's cell phone number, but received no answer either. Finally I tried their apartment phone number, expecting no one to pick up. By an amazing stroke of luck, my brother answered the phone. It was pure joy to hear his voice and speak with him directly. He said that he was allowed to go home and had just been released from the hospital. For a few blessed days everything seemed to be under control—he was feeling well enough to cook a meal for his granddaughters and even drive his car. By the time the Jewish High Holidays had arrived, he had started experiencing high fever, severe stomach pain, and diarrhea. I called to wish him the best for the Jewish New Year, only to hear from his wife that he was back in the hospital. On September 30, the second day of Rosh Hashanah festival, I received a sad email from him, saying, "I am still in the hospital, under the hands of the doctor, getting antibiotics and blood transfusion, till now no improvement. Love, Shimon." This was the last written message that I would ever receive from my brother. From that point on, he stopped answering my emails and phone calls, and my contact with him was solely through his wife.

Graft-versus-host disease (GVHD), a complication that can occur after a stem cell or bone marrow transplant, is a condition in which the newly transplanted material attacks the recipient's body. The difference between the donor's cells and the recipient's tissues often causes T cells (a type of white blood cells) from the donor to recognize the recipient's body tissue as foreign. When this happens, the newly transplanted cells attack the recipient's body. Acute GVHD usually happens within the first three months after the transplant. Chronic GVHD usually starts more than three months after the transplant and can last a lifetime. Rates of GVHD vary from between 30–40 percent among related donors and recipients to 60–80 percent between unrelated donors and recipients. My brother's situation was further complicated by his heart condition: fifteen years earlier he had undergone open heart surgery to fix a rare heart valve problem and subsequently had a pacemaker implanted in his chest to regulate the rhythm of his heart. The prognosis of beating GVHD depends on the severity of the condition. While some cases of GVHD can lead to death, many cases, whether acute or chronic, can be treated successfully. Successful treatment of GVHD does not guarantee that the transplant itself will succeed in treating the original disease. In my brother's case, the transplanted stem cells succeeded in treating his blood cancer but then they turned against his body, causing severe damage to his lungs, liver, and digestive tract. I knew none of these grim facts at that time. Only after the complications had started to emerge, did I learn all this information.

When October came and my brother's condition had still not improved, I felt conflicted about leaving for Jordan. I wanted to go to Israel instead, to see my brother. When my departure date was moved up by a few days, I thought that if I left as planned, I would already place myself across the Atlantic Ocean, in the Middle East, within a short distance from Israel. There were daily flights from Amman to Tel Aviv and the flight duration was merely half an hour. I could easily arrange to fly over to see him. I had no doubt that the Peace Corps would allow me to do so.

As I carried on with the preparations for my departure, the issue of my Jewish identity suddenly came up. A few days before I was scheduled to leave, I received a phone call from the then-Peace Corps country director in Jordan, Alex Boston. After exchanging pleasantries, he went straight to the point. "Cohen is an easily recognizable Jewish name," he said. "Jordan is an Arab Muslim country. Perhaps you would feel more comfortable using another name." Surprised, I said, "Cohen is my married name. I'm now divorced and I don't mind changing it, but this is a lengthy process which can't be completed in time for my departure." He said, "You don't need to do this legally. You can keep your last name on your passport but use a different name, perhaps your middle name or maiden name, when you introduce yourself to your Jordanian host family, to members of your Jordanian host community, and to teachers and students at the Jordanian school to which you will be assigned. We have several volunteers who have done this in the past." I had no idea that adopting another name was an option. "I don't have a middle name," I said. "And my maiden name, Abudi, can mislead my host family into thinking that I am an Arab. This would put me in an untenable position. Let me think of another, neutral name. When do you need to have it?" "When you arrive in Amman for your pre-service training orientation," he replied.

As soon as I got off the phone, I started looking for a substitute for my last name. I went online and searched various sites for popular last names but none of them appealed to me. I wanted a name that would mean something to me and at the same time disguise my identity. My pen name on my books was Cohen-Mor. Sometimes I abbreviated it to C. Mor. What about joining the two together and changing the spelling slightly, like Seymour or Seymore? Seymour is an old English name, and Seymore a variant spelling of it. Dalya Seymore. Yes, this sounded okay to me. I would recognize this name if someone called it out and could relate to it.

The remaining days before my departure were hectic. I contacted Verizon and requested to disconnect the telephone, television, and Internet services to my home. I prepared my car for long-term parking and gave a set of my house keys to my trusted friend, Miri. I packed, unpacked, and repacked two medium-size suitcases, a carry-on bag, a laptop bag, and a handbag. Peace Corps reporting instructions included paid transportation by train from Washington, DC to Philadelphia, where the departure orientation was set up. I realized that I wouldn't be able to handle all the pieces of my luggage by myself while changing from cab to train to cab and arranged for a taxi ride, at my own expense, from my home straight to my destination in Philadelphia.

At long last—almost a year and a half after submitting my application—the day I had been eagerly awaiting had arrived. I was about to begin my journey in answer to the challenge, "Life is calling. How far will you go?" I was brimming with anticipation and excitement.

3 . STAGING

IN THE EARLY HOURS OF TUESDAY MORNING, OCTOBER 18, I climbed into the back of a Barwood cab and began the three hour ride from Potomac to Philadelphia, where the so-called "staging" or departure orientation was set up. We were instructed to check into the Hampton Inn–Center City, where the Peace Corps office had made reservations for the entire J15 group. The staging, as the reporting instructions stated, was meant to offer the volunteers a chance to meet each other, review important policies and procedures, and complete various registration forms. Then we would receive our Peace Corps passports and airline tickets and fly together to Jordan.

There was little traffic on the road and the ride went without a hitch. I arrived at the Hampton Inn in good time and checked in quickly. The bellboy helped me carry my luggage to a modest double bedroom on the upper floor. After organizing my stuff, I changed from my travel clothes into business casual attire, as required, and settled into a chair to eat an apple. Suddenly, there was a knock on the door. I opened it to a middle-aged woman with a shock of white hair. "I'm Lora, your roommate," she said. "I'm Dalya," I replied, and held out my hand to shake hers. I helped her bring her bags into the room and then we sat opposite each other on our beds and started to chat.

Lora was a special education teacher from Florida. A fair-skinned, blue-eyed, single woman who had raised her two children by herself after her divorce, she was looking for something new and exciting to do now that they were both adults. She had gotten the idea of serving in the Peace Corps from her daughter, who had been a Peace Corps volunteer a couple of years before and had loved it. Lora was fifty years old but her white hair, which she wore loose around her shoulders, made her look older. I took an instant liking to her, feeling reassured by the fact that she was an older volunteer, like me. I told her that I was single too but didn't mention my recent divorce. I decided in advance that I would keep my personal life private. I also decided not to mention that I was born and raised in Israel, preferring to say instead that I was from the Netherlands. I felt safer this way. Israel does not fare well in world public opinion and many people harbor anti-Israeli sentiments. By contrast, the Netherlands is a neutral country that no one has issues with—even Arabs. I had lived in the Netherlands for many years and it was easy for me to adopt it as my background. I didn't worry about my Hebrew accent—I could say that it was Dutch. During the many years that I had lived in the United States, I discovered that Americans cannot guess the country of my origin by my accent. The reason is that most Americans don't speak Hebrew, or Dutch, or any other foreign language for that matter. I was confident that no one would discover my secret.

After chatting for a while, we went downstairs to the lobby and headed for the conference room to meet the rest of the J15 group. The schedule that we had received prior to our arrival outlined the activities for the day. First, we would go through official registration as Peace Corps volunteers, which meant more forms to fill out. Then we would receive our Peace Corps passports, airline tickets, and a small allowance to cover our meals and travel expenses. We pinned our nametags to the lapels of our jackets to facilitate the process of getting to know each other, and began to mingle. I discovered that J15 was a fairly large group of thirty-eight volunteers from across the United States, most of them in their early to late twenties. There were three African Americans, three Hispanic Americans, two Asian Americans, one Arab American, and one Sabra—me. One volunteer stood out: a gray-haired man in his early seventies who wore a big silver hoop earring on the right side. I wondered whether he had familiarized himself with the values of traditional Arab culture. Didn't he know that in this conservative society such an ornament—and statement—was totally unacceptable? I had no doubt that he would be told to take the earring off on arrival in Jordan.

I submitted all the required registration forms except for the "Privacy Act Waiver" and "Authorization to Use Personal Material," both of which were presented as optional. With regard to the first form, I wanted to protect my identity and avoid the risk that my real last name would appear in blogs or newsletters and compromise my efficacy and safety as a Peace Corps volunteer. As for the second form, I wanted to reserve the exclusive right to draw on my experiences in Peace Corps service in my future research projects and publications. There were a few other volunteers who objected to this form and didn't sign it.

As soon as we had completed the official registration, our orientation began. We sat around big round tables in the conference room, facing the staging director, Emily, who was assisted by the staging coordinator, Hannah. Both were former Peace Corps volunteers. Each of us received a staging workbook with questions that focused on the Peace Corps history, mission, and core expectations, as well as on the general principles of being an effective and safe volunteer. The discussion proceeded from volunteer to volunteer, table to table, or workgroup to workgroup. At the end of the orientation five hours later, we had already formed first impressions of each other and of what was expected of us.

Some volunteers had distinguished themselves from the outset: Armando, with his gigantic frame and funny jokes; Theresa, with her good looks; Marc, with his hoop earring; Anna and John, in being the only married couple in the group; and Ben, with his German background and hoarse voice, the result of a car accident. There was a girl named Mona who painstakingly defended aspects of Arab culture that came under criticism during the discussion. I realized immediately that she was an Arab.

Later in the evening I ran into Mona in the hotel's computer room. She seemed eager to talk with me. She told me that she was working on getting her master's degree in English. Born to a Palestinian mother and a Yemenite father, she grew up in a predominantly Arab community in Dearborn, Michigan. She could speak the Palestinian dialect but could not read or write modern standard Arabic. She asked me if I knew Arabic. I said yes, a little. I didn't want to draw attention to myself with my doctorate. She inquired whether I was married. I replied that I was single. She said that she was thirty years old and still single. She was worried that her host family and host community in Jordan wouldn't understand why she wasn't married yet and would give her a hard time about it. I got the impression that she was torn between conflicting choices: pursuing marriage or a career; finding an American or Arab husband. A tall, soft-spoken girl with a meek demeanor, she came across as being affable and was surprisingly open. I assumed that my age and Middle Eastern appearance made her feel at ease with me.

That evening, I joined Lora, Marc, and a few younger volunteers for dinner. We walked a good distance looking for a restaurant that would appeal to all of us. At home, I followed a low-fat diet based on fish, dairy products, fruit, and vegetables. I would have been content with a sandwich and a yogurt at the deli across the street from the Hampton Inn, but I had never been to Philadelphia before and we had just this one night here. Our hotel was situated in downtown Philadelphia, within walking distance from the historic district. As we roamed through the streets, historical attractions seemed to grace every corner. The downtown area abounded with shops, cafés, restaurants, and bars, and pulsated with nightlife. We selected a traditional Philly cheesesteak joint. I ordered a hoagie sandwich, which is a local version of a sub, with a soda. I noticed that Lora, who sat opposite me at the table, hardly touched the food on her plate. When I asked her if she didn't like it, she replied that she wasn't hungry. It seemed that she was there for the company, much like me. After dinner, those who wanted to continue exploring the city went in one direction, and the rest, including myself, returned to the hotel.

It had been a long day and a much longer—and arduous—day awaited us. The following morning we had to check out of the hotel by 11:00 a.m. and board the bus to New York's JFK International Airport at 1:00 p.m. Our flight to Jordan was scheduled to depart at 9:40 p.m., with an eight-hour layover in Frankfurt. We would depart from Frankfurt at 8:50 p.m. local time and arrive in Amman at 1:55 a.m., provided there were no delays. This meant a grueling, nighttime trip. For those who could sleep on the plane it wasn't so bad. For me, who found it difficult to sleep during flights, it meant a tough time. I took a shower and went to bed. Lora stayed out late. I hoped that she would be quiet and considerate when she returned to the room, but she wasn't. She came back well after midnight, slammed the door shut, turned on the lights, fiddled noisily with her bags, and then took a long shower. I said nothing. It was just one night and I assumed that I would get another roommate at the next hotel.

The next day I got up early and started organizing my things. I was worried—as many of us were—about the weight of my baggage. I didn't pack a lot of stuff but somehow it all added up and exceeded the weight limit of 100 lbs. All my worldly possessions for the next two years were inside these two suitcases and one carry-on bag.

I didn't know how, with just two hands, I would be able to carry them around. Many volunteers faced the same problem but I was older. I was concerned that I might hurt my wrists, which were thin and fragile, or my back.

Bursting with energy, I went downstairs to the lobby, checked out of the hotel and closed my credit card account, before stepping into the dining hall for breakfast. Only a few volunteers were around as most of them were still in bed after a late night out. I smiled to myself. You really can't beat youth. After two cups of coffee and some cereal, I headed for the nearest post office to mail a couple of personal documents that I no longer needed back to my friend Miri for safekeeping. I didn't want to shoulder the burden of carrying them around in Jordan. It was raining heavily outside and the small umbrella that the hotel's concierge loaned me offered little protection from the strong wind and pouring rain. By the time I got back to the hotel, my jeans and sneakers were soaking wet.

I went up to my room to change my outfit and fix my hair, which had become frizzy from the moisture. Lora was nowhere to be seen. I put my wet clothes in a plastic bag and called the bellboy to help me carry my baggage to the lobby. A large group of tourists had just arrived and the lobby was bustling with activity. Many volunteers were already in the lounge, drinking coffee and chatting while waiting for the bus. I headed for the lounge to join them, feeling a little nervous and insecure. I was quiet and reserved by nature, and having to socialize all the time exhausted me. Marc came over and sat beside me, looking lost and ill at ease. He told me that he was from San Francisco, that he had a law degree, and that he had worked at various jobs, including teaching and filmmaking, before volunteering for Peace Corps service. Rob, a serene-looking guy from Nashville, Tennessee, joined the conversation. Slightly older than the average volunteer, perhaps in his mid-thirties, he was interested in going into public service and this was why he had committed to the Peace Corps mission. The more I talked with members of my group, the greater variety of motives I discovered for their joining the Peace Corps. Some were idealists, others opportunists; some looked for adventure, others for professional experience; and still others sought a temporary employment during a time of economic crisis. There were also those who were running away from something unpleasant in their lives—a failed relationship, a drab job, or the rat race.

At long last the bus arrived. We loaded our bags and took our seats for the two-hour ride to New York's JFK International Airport. Much to our surprise, neither the staging director, Emily, nor the staging coordinator, Hannah, accompanied us on the bus ride. We were going to travel by ourselves, without a Peace Corps escort, all the way from Philadelphia to Amman. At Amman International Airport, Peace Corps staff would meet us, help us through customs, and take us to a hotel. Some volunteers attributed this arrangement to recent cuts in the Peace Corps budget. Others remarked that the salaries of top Peace Corps officials should have taken the cuts, rather than the overall budget. We weren't the least bit concerned about traveling by ourselves; after all, we were all adults.

I hoped to nap on the bus in order to gain strength for the long nighttime flight, but I couldn't. There was too much noise and too many conversations going on around me all at once. I listened with interest to Mona, who sat a couple of rows across the aisle from me, talking with a group of girls about her lifestyle as an Arab American: "I don't have any restrictions on my freedom," she declared. "I can date guys, travel, and live by myself." They asked her if she was Muslim. "Yes, I am. But I don't wear a hijab and I don't pray five times a day." This would be frowned upon by members of her host community in Jordan, I thought to myself, as I closed my eyes and tried to doze off.

We arrived at JFK Airport around 3:30 in the afternoon. The bus driver dropped us off by the entrance to the United Airlines terminal and hurriedly unloaded our bags onto the pavement. I wheeled in one suitcase at a time, leaving the first at the line of volunteers by the check-in desk before getting the second. I was burdened not only by my suitcases but also by my laptop, which I watched carefully lest it should get banged about and damaged. The Peace Corps office had provided us with vouchers to pay for any extra fees charged on the second suitcase, but we had to stay within the total baggage weight permitted. We waited anxiously in line, preparing ourselves for the worst case scenario. But when the check-in process began, we were all pleasantly surprised. The airline didn't charge us for the second suitcase or for extra weight and we didn't have to use our vouchers. Our bags were checked right through to our final destination and we would see them again only at Amman International Airport. Breathing a sigh of relief, I asked the check-in clerk to change my seat, which was at the back of the plane, to the front section. I wanted to be in a quiet cabin where I would be able to get some sleep.

With our boarding passes in hand, we proceeded through security check to our departure gate. It was about 5:30 p.m. and we had four hours to kill until our boarding time. Some volunteers ate in the cafeteria, some went shopping, and some remained in the departure lounge to read or play games on their laptops or smartphones. The minutes crept by slowly. At 9:30 p.m., it was announced that our flight was delayed. It was close to midnight when the plane finally took off. I squeezed my weary body into my narrow seat and tried to sleep. I couldn't. My mind refused to switch off. I got up and started to pace up and down the aisles. The plane was packed full. The last cabin, where I had been originally assigned to sit, was very hot and noisy. Many volunteers were already fast asleep, their bodies curled up in various positions. I looked at them with envy. After stretching my legs for a while, I returned to my seat, put my ear phones on, closed my eyes, and abandoned myself to the sounds of music.

Nine hours later, the plane touched down at Frankfurt International Airport just before noon, local time. The Peace Corps office had arranged for us to rest at the Steigenberger Airport Hotel until our next flight, scheduled to leave at 8:50 p.m. For some reason, we couldn't find the hotel. We dragged ourselves from one hall to another, only to be told to retrace our steps. After shuffling back and forth several times, we learned that the hotel was located about half a mile from the airport and that we had to use the shuttle bus service to get there.

When we finally arrived, all exhausted, we lined up in the lobby to show our passports to the desk clerk, sign our names, and get the keys to our rooms. I could barely keep my eyes open. All I wanted was to crash out on a flat surface. I hurried up to my room, closed the curtains on the window, and flung myself down on one of the beds. Just as I was drifting into a blissful sleep, Lora opened the door and walked in. "Oh," she said. "I see that you got here before me!" She went straight to the window and pulled the curtains wide open. The bright sunlight flooded the room and blinded me. I instinctively covered my eyes. "Please close the curtains," I muttered in a choked voice. "I need to get some sleep. Aren't you going to sleep too?" "No," she said. "I slept on the plane. I want to take a shower and wash my hair. Then I want to iron my clothes for the flight tonight and watch television." I listened to her in disbelief. She was acting as if there was no one else with her in the room. "I didn't sleep at all on the plane," I explained. "Can't you wash your hair and iron your clothes later?" She rolled her eyes. "But this is my room too! What do you expect me to do while you sleep?" Quietly, I replied, "I expect you to be considerate. I would do the same for you." There was a moment of silence. "Okay," she said. "First I want to iron my clothes and then I'll go for a walk." I turned my face toward the wall and inserted earplugs into my ears. I tried to ignore her and stay calm, but I was upset. After what seemed like an eternity, she finished ironing her clothes and left, slamming the door hard behind her. I remained stretched out on the bed, my peace of mind totally destroyed, and sleep eluded me.

I lay in bed feeling miserable. I was stuck with a roommate who had been living by herself as a single woman for many years and simply didn't know how to share space with another person. It was obvious that Lora and I were incompatible: I was a light sleeper whereas she was a heavy sleeper; I went to bed early whereas she went to bed late; I couldn't sleep on a plane and was dead beat after a long-haul flight whereas she could sleep on a plane and was hyperenergetic after such a flight. Was it possible to reconcile such differences? I laughed at the naive assumption of the Peace Corps staff who had paired us together—just because Lora and I were close in age didn't mean that we were compatible. I wondered if we were destined to remain roommates throughout the pre-service training.

I got up and took a long hot shower, then put on a fresh set of clothes and went downstairs to the lobby. I spotted two girls, Megan and Michelle, having dinner in the hotel's café and joined them at their table. They told me that almost all the members of our group crashed out in their rooms, except for a few guys who took a cab to tour the city of Frankfurt. As we were eating and chatting, Lora arrived, saying that she had gone for a walk to get rid of her pent-up energy. We were polite to each other but there was an undercurrent of tension between us.

We checked out of the hotel at 7:00 p.m. and took the shuttle bus back to the airport. Mat, a bearded guy of Italian background, helped me carry my heavy backpack, where I had put my laptop, to our departure gate while I wheeled my carry-on bag. When we arrived at the security check, we were separated into two different lines by German security officers. My line moved faster and I lost sight of Mat. Suddenly, I remembered that I had forgotten to tell him that my laptop was in my backpack. I became alarmed. Security regulations require taking a laptop out of its case and placing it in a separate bin before it goes into the screening machine. Mat would fail to comply with this regulation because he didn't know that there was a laptop in my backpack and he might get into trouble. What a terrible mistake! I completed the security check and waited anxiously for him to emerge from his line, but he was nowhere to be seen. When he finally appeared, he looked pale. I rushed toward him and apologized profusely. He told me that he had been taken out of the line and questioned by two German security officers about the laptop in my backpack. They asked him if the backpack belonged to him, which he confirmed. They examined the laptop, put it through their screening machine, and after ascertaining that it was harmless, let him go. Mat insisted that he wasn't the least bit worried, but he looked visibly shaken. We both learned a valuable lesson from this incident: accepting a package at the airport, *even* from a friend, is risky.

The flight to Amman departed without delay at 8:50 p.m. I was seated with the rest of my group in the back of the plane. It seemed to me that I was the only one among them who had suffered sleep deprivation on the previous leg of the trip and was near exhaustion. I hoped to nap soon after takeoff, when the cabin lights would be switched off to allow passengers to sleep, since this was a nighttime flight. I had no inkling of what was about to happen. I had an aisle seat, a volunteer named Zack sat in the middle, and an elderly Jordanian occupied the window seat. Natalie, a corpulent, middle-aged volunteer who sat in the row behind me, asked Zack to change places with her. As soon as she settled in her new seat she started complaining that her leg room was too small and that her feet hurt, hinting that I should offer her my seat. I told her frankly that I had problems with my left knee cap and that I had to keep that leg stretched out in the aisle during the flight. Suddenly, the elderly Jordanian next to her got up and exchanged seats with his relative, a young man who seemed eager to practice his English with us. At first Natalie treated him coldly, but when he suggested giving her an Arabic lesson, her aloofness vanished and she became extremely nice and friendly. Their loud voices could be heard from one end of the cabin to the other—the Jordanian with his broken English and Natalie with her broken Arabic. It was past midnight. The lights had long been switched off in all the cabins and almost all the passengers were fast asleep. Natalie and her self-appointed teacher were making a hell of a racket. I thought that they would soon get tired and stop, but they didn't. When I reached the end of my tether, I turned to them and said, "Can you please lower your voices?" Natalie gave me an icy glare. I looked at the Jordanian guy and repeated my request. He was more responsive—perhaps he was already exhausted—and apologized to me. Sullen, Natalie rose to her feet, jerked the top of my chair roughly as she passed me and walked down the aisle. I knew that she would do the same thing again upon returning to her seat, so I got up too and went to the kitchen to get a cup of water. To my chagrin, I found her standing there with Anna, the married volunteer. When she saw me, she leaned over Anna's head and whispered audibly in her ear, "She was jealous that I was getting a private Arabic lesson!" Anna gave me a disapproving look. I felt like saying to Natalie, "I have no reason to be jealous. I speak and read Arabic fluently." But I didn't. It would serve no purpose. Let her think whatever pleased her. I drank a cup of water and returned to my seat.

The grueling flight finally came to an end. At 1:55 a.m., the plane touched down at Amman Queen Alia International Airport and slowly taxied toward the terminal. We were instructed to be dressed neatly and modestly—no jeans, no bare arms or legs, and no open necklines. Some volunteers had brought a change of outfit with them and rushed to the bathroom to put it on before landing. The girls fixed their hair and makeup. The guys adjusted their ties and smoothed their jackets. The plane stopped at a distance from the terminal and we were bussed to the gate. We entered an old building that was almost deserted this early in the morning. Every sign was in Arabic and English. We walked quietly through empty hallways toward Passport Control. Two Peace Corps staff members were waiting for us there: Samir Dahshan, the safety and security coordinator, and Bryan Butki, the programming and training officer. We exchanged greetings with them and shook their hands, grateful that they had come to meet us at this ungodly hour.

I was nervous when I stood in line to have my passport checked and stamped. This was my first encounter with the Jordanian authorities: Would they question me on seeing my last name and place of birth, or would they process me smoothly? I noticed that the face of each arriving passenger who was cleared for entry was photographed by a camera that was installed on the Passport Control desk. When my turn came, the Jordanian officer processed me mechanically, without any comment or question. I felt a huge surge of relief. My ears and eyes were wide open and absorbing every sound and sight around me. The security guards and airport clerks were friendly and relaxed, the baggage personnel courteous. They laughed and joked as they helped us grab our bags from the carousel and passed them through the X-ray machine by the exit—a security measure that baffled us. Outside, a truck and a bus awaited us in the street. The truck would take the bags that we didn't need for immediate use to a storage facility at the Peace Corps training site on the campus of Al al-Bayt University in Mafraq, while the bus would take us to Palmyra Hotel in Amman. I got on the bus and sat by the window, gazing, mesmerized, at the evolving scenery in the dim light of dawn. My heart was pounding with excitement. Softly, I said to myself: "Welcome to Jordan, Dalya."

4 . ALICE IN WONDERLAND

WE ARRIVED AT PALMYRA HOTEL IN AMMAN AT DAYBREAK AND
gathered in the lobby by the reception desk to check in. It was
Friday, October 21, and we had been on the road for three consecutive days. Checking in was a slow and tedious process: each
volunteer had to present his or her passport for identification,
the desk clerk made a photocopy of the picture page of the passport, checked the volunteer's name on his list, and only then
handed the volunteer a key to a room. I was assigned a room on
the second floor, with Lora, again, as my roommate.

The Palmyra is a two-star hotel located within walking distance
from the main gate of the University of Jordan, about 10 km north-
west of downtown. It is an old building with limited amenities and
no Internet services. We were urged to try to get a few hours of sleep
before the orientation session, which was set to begin at 1:00 p.m. in
the ballroom on the seventh floor.

Lora and I went up to our room, a cramped space furnished with shabby furniture. Lora said that she had slept enough on the plane and was going to explore the neighborhood. As soon as she left, I crashed out on the bed. When I woke up it was almost 11:00 a.m. I found myself staring at an old wooden dresser and tattered patches on the carpeted floor. It took me a few moments to connect the dots and figure out where I was. Amman, Jordan! I jumped excitedly from the bed and flung the frayed curtains open to look out the window. No view. High buildings obstructed my vision in every direction. I took a quick shower and got dressed fast so I could take a walk outside before the orientation session. I wore an ankle-length skirt, a long-sleeved blouse, and a loose-fitting cardigan, and tied my hair back in a ponytail. I smiled at my reflection in the mirror. In this outfit, with my Middle Eastern features, I could pass for a Jordanian woman. I bounded down the stairs to the lobby to leave the key at the front desk—we had received only one set. I greeted the Jordanian clerk in Arabic and he returned my greeting. We started chatting about the weather and where I could go for a walk. He was amazed to learn that I was a member of the Peace Corps group. "You speak Arabic so well. Are you an Arab?" he asked. "No," I said. "But I have Middle Eastern roots." "Syrian?" he tried to guess. "No. Iraqi," I replied. In fact, my mother's maiden name was Shami, which means "Syrian." Her family must have emigrated from Syria to Iraq. Formerly, there were 600,000 Jews who lived in Arab lands, until their expulsion—or forced emigration—in 1948, when the State of Israel was established. These Jews are sometimes called "Arab Jews," which, in my view, is a contradiction in terms. You can either be a Jew, which denotes a specific ethnoreligious group, or an Arab, which denotes another, entirely different ethnoreligious group. How can you be both, especially when these two ethnoreligious groups have been at war with each other for the past one hundred years?

I went for a walk along Jordan University Street, my mind and senses avidly absorbing everything around me. Amman, a bustling

metropolis, home to 2.5 million people, is largely a modern construction lacking grand Islamic architecture. I was amazed to see the
large number of malls, boutiques, and Western fast-food restaurants
that lined both sides of the street. Most of the signs were in Arabic
and English—the dominant second language here. The sidewalk was
uneven and frequently interrupted by unpaved side streets, where
waste water flowed on the surface of the ground. An endless stream
of buses, cabs, and cars passed me by, blasting their horns. I noticed
many women in the driver's seat, some of them were veiled, others
wore hijabs (headscarves), and still others had no head covering at
all. The young men on the street wore Western-style clothes, their
faces mostly clean-shaven. The mustache—that archetypical symbol
of Arab manhood—seemed to have lost its popularity with the young
generation. Many young female pedestrians wore fitted jackets, tight
pants, and high-heeled shoes or boots. If it were not for the hijab, you
couldn't tell them apart from young American women. I smiled to
myself, recalling the conservative dress code that the Peace Corps had
instructed us to abide by. Those wide, loose-fitting garments that we
were told to bring with us seemed awfully old-fashioned and unstyl-
ish compared to these tight pants and jackets. I noticed that the color
of a woman's hijab matched the color of her jacket or sweater, and
that the color of her belt matched the color of her shoes or handbag.
It was obvious that a lot of care went into putting together each outfit. Unveiled women tended to have heavy makeup on: kohl around
the eyes, mascara, eye shadow, rouge, and lipstick. Next to them were
also traditional women who were covered from head to toe in black
veils and abayas (outer wraps).

I was fascinated by the sights and sounds around me. I felt as
if I had gone "down the rabbit hole" and landed in an unknown
realm filled with amazing things. I didn't know why I felt this way.
After all, I had traveled in the Arab region before: I had been to
Morocco, Tunisia, and Egypt—the three Arab countries that, as a
Sabra, I could visit safely. I was intimately familiar with Arab culture

and had published several successful books about it. Why, then, all this excitement about Jordan? Perhaps it was because my intellectual curiosity and sense of adventure were at their peak at this juncture in my life. Perhaps it was because deep in my subconscious I perceived myself as an "alien from across the border" who had ventured into the "forbidden zone." And perhaps it was because I was going to stay in Jordan for two whole years as a Peace Corps volunteer.

Prior to my departure to Jordan, I had read in the Peace Corps *Volunteer Handbook* that volunteers' communications abroad are monitored by the local authorities: "Volunteers should assume that other persons or entities may be interested in the Volunteer's communications overseas, regardless of the method of communication the Volunteer uses. Landline and cell phone calls, email, personal mail, blogs, websites, or other forms of communication may be monitored either in a country of assignment or elsewhere. The concept of privacy that is accorded to private communications in the U.S. is not necessarily recognized or strictly respected in all countries" (p. 55). Aware that Jordan is not a democratic country, I had agreed with my friend Miri before I had left that I would never use the word "Jewish" in my letters. Instead, I would use the words "my sensitive skin" or "my freckles." When I came across an Internet café called Evolution opposite the main gate of the University of Jordan, I went inside and dropped her a note, saying: "Hi Miri. What is a little freckled girl like me doing on Jordan University Street in Amman? I have to pinch myself to make sure that I'm not dreaming and that this is all real. Everything is so fantastic. I feel like Alice in Wonderland." It was an innocent message expressing my sense of wonder and excitement, but I still had to be careful.

It was past noon and I hastened to return to the hotel to attend the J15 Amman orientation. When I arrived, all the volunteers were already gathered in the ballroom on the seventh floor, looking fresh and spruce. After a welcome speech by our programming and training officer, Bryan Butki, we were sent to various processing stations. First we signed documents for cell phone service and received basic cell phones. Then we posed for a head shot for Peace Corps Jordan identification. At lunch break, a lavish buffet was laid out for us in the dining room. After spending three days on the road, we were hungry for a hot meal and eager to taste Jordanian food. It was plentiful and delicious: soup, green salad, *kofta* (meatballs in a stew), *maqlubeh* (casserole consisting of layers of rice, vegetables, and chicken), and *muhalabiya* (rice pudding, made with rose water) for dessert. We sat in small groups around circular tables and chatted as we ate, getting to know each other's names and backgrounds.

After lunch, we felt energized and ready to resume our orientation. We received a review of the pre-service training program and ground rules, and went through five more processing stations. The first was a medical interview with Laurene Abu Anza, the Peace Corps nurse and medical officer. Canadian by origin, she was married to a Jordanian and had been living in Amman for many years. She asked me if I had any allergies or special requests. I told her about my G6PD deficiency and requested to be placed in a nonsmoking host family—Jordanians are known to be heavy smokers—and in a house that was equipped with a commode. My left knee cap was worn out and I was worried that having to bend constantly when using a squat toilet would worsen its condition. She wrote this down.

The second interview was with the country director, Alex Boston, and the safety and security coordinator, Samir Dahshan. Alex repeated what he had told me on the phone when I was in the United States: for the sake of my safety and efficacy it would be better for me to use a different last name. *Cohen* is simply too Jewish and thus risky, considering that the overwhelming majority of the people in Jordan are Palestinians. Samir nodded his head in agreement, his expression grave. Alex asked if I was willing to accept his recommendation and conceal my Jewish identity. I said yes. I was committed to doing whatever was necessary to carry out my work as a Peace Corps volunteer effectively. Assuming a different last name seemed like a small sacrifice—or so I thought. If I were to be asked this question three months later, I doubt that I would have given the same answer. But at that moment, my main objective was to *fit in*, just like everyone else.

My next interview was with the Jordanian training manager, Sultan Abu Dulbouh, and the programming and training officer, Bryan Butki. They both shared Alex's concern about my last name and wanted to know if I agreed to use a different name. I confirmed that I did. They asked if I had a middle name or a maiden name that I could use instead of Cohen. I replied that I had no middle name, and that my maiden name, Abudi, was unsuitable because it might mislead Jordanians into thinking that I was an Arab and thus put me in an untenable position. My parents were born in Iraq, where their families had lived for generations, adopting local proper names and surnames to avoid discrimination and persecution by the authorities. This was a common practice among Jews who had lived as an oppressed minority in the Diaspora, whether in the Middle East or elsewhere. I didn't want to pass myself off as an Arab. I wanted a neutral name, not Jewish and not Arab, a name that would sound American and would be easy for me to relate to. "What about *Seymore*?" I asked. Sultan objected. "It sounds too Jewish to me," he said. "Why?" asked Bryan. "*Simon* is a common Jewish name. Jordanians would recognize it immediately," he explained. "No, not *Simon*," I corrected him. "*Seymore*. I researched it on the Internet. It's an English name, originally spelled as Seymour." Sultan looked embarrassed. "I thought you said *Simon,*" he apologized. Bryan had no objection to Seymore. "How would this be done?" I asked. "You will use the name Seymore whenever you interact with Jordanians; for example, when you are with your host family in the village or with teachers and students at the village school. But to the Peace Corps staff you will be known by your real last name," Bryan explained. "What about the Jordanian LCFs (language and culture facilitators) who will be teaching us?" I asked.

"We will make sure that you will appear on their lists as Seymore," he said. "Do you have any other questions?" Actually, I did have one pressing question. I wanted to know if they had a language class that suited my level. I was eager to advance my Arabic skills and hoped to be placed in a class that would challenge me rather than bore and bog me down. But I hesitated to ask. I didn't want to come across as being pushy or arrogant. I said to myself: "Surely they have read my resume and know that I have a doctorate in Arabic. Why bother them? They have been doing this for years." So I refrained from asking, shook my head, and the interview came to an end.

When I rejoined my group, I learned that two other female volunteers had been approached by Alex regarding their names. Judith, of Hispanic background, was asked to adopt a different first name because Judith sounded "too Jewish." She refused. Claire, of Anglo-Saxon background, was asked to adopt a new last name because her own name, Goodman, sounded like a Jewish name. She agreed to replace it with her middle name. Both girls were Christians and had no trace of Jewish blood in their families. When I examined the list of all the volunteers' names that we had received, I realized that I was the *only Jewish* person in the entire J15 group.

The next processing station was an administrative one. Our passports were collected to be kept at the Peace Corps office in Amman. We would not be in possession of our passports throughout the pre-service training period; instead, we would carry a photocopy of the picture page and visa page as a form of identification. We had to fill out forms to set up a bank account and to sign for our bimonthly walk-around allowance. We were also required to sign the Peace Corps "Authorization to Use Personal Material" form. It was the exact same form that we had received during staging in Philadelphia, except that then we were told that it was *optional* and now were told that it was *obligatory*: unless we signed it, we would not receive our walk-around allowance. I told the financial assistant, Rania, that I couldn't sign this form. She said that I needed to speak

with Alex about this matter and obtain his approval. I approached
Alex and told him that I was a scholar and intended to use my personal material in my future publications. He accepted my explanation and I was exempted from signing the form.

We had supper at 7:00 in the evening. In Jordan, lunch is the
main meal of the day, and supper is a light, mostly dairy meal. We
had sliced tomatoes and cucumbers, *jobna* (cheese), hummus, *labaneh*
(yogurt cheese), olive oil, zaatar, baloney, and pita bread. We were free
to go out after that, but had to be back in the hotel by 10:00 p.m.
Most of the girls rushed to the malls to buy scarves, hair dryers, and
power adaptors for their laptops, while the guys preferred to explore
the city. I headed for Evolution Internet café on Jordan University
Street to check my email account and send letters.

Our orientation resumed the following day. In the morning,
we had a safety and security overview, a review of Peace Corps core
expectations and volunteer rights, a medical session, and a sector-based technical session (SE—special education, YD—youth
development, and TEFL—teaching English as a foreign language).
We were introduced to the Peace Corps staff in Jordan, including
the local instructors (LCFs) who were hired to teach us Jordanian
Arabic and traditional customs. The sessions were long, intensive,
and exhausting. At lunch, we were again served a lavish meal, which
consisted of a variety of salads, lamb with long-grained white rice,
grilled vegetables, and sweet desserts. In the afternoon, we had a
pleasant outing: a visit to Amman's citadel, where we had a picnic.
The weather was warm, the sky clear, and the view breathtaking. The
ancient citadel (Jabal al-Qala'a) sits on the highest hill in Amman,
offering sweeping views of the city and its vast urban sprawl. It is an
archeological site rich in remains dating back to the Bronze and Iron
Ages, as well as to the Hellenistic, late Roman, and Arab-Islamic
Ages. We strolled to the site of a small Byzantine church, gazed at
the temple of Hercules, which was built in the reign of the emperor
Marcus Aurelius, and roamed around the ruins of the Umayyad

palace complex. We visited the small museum on the citadel, which houses antiquities from prehistoric times to the fifteenth century, among them an exhibit of the Dead Sea Scrolls, a copy of the Mesha Stele, and four rare Iron Age sarcophagi. It was an enjoyable excursion and a chance to relax and get to know each other and members of the Peace Corps staff. We watched the beautiful sunset as we sat on the scattered rocks, snacked on kebab sandwiches, and refreshed ourselves with soft drinks.

It was already dark when we returned to the hotel, but the night was still young. Some volunteers wanted to go to a restaurant to have dinner, others to a café to have a beer and smoke sheesha (water pipe), and still others preferred to go shopping. Lora and I didn't join the same group. We agreed that whoever came back last to the room would enter quietly so as not to disturb the one already asleep. We were in two different sectors—she was in SE (special education) while I was in TEFL (teaching English as a foreign language), and we hardly spent any time together. I went with five other girls to a mall near the hotel. I was eager to look at *thoobs* (traditional robes or gallabiyas) for women. I found a couple of stores and tried on a variety of *thoobs*. They were beautiful, but even the smallest size was too big for me. My figure was slim, and I seemed to vanish inside these flowing robes. Perhaps they were meant for large and buxom women. I loved the colorful embroidery on the front and sleeves of these robes and hoped to get one for the swearing-in ceremony. Many volunteers, guys as well as girls, intended to wear the traditional Arab robe for the ceremony. We thought we would look cool in them.

I was impressed by the shopkeepers' friendly and relaxed attitude. They didn't pressure us while we browsed and didn't get angry if we left their shops without buying anything. The greeting *ahlan wa-sahlan* (welcome to Jordan) was repeated to us numerous times. I felt an affinity for the local people; after all, Arabs and Jews are "first cousins"—the descendants of the two sons, Ishmael and Isaac, of the patriarch Abraham. How ardently I wished that the Arabs would accept the existence of the tiny Jewish State. Imagine what Israeli know-how and technology combined with Arab oil and petrodollars could achieve. The Middle East would become the most prosperous place on the face of the earth!

I left the mall and walked along Jordan University Street toward Evolution Internet café. I had not heard anything about my brother since I had left the United States and I was worried. As on my previous visits, the Internet café was filled with Jordanian men who were smoking heavily. I sat at a computer terminal and logged onto my email account, hoping to find a message from my family about my brother. There was none. I wrote to my sister-in-law, asking how my brother was doing, and emailed the same query to my sister in Australia. I realized that from now on it would be difficult for me to communicate with them because I would have only sporadic access to the Internet during the entire period of pre-service training; it would be limited to the days when we would come from our villages to the Peace Corps training site on the campus of Al al-Bayt University. This meant that I would be out of touch for many days in a row during a stressful time in the life of my family. I hadn't foreseen this problem, and it worried me.

It was already curfew time when I got back to the hotel. Exhausted from the long day, and still jet-lagged, I decided to turn in, falling asleep as soon as my head hit the pillow. A couple of hours later, I was awakened by Lora's return. I thought that she would go to bed quickly, but she didn't. She started zipping and unzipping her bags, searching noisily for something, before she went to the bathroom and took a long shower. I heard the water running for at least half an hour. I was flabbergasted. Earlier, we had clearly agreed that whoever returned last to the room would be quiet and considerate toward the other. I looked at my watch; it was after midnight. I told myself that I wasn't going to start an argument in the middle of the night. Whatever needed to be said could wait until the morning. I inserted my earplugs into my ears, turned

my face to the wall, and waited for Lora to finish with her noctur-
nal activities. When she finally went to bed, I was wide awake and
unable to fall asleep again. I lay quietly, reviewing the details of our
schedule in my head. We had one more night at the Palmyra Hotel
before we would travel to the Peace Corps training site at Al al-Bayt
University in Mafraq, where we would stay for three days. I realized
that if Lora and I were destined to remain roommates, we needed to
establish some ground rules.

In the morning, I discovered that Lora had done her laundry at
night and hung it on the towel rod in the bathroom to dry. So this
was why I had heard the water running for so long. I waited until
she got dressed, then said, "Lora, we need to talk." She looked at me
questioningly. I went straight to the point. "It was inconsiderate of
you to make so much noise when you returned to the room late last
night." She snapped back, "What do you want me to do? Go to sleep
at 10:00 p.m. like you?" "No, of course not," I said. "You can go to
sleep whenever you feel like it. But please be considerate when you
come back late at night. Why not take your shower and do your laundry in the morning? We are both early birds." She turned red in the
face. "You know what? I'm going to tell the Peace Corps staff that
we don't get along and can't be roommates!" Calmly, I responded,
"That's not a productive approach. What kind of impression will this
make on them? As older volunteers we have to show that we can solve
our problems in a mature way." She pondered for a moment, then
said, "You're right. I'm sorry that I woke you up last night. I didn't
mean to wash my hair and do my laundry. It was an impromptu decision." I readily accepted her apology. "Never mind. It looks like you
don't need much sleep. Do you?" "No," she admitted. "Five hours of
sleep per night are enough for me." "You're lucky," I said. "You're
also a heavy sleeper and can sleep on a plane. I'm a light sleeper,
I can't sleep on a plane, and I need seven hours of uninterrupted
sleep at night." We laughed at our different natures, and then we
hugged each other and made peace. We never had another argument

after this, and we remained roommates throughout the period of our pre-service training.

That morning, the dominant topic of conversation at breakfast was Muammar Gaddafi's demise. On October 20, 2011, after eight months of bitter fighting, Libyan rebels captured and killed the dictator, liberating Libya from forty-two years of brutal one-man rule. We wondered how this development would affect the civil unrest in Syria, and whether this unrest would spill over into Jordan. Although Jordan is a relatively peaceful Arab country, it was impossible to predict what would happen. The entire Arab region was convulsing with revolutionary fervor. One thing we knew for certain: if the political situation in Jordan became unstable, we would be evacuated from the country at once. We hoped that this scenario would not take place—none of us wanted to go back home.

We were already familiar with each other's first names and there was a strong sense of camaraderie among us. We knew that for the next two years we would be each other's family, so we had better be nice to each other. Nevertheless, from the outset, certain preferences and alliances began to emerge, reflected in who we chose to sit next to in the dining room or in the classroom, and who we went out with in the evening. I didn't bond with anyone in particular, though I enjoyed the company of some volunteers more than others.

A long day crammed with technical sessions awaited us. We had discussions about the goals of pre-service training and a review of the entire schedule, we got the first shot in a series of immunizations, beginning with rabies, and we received informative handouts, including a phone list of all the J15 volunteers. I looked for my name. I saw that I appeared as Dalya Cohen on the list, not as Dalya Seymore.

In the evening, I went for a walk in the residential area surrounding the hotel. There was no sidewalk and a lot of construction material lay on the ground alongside the road. I moved slowly around piles of iron rods, building blocks, and wooden beams, careful not to trip and sprain my ankle—this was a common accident among volunteers, and one that the Peace Corps nurse had warned us against in our medical sessions. I was about to end my walk and retrace my steps when I saw a food store. Lo and behold! It was Safeway, my favorite American supermarket. I went inside and browsed around the aisles to see what items were available for their local customers and was pleased to discover that the shelves were well stocked; they even carried Colgate toothpaste and Listerine mouthwash. This meant that during future visits to Amman I would be able to replenish many of my basic necessities.

When I returned to the hotel, I sat in the lobby to watch television. I enjoyed listening to the sounds of colloquial Jordanian, trying to compare its pronunciation and vocabulary to colloquial Egyptian on the one hand, and to modern standard Arabic on the other hand. As I was sitting there, a large group of new guests arrived in two buses that pulled up by the hotel entrance. They were fair-skinned and blue-eyed and looked European, but the women wore hijabs and some of the men wore traditional Arab robes. They lined up by the reception desk to check in, speaking in a strange language. My curiosity got the better of me and I asked one of the women in English where they were from. She replied that they were Muslim pilgrims from Serbia on the way to Mecca to perform the hajj. They were traveling by bus to Saudi Arabia, and had stopped in Amman for a couple of days to rest. The men turned out to be a rowdy bunch. They made a lot of noise in their rooms and smoked heavily in the lobby, hallways, and even in the elevators. They noticed that we were an English-speaking group and eyed us with curiosity. One of them approached me and asked who we were and what we were doing in Jordan. I replied that we were American volunteers who had come to Jordan to promote world peace and friendship by helping to train the local people in various areas of work. He looked incredulous, even suspicious. He had never heard of the Peace Corps before, and the notion of young American men and women who would be willing to work without being paid for two whole years sounded utterly absurd to him.

Monday, October 24, was our last day in Amman. In the morning we had two language classes to introduce us to colloquial Jordanian. After lunch we checked out of the Palmyra Hotel and boarded a bus to the Peace Corps training site on the campus of Al al-Bayt University, which is located in the Eastern Desert, in the town of Mafraq, about 70 km to the northeast of Amman. We would stay there three days and then disperse in small groups to various villages in the area. The pace at which we moved from place to place was dizzying and the activities strenuous and challenging, but we were all in amazingly good spirits.

Mafraq is the capital of the governorate of Mafraq, which lies in the northeastern part of Jordan. It is the only governorate that has borders with three countries: Iraq to the east, Syria to the north, and Saudi Arabia to the south. Mafraq means "crossroads," because the town is located at the intersection of the road leading from Jerusalem to Damascus and the road from Tel Aviv to Baghdad. This strategic location is the reason that Mafraq is known for its military bases and has been used in the past in various military operations, notably the campaign by the legendary Lawrence of Arabia. Mafraq is also famous for Al-Noor Sanatorium for lung diseases, which is the only site for treatment of multidrug resistant tuberculosis in the Middle East. Al al-Bayt University, one of the public universities in Jordan, is located on the outskirts of the town. Opened in 1994, this institution of higher education, whose name means "People of the House of the Prophet," is renowned for Islamic studies. The Peace Corps began using the university campus as a training site for volunteers just two years earlier and was still in the process of adapting to its new location.

I sat by the window, watching the changing scenery. Amman's suburbs gradually disappeared, giving way to the *Badia,* a stony, arid, and desolate desert that extends to Iraq and Saudi Arabia. We passed by Zarqa, located 19 km northeast of Amman. Zarqa is Jordan's industrial center and the third largest city after Amman and Irbid. Currently, it is famous as the hometown of the Jordanian terrorist Abu Musab al-Zarqawi, who led a brutal insurgency in Iraq, including homicide bombings and kidnappings, before he was killed in an air strike in Baghdad in 2006. Beyond Zarqa, the desertscape—flat, barren, and bleak—surrounded us, merging with the horizon. Steel transmission towers carrying power lines and telecommunication cables crisscrossed into the wilderness. Jordan's deserts make up 80 percent of the country's land, but support only 5 percent of its population. While the governorate of Mafraq covers the second largest area in the Kingdom, it has the second smallest population density. The harsh desert climate, barren soil, and scarcity of water make it uninhabitable.

After a ride that lasted about two hours, we arrived at Al al-Bayt University. The campus, nestled amid graceful olive trees, looked like an oasis in the desert. It was clean, peaceful, and spacious. Long walkways shaded by blue, arched awnings connected the various faculty buildings. The Peace Corps training site comprised two double-story buildings accessible through a gated, rectangular courtyard. One building served as the women's dorm, and the other housed the Peace Corps offices on the first floor and the men's dorm on the second floor. An additional building, at a five-minute walk from the dorms, served as the Peace Corps classrooms. In front of the training site was a large open square that was utilized for social events. To the right of the training site was the Islamic Cultural Center, and facing it from across the square was the Faculty of Islamic Law.

The bus dropped us off at the square. We picked up our suitcases and rushed to the dorms to see our rooms. The rooms were pre-assigned, each one to be shared by two volunteers whose names were posted above the doors. Lora and I were given a room on the ground floor, close to the dorm entrance. It overlooked the inner courtyard and the communal kitchen, which was located across the walkway that connected the two buildings. We didn't expect to find any luxury in our rooms—we knew that our living conditions would be similar to those of our host community. But we didn't expect the women's dorm to be in such a state of neglect: soiled rugs on the floor, broken desks and chairs, stained foam mattresses, wardrobes smeared with graffiti, dirty walls and curtains, and thick layers of dust everywhere. Worst of all were the communal bathrooms: the toilets were filthy and downright gross, the sinks were full of grime, and all the faucets were broken, their handles missing; in the showers, the floors were covered in soap scum, slime, and hair, and all the drains were clogged, thus creating a breeding ground for germs and bacteria. It was quite obvious that the women's dorm was in a poor condition because of age and lack of care. This run-down place was going to serve as our second home for the next couple of months— once a week we would come here from our villages for what was referred to as "center days" in Peace Corps lingo, which entailed further training. Some volunteers had brought sheets from home; others, myself included, had brought sleeping bags. I realized that I had to be very careful not to catch a disease under such unsanitary conditions. Despite every precaution, within a couple of weeks I had contracted a nasty eye infection.

Our days at the training site were extremely structured: breakfast from 7:00 to 8:00 a.m., warm-up exercises and announcements from 9:00 to 9:30 a.m., language class from 9:30 to 10:45 a.m., discussion of cross-cultural information and homestay etiquette from 11:00 a.m. to 12:30 p.m., an hour lunch break, followed by another language class from 1:30 to 2:45 p.m., and a closing session either on health or on safety and security from 3:15 to 5:00 p.m. In the evenings we were free to do whatever we pleased. Usually, most of us rushed to connect to the Internet in order to read the news, check our email accounts, or use Skype to call home, which was a time-consuming activity with unpredictable results. Some of us would go for walks around the campus or visit the convenience store to buy snacks, even though we were well fed at the training site. For lunch, we were served a hot meal, buffet-style: we would scoop spoonfuls of salad, pieces of lamb or chicken cooked with long-grain rice, and dessert onto paper plates, and sit around the olive trees in the sunny courtyard to eat. For supper, we had a cold buffet consisting of pita bread, hummus, tahini, halva, apricot jam, yogurt cheese, baloney, and slices of tomatoes and cucumbers.

After supper, many volunteers would gather in the kitchen to drink coffee, listen to music, and play card games. Those who had brought a musical instrument from home would sit in the courtyard to play music. We had a guitarist, a saxophonist, and a harmonica player in our group, who would entertain us with their merry-making. But when the partying continued past midnight, the noise became a problem for those whose rooms were close to the kitchen or overlooked the courtyard.

I couldn't sleep until 2:00 a.m. the first night. Only when the lights were finally turned off in the kitchen and the partying ended did I get to sleep. I woke up the next morning feeling tired and cranky. I realized that this pattern of social activities would repeat itself night after night. Perhaps I had better move to another room on the other side of the building—there were plenty of spare rooms in the women's dorm. At lunch break I went to Stephanie, a J13 volunteer who was assigned to assist us during our pre-service training, and asked her to move me to a quieter room. Later that day she informed me that the homestay coordinator, Rifaat, had approved my request, but the new room would have to be cleaned first and therefore would only be available on our next visit to the campus. This meant that I would have to spend two more nights in my noisy room. Knowing that it would be a torture, I went to Maggie and Kasumi, who had a quiet room in the back of the dorm, and asked if I could bunk up with them for two nights. They had an extra bed in their room—all the rooms were furnished with three beds—and they didn't mind. At 11:00 p.m., I would move over to their room with my sleeping bag, and at 6.00 a.m. I would sneak quietly back to my own room. Lora, who was a heavy sleeper, slept through everything.

The language classes proved to be way below my level. It was uninspiring to sit with a group of beginners who were learning the Arabic alphabet and basic vocabulary. I wondered if Sultan and Bryan had really read my resume and aspiration statement. I approached Bryan and told him that I was getting bored in the language classes. "Imagine that you have a PhD in English language and literature and are placed in a class of beginners who have just started to learn the English alphabet," I explained. "I really want to use this time productively." Bryan said that he had a shortage of teachers and that he would see what he could do for me after we moved to our villages.

I wondered if I was I drawing unnecessary attention to myself. I felt like I was walking a tightrope. On the one hand, I was eager to excel in the acquisition of colloquial Jordanian. On the other hand, I was standing out from the group instead of blending into it. I noticed that on all the lists of volunteers' names that were posted on the bulletin board, above the classrooms doors, and above our dorm rooms' doors, I appeared as Dalya Cohen and not as Dalya Seymore. This bothered me. The Jordanian language instructors, who would accompany us to our villages, were not supposed to know my last name and, through it, my identity. Were Sultan and Bryan aware of this situation? Should I bring it to their attention? I hesitated. I didn't want to appear apprehensive.

Of all the technical sessions, I enjoyed most the ones on Jordanian culture and homestay etiquette. While Arab cultures share the same core values throughout the Arab region, local customs and traditions vary from country to country and even within the same country from urban to rural to Bedouin settings. We had fascinating presentations on how to interact with members of our host families and host communities. A lot of the restrictions on women have to do with gender segregation. When a woman is introduced to another woman, she can shake hands with her or kiss her on the cheeks: once on the right cheek, twice on the left cheek, and possibly once more on the left for good measure. But when a woman is introduced to a man, she is expected to put her right arm across her chest as a form of greeting instead of shaking (and thus touching) his hand. A woman should avoid eye contact with men when she is out on the street; she should lower her head and look at the ground. A female volunteer should not sit alone in a room with her host father and should not go for a walk unescorted. Some rules of homestay etiquette apply to both sexes: when you enter a Jordanian home, you should take off your shoes and leave them by the front door; when you sit on pillows on the floor, you should tuck your feet behind you or cover them with a small blanket; it is offensive to stretch your feet in front of you; it is offensive to sit on a chair and cross your legs; it is offensive to point the soles of your shoes in the direction of someone's face. As for table manners, you are expected to refuse food once or twice before accepting it; you should accept at least a small amount of food when offered; you should accept a cup of tea (or coffee) with the right hand only and eat with the right hand only (the left one is used for ablutions). With respect to private and public transportation, a woman should not ride alone in a car with a man, unless he is a close relative; when riding in a bus, women should sit in the back, men in the front; a woman should sit only next to a woman and she can ask a man to change his seat so that she will not have to sit beside him.

I was struck by the similarities between the rules of public conduct for women in a conservative Jordanian milieu and an ultra-orthodox Jewish milieu. In 1998 I spent a year in Israel and taught at the Hebrew University of Jerusalem. I used to travel by bus from Ramat Gan to Jerusalem International Convention Center (Binyanei Ha-Uma), and from there catch another bus to Mount Scopus. On these rides I often witnessed seat-shuffling taking place to ensure that ultra-orthodox passengers would not sit next to members of the opposite sex. Sometimes I was asked by an ultra-orthodox man to move to a vacant seat next to another woman so that he would not have to sit next to me. As for modest appearance, ultra-orthodox Jewish women are expected to cover their hair, arms, and legs, much like women in a conservative Jordanian milieu.

There were two taboos that we had to pay close attention to: sex and alcohol. A female volunteer was not allowed to socialize with a male volunteer, even if they lived in the same village. The consumption of alcohol, which is forbidden is Islam, had to be discreet; a volunteer found guilty of drunken behavior in public would be dismissed from Peace Corps service. We were told to examine every item that we threw into the garbage can because at night stray cats and dogs might tear up the trash bags and scatter their contents in the street. It so happened that a Peace Corps volunteer threw a *Sports Illustrated* magazine with pictures of models clad in skimpy swimsuits into the garbage can; in the morning the magazine was found lying in the street with the provocative pictures in plain sight. The village people, regarding it as pornographic material, were outraged, and the volunteer was expelled from the village.

Along with general guidelines that prepared us for living with a traditional host family in a village, we were also taught strategies of coping with inquisitive questions about our private lives, particularly our marital status, age, religion, and political orientation. We were told that Jordanians ask everyone such questions, even each other: Are you married? Why aren't you married yet? Do you have a boyfriend? How old are you? Are you a Christian? Do you drink alcohol? How much money does your camera cost? Can you get me a visa to America? Why does America support Israel all the time? Many of the answers that we were advised to give to such questions required that we *lie*: "No, I've never had a boyfriend. I'm still a virgin. I never drink alcohol. I don't know how much my camera costs—it was a gift from my father." There were two details of personal information that we were instructed to keep secret at all times: don't tell anyone if you are gay, and don't tell anyone if you are Jewish. As for politics, we were urged to avoid discussing it altogether by saying, "I don't know much about politics. It's not my area of interest." And if that failed, to use the ultimate excuse: "The Peace Corps *does not allow* me to discuss politics" (or do anything that was beyond the volunteer's call of duty).

It felt reassuring to have a stock of ready-made answers. My favorite reply to the question "Why aren't you married?" was "*nasib*," that is, fate. This response was guaranteed to stop any further questions and at the same time elicit sympathy. The belief in fate is deeply rooted in Arab culture. I was thoroughly familiar with this intriguing concept: in 2001 I published a book on the topic that won a prestigious academic award. Still, no amount of knowledge or preparation can predict real-life situations. As we later found out, we all had to use our wits, tact, and a good sense of humor to deal with unexpected personal questions, as well as stereotypes and misconceptions about Americans, which we encountered among our host families and host communities.

The highlight of our stay at the training site was the "culture night" that was held on October 25. That evening, a big tent was erected on the square in front of the Peace Corps buildings and a large crowd had gathered, including Jordanian dignitaries, Peace Corps staff members, J13 and J14 volunteers, and our J15 group. A troupe of Jordanian dancers dressed in traditional Bedouin garb performed a variety of debka dances to the rhythm of Arabic music. Then we joined the dancing, holding hands and forming a long line that wound around the square as we moved to the beat of tambourines. Afterward, we were introduced to the custom of henna staining: the girls had their hands and feet dyed with henna (a reddish-brown color) in exquisite patterns. I was already familiar with debka dancing and henna staining from my youth in Israel and my trips to Egypt. Finally, we were treated to the most popular Jordanian dish, *mansaf*: large round trays of steamed rice topped with pieces of lamb, along with pitchers of yogurt sauce, were placed on small round tables. We were invited to eat in the traditional way, that is, by scooping the food with our fingers (right hand only), or in the "modern" way, by using a spoon (with or without an individual plate). The evening was remarkable for both its cultural and social aspects, as it gave us the opportunity to meet Peace Corps volunteers from the two previous years and to hear their stories. I was struck by the significant number of elderly volunteers, who were in their late sixties to early seventies, in the J13 group. One of them, Sharon, looked particularly delicate and elegant. She told me that she was at the end of her Peace Corps service in the village of Taybeh near Petra in the south of Jordan. I was impressed by her stamina, totally unaware that our paths would soon cross again.

At night, our dorm rooms were hot and some of the girls slept with their windows open. In the morning, they discovered that it was a bad idea—their faces were covered with mosquito bites. I was spared this unpleasant experience because the windows in Maggie's and Kasumi's room remained shut at night. But Mona had slept with her window open. She looked awful, with red bumps all over her face. I noticed that she was staring at me in a peculiar way during our technical sessions, and wondered why. When we ran into each other in the kitchen, I asked her how she was feeling. She said that the nurse had given her some lotion to rub on the mosquito bites and an insecticide to spray in her room. Scrutinizing my face, she asked in a strange tone, "How come you don't have any mosquito bites?" I smiled and said, "Apparently my blood isn't sweet enough." She gave me a suspicious look and said, "I think someone has given me the evil eye. That's why I've got the worst mosquito bites in the whole dorm!" I gasped in surprise. A university-educated Arab American woman who believes in the evil eye! So that was why she was staring at me so peculiarly during our technical sessions. "The best way to keep the evil eye away is to keep your window shut at night," I advised her, trying hard to keep a straight face.

The incident with Mona and the "evil eye" reminded me of a similar affair that I had heard about from an English woman who was married to a Jordanian. I had met her when I had lived in the Netherlands. Her son had been in the same class as my son at the British School in the Netherlands and they had become close friends. Once, I had been invited to dinner at her house and she had told me an anecdote about her husband. She had gone with him on a trip to Seattle to visit his relatives and they had stayed in a hotel there. Soon after they had returned home, her husband discovered that he had forgotten his white jacket in the closet of their hotel room. He accused her of casting the evil eye on his jacket because she had not liked it from the day he had bought it. A couple of weeks later the hotel manager found the lost jacket and sent it back to its owner. I asked her what her husband's reaction was when the lost jacket had arrived. Did he still think she had given it the evil eye? "Absolutely!" she said, in all seriousness.

In the late afternoon of October 26, the names of our host villages were posted on the bulletin board of our classrooms building. Divided into small groups of four to six volunteers, each group with its own Jordanian language and culture facilitator (LCF), we were assigned to several villages in the Mafraq area. Mona and I were placed together, along with four guys, in the village of Hamadiyya. From that moment on, each and every one of us was preoccupied with a single thought: What would my host family and host village be like?

5 . VILLAGE LIFE

FILLED WITH NERVOUS ANTICIPATION, I BOARDED THE BUS THAT took me and five other volunteers the next morning to the village of Hamadiyya,[2] located in proximity to the town of Mafraq. I had one suitcase with me and a carry-on bag. We were instructed not to bring too much personal stuff to our host families—it might create a bad impression. After all, these were poor villages. Since we intended to travel back and forth between our training site at Al al-Bayt University and our host villages, we needed a carry-on bag in which to pack the basic necessities for our weekly overnight visits to the campus.

As usual, I sat by the window. The vast desert, harsh and unforgiving, was everywhere I looked. It brought to my mind several Arabic desert novels that I had read: Hanan al-Shaykh's *Women of Sand and Myrrh,* which is set in the Saudi Arabian Desert; Miral al-Tahawy's *The Tent,* which is set in Egypt's Eastern Desert; and Ibrahim al-Koni's *Anubis,* which is set in Libya's Tuareg Desert. These unforgettable novels offer a rare glimpse into the changing world of the Bedouins, whose traditional values and way of life have been altered under the impact of modernization. I wondered if I would see the effects of social change in my village too. Would I be welcomed into this still closed society?

After a relatively short ride the bus turned from the highway into an unpaved road, entering the outskirts of the village of Hamadiyya. Long, narrow streets lined with houses with flat rooftops and gated courtyards came into view. Unfinished foundation columns and iron rods rose from the rooftops into the air—a common sight in Jordanian towns and villages—indicating the owner's intention to build another floor one day. The rooftops were equipped with water tanks and television antennas and enclosed by three-foot-high walls to hide the laundry hanging to dry on clotheslines. There were animal pens and chicken coups in the courtyards, and sheep, goats, and chickens roamed freely in and out of them. Little vegetation met the eye except for olive trees, their branches heavily laden with olives, for it was the harvest season. The size of the houses, as well as of the land they stood on, varied, ranging from small to large. Some houses had a shabby exterior, others were whitewashed, and still others looked brand new. All the windows were protected by metal bars painted black or green. Three transmission towers loomed in the distance, and five minarets marked the location of five different mosques. The bus turned into a narrow dirt road, raising a cloud of dust behind it, and a few minutes later pulled up in front of a small house with an old white Fiat parked beside it. My LCF, a young Jordanian of Palestinian origin named Walaa, turned to me and said, "Dalya, this is your host family's house." I picked up my bags and got off the bus. She walked with me to the front door and rang the doorbell. A fair-skinned man in his mid-forties, dressed in Western-style clothes, opened the door.

"Good morning, Abu Omar," Walaa said in Arabic. "How are you? This is Dalya."

"Welcome, welcome," Abu Omar replied with a smile. He held out his hand to shake mine and invited us to come in. Walaa excused herself, saying that she had to take the other five volunteers who were on the bus to their host families, and hastened to leave. Abu Omar picked up my bags and led me inside the house. The front door opened into a small sitting room furnished in a traditional style with farshas (mattresses) and pillows on the floor, which was covered with a thick oriental rug in shades of blue. A sliding door on the right connected the sitting room with a small hallway leading to the kitchen on one end, the master bedroom on the other end, and the bathroom in between. Another door, directly opposite the front door, led from the sitting room into a small bedroom furnished with a bed and a wardrobe. The layout of the house reminded me of a passenger train in which the first car provides access to all the others.

"This is your room," Abu Omar said. He placed my bags in one corner and invited me for a cup of coffee in the sitting room.

I sat on the farsha, my legs stretched out in front of me, and Abu Omar sat opposite me.

"Nawal," he called out.

A woman in her early thirties, wearing a hijab and a traditional Arab robe, walked in through the sliding door.

"This is Umm Omar," the husband introduced her.

"Pleased to meet you," I said in Arabic as I rose to shake her hand.

"Oh, you speak Arabic," she said, surprised. She was tall and had a full figure. Her complexion was fair, her eyes dark, and her face was fully made-up.

"Yes, I do. I speak Egyptian Arabic and modern standard Arabic. Now I need to learn Jordanian Arabic," I said nervously.

She smiled and retreated behind the sliding door. Moments later she returned, carrying a tray with two cups of coffee and a small bowl of chocolates. She offered them to us, then set the tray on the floor and left the room. Abu Omar took a packet of cigarettes out of his pocket and asked if I minded if he smoked. I shook my head. Was I at liberty to object? He was the master of the house and I was a guest. He lit a cigarette and began to puff the smoke into the air. I tried to avoid breathing it directly, but failed. The room was too small and he was sitting close by. Ruefully, I realized that my request to be placed with a nonsmoking family had been ignored by the Peace Corps nurse.

"Well, Dalya, how do you like Jordan so far?" he asked in Arabic, mixing a few English words into his speech.

"I like it a lot," I replied in Arabic.

"How long have you been here?"

"One week."

"That's all?" He sounded astonished.

"Yes, we arrived in Amman on October 21."

"Is this the first Jordanian house you've been to?"

"Yes."

He paused for a moment. "Would you like me to teach you about us? Do you want to learn?"

"Yes, of course!"

"Let me tell you about our customs. First, when you enter a Jordanian house, you have to take your shoes off and leave them outside by the door."

Oh my God! I looked with dismay at my shoes.

"Then, when you sit on a farsha, you should tuck your feet behind you, or cover them with a little blanket if you want to stretch them in front of you."

Oh my God! I got off on the wrong foot with my host family! I was so nervous about meeting them that I had forgotten the basic rules of homestay etiquette that we had been taught!

I apologized to Abu Omar. "I'm so sorry. This won't happen again." I got up at once and rushed toward the front door. I opened it, took my shoes off, and placed them outside. Then I resumed my seat on the farsha, carefully tucking my feet behind me.

Abu Omar smiled. "You can put a pillow behind your back or under your arm to make yourself more comfortable."

"I'm okay," I said, terribly embarrassed.

"Don't worry. You will learn everything in no time."

Abu Omar proceeded to tell me that they had four children, two girls and two boys. The eldest, Latifa, was twelve years old, Omar, ten, Hasan, nine, and Zahra had just turned one. The older kids were still at school, and the baby must have been asleep because I didn't hear her make a sound. Abu Omar said that they were Syrians in origin and that they had lived in Saudi Arabia for many years prior to settling in this village. His parents and his wife's parents, who all resided in this village, were closely related: his father and his wife's father were brothers, which meant that he and his wife were first cousins. I wasn't surprised—cousin marriages are customary and common among Arabs. Abu Omar asked me about my religion. I said I was Christian. He said that he belonged to a religious brotherhood whose slogan was "Love for all and hatred toward none." Inwardly, I wondered if that included Jews as well.

There was a knock on the door and Abu Omar rose to open it. Bryan, our programming and training officer, was standing on the stoop. He had come to meet the host families of the six volunteers who were assigned to this village. Bryan didn't speak Arabic, so the conversation switched to English. After the handshakes and greetings, Abu Omar invited both of us for a cup of coffee in the formal reception room.

The reception room was attached externally to the main house and had a separate entrance. We followed Abu Omar as he exited the front door, walked to the far right end of the stoop, and unlocked a side door. We entered a large, sunny room furnished elegantly in a traditional style with farshas and pillows, a thick oriental rug, and decorative window treatments, all in matching colors of gold and brown.

"What a lovely room!" I exclaimed.

"Thank you," Abu Omar said, pleased.

We sat down on the farshas, and Bryan and Abu Omar engaged in small talk. A few minutes later Umm Omar appeared, carrying another tray with cups of coffee and chocolates. She served us courteously, then set the tray on the floor and left the room.

"How long have you lived in this village?" Bryan asked Abu Omar.

"We moved here about two years ago, when I finished building this house. We lived in the town of Mafraq before."

"What do you do for a living?"

"I work at the local municipality."

"And what do you do there?"

"I help them," Abu Omar answered vaguely. Bryan looked mystified. I tried to keep a straight face but inside I was shaking with laughter. The Yiddish term *gescheften* (literally, "air businesses"), meaning "obscure wheeling and dealing" sprang to my mind and triggered this reaction. There was an awkward silence.

"How big is the village?" I asked, steering the conversation in a different direction.

"It has about twenty-five hundred people."

"How many schools does the village have?"

"Two elementary schools, one for boys and one for girls, and two high schools, one for boys and one for girls."

"Where do the people of the village work?" Bryan inquired.

"Many work for the army or the government. Some have jobs in the town of Mafraq."

Bryan finished his coffee and placed the cup back on the tray. Glancing at his watch, he said, "It's getting late. I must move on. I have five other families to visit." He rose to his feet.

"Thank you very much for your hospitality," he said to Abu Omar and shook his hand.

"You're welcome," Abu Omar replied.

"Goodbye, Dalya. You have a great host family," Bryan said to me.

"Yes, indeed. Thank you for stopping by. Goodbye, Bryan."

Abu Omar locked the door of the reception room and took me back to the main house. Umm Omar was still out of sight. I followed him into the kitchen, where we found her busy cleaning up. He told her that he had to return to his work and left. We heard him start his car and drive off.

I looked at Umm Omar in astonishment. Her outward appearance had completely changed. Gone were the hijab and robe; instead, she was wearing a knit blouse and a pair of pants. Her hair hung loose around her face, its dark color contrasting with her fair complexion. Later on, I learned that this was how she always dressed around the house. Only when she went out did she put on the traditional Arab garb. If family members dropped by for a visit, she didn't bother to cover her hair or arms. But if a stranger knocked on the door, she immediately covered up. There were different rules and degrees of revealing and concealing, according to the type of social interaction.

Now it was Umm Omar's turn to talk with me and figure me out. She was clearly bursting with curiosity.

"Do you know that Dalya is an Arabic name? It means 'a hanging vine' in Arabic."

I nodded in acknowledgment, thinking of the famous Druze village, Daliyat al-Karmel, on the slopes of Mt. Carmel in Israel. "Yes, I know. But I'm named after the flower. It has many colors and grows in many countries around the world." I actually meant to bring pictures of dahlias with me to show to my host family, but I forgot.

"Are you married?" She cut straight to the chase.

"No, I'm not."

"Why?"

"*Nasib,*" I said with a shrug. "I haven't been lucky."

She looked at me sympathetically. "Do you have children?"

"How can I have children if I'm not married?" I asked, feigning ignorance.

"But I saw on television that American women get pregnant and have babies without getting married."

"*Some* women do, not all women. Most women want to get married first. I personally believe that a child needs both a mother *and* a father to grow up well-adjusted."

She nodded her head in agreement. "Do you live with your parents?"

"No. I live alone. In the United States single women can live alone if they want to."

"How old are you?"

"Thirty-six."

She stared at me in disbelief.

"I stopped counting the years after my thirty-sixth birthday," I explained with a wide grin.

She laughed, then moved on to the next question. "Are you a Protestant or a Catholic?"

"I'm a Protestant." I replied cautiously, sensing danger. I wasn't well versed in the differences between the various Christian denominations.

"Do you go to church to pray?"

"No. I pray in my heart. I go to church on the major holidays."

"The Prophet Muhammad said, 'Christians are the closest in friendship to Muslims,'" she said, attempting to put me at ease.

I was familiar with this Koranic verse. The fact that she recited it and mentioned several other sayings and traditions attributed to the prophet Muhammad indicated to me that she was a devout Muslim. I assumed that this was closely related to her having been raised in Saudi Arabia. Later, I also saw her pray whenever the muezzin's call to prayer sounded from the mosque.

She stood at the sink, washing some cups and dishes and putting them on the dish rack to dry. My eyes roamed around the kitchen, a cramped space equipped with the bare necessities: an old refrigerator, an old cooking top with three burners, and a traditional Arab stove. The heavy metal cylinders that supplied buta gas to the stove and cooking top were in plain sight. There were no cabinets—all the pots and pans, dishes and bowls, as well as canisters of rice, flour, oil, sugar, etc., were kept on a shelf underneath the countertop and a frayed curtain hid them from view. The kitchen floor was covered with small square tiles in mottled gray. A white plastic table, the kind that is used as patio furniture in the United States, stood in the middle of the kitchen, and six plastic chairs were stacked up against the wall. Pale light filtered through the sheer floral curtain that covered the small window overlooking the street, and a buzzing fluorescent tube on the opposite wall was the main source of light.

The sound of a baby crying suddenly came from the master bedroom. Umm Omar dried her hands quickly and rushed out of the kitchen. I heard words of endearment followed by noisy kisses, and then she emerged with Zahra in her arms. Zahra was a skinny, redheaded baby who could babble a few words and walk on her own. Her eyes were brown, her hair was short and curly, and her ears were pierced with tiny pink studs. She was still breastfed, even though she already had eight front teeth, four on each gum. Umm Omar brought her close to me and said, "Look who's here! This is Dalya." Zahra turned her head away and then buried it in her mother's breast.

"She's so sweet!"

"She is the apple of my eye," Umm Omar said. "Before she came, my other three kids were already big and in school, and I was free to do with my time whatever I pleased. But I missed having a little baby to cuddle and keep me company. So I decided to have another child." She nicknamed her *dubba* (literally, "a female bear"). It was clear that Zahra was a much loved—and spoiled—baby. She was teething—her first molars were coming out—and the pain made her cry at lot, especially at night.

Suddenly, the front door was flung open and three excited kids burst in. Latifa, the eldest, looked exactly like her mother, with big black eyes, dark hair, and fair skin. Although she was only twelve, she wore a hijab, which meant that she had already had her first period.

She hugged and kissed me, saying that she was very happy that I had come to live with them. Omar, the older boy, shook my hand and smiled shyly, and so did Hasan, who had a much darker complexion than his siblings. Latifa couldn't wait to tell me that she was a student at the girls' elementary school where I was assigned to do my practicum. She hoped that I would come to her class to observe and teach. She had already told all her classmates that an American teacher was coming to live in her house. She was proud, as her two brothers were, to be my host family.

They were a nice bunch of kids. Of course, they immediately wanted to show me all their games, vying with each other for my attention. They took me to a corner of the sitting room where an old computer, with no connection to the Internet, rested on a stand, and showed me their favorite video games. We played together, shooting a villain, then racing a car, and they were delighted to score more points than me. Afterward, they insisted on showing me a video of funny Arabic cartoons, each of which elicited peals of laughter from them. I watched the cartoons and the children's reactions to them in amusement. Suddenly, there appeared an image of two airplanes crashing into twin towers, causing them to explode and collapse to the ground in piles of rubble. My host family's children roared with laughter. I stared at this image in horror, unable to believe my eyes. Before I could recover from the shock, there appeared an image of an Arab boy riding on a donkey that had a patch with the Star of David and the word "Yahudi" (Jew) attached to its neck. My heart sank and my stomach was in knots. I wondered if Abu Omar and his wife were aware of the "funny" cartoons that their children were watching. Was the Jordanian Ministry of Education informed of the videos that were made for children's entertainment? Surely these negative images were bound to leave a permanent mark on the children's minds. But, however upset I was, I wasn't at liberty to say anything. In our technical sessions, we were emphatically told *not* to criticize any negative aspect that we might encounter in the homes of our host families, and *not* to interfere in their lives, even if we didn't like what we saw. We were there as *guests*, not as jurors or judges.

I excused myself to go to the bathroom to extricate myself from this unpleasant situation. I had heard that some village houses were equipped with a commode and had specifically asked the Peace Corps nurse to place me in such a house. But when I opened the door to the bathroom I was disappointed: it had a squat toilet. The cartilage in my left knee was worn out and my knee hurt when I bent it. I made many trips to the bathroom during the day. How long would I be able to assume the squatting position without developing a serious problem? The bathroom was small and its location did not afford a sense of privacy because it was directly across from the sitting room sliding door, which was kept open all the time. The hole in the floor had a trap door that flipped open when something heavy, like stool, dropped on it and then clapped shut so noisily that it sounded like an explosion. The sudden loud bang reverberated throughout the small house, announcing to everyone what had transpired in the bathroom. For a self-conscious person like me, it was a mortifying experience.

Umm Omar had finished preparing lunch and called us to eat. To my surprise, we ate seated around the kitchen table, which was laid out with spoons and plates. She placed on the table a round tray full of white rice topped with a few pieces of chicken and served us portions. Traditionally, village people eat seated on farshas on the floor, using their right hands to scoop food from the communal tray. Perhaps Umm Omar thought that since I was a foreigner, it would be easier for me to sit at a table and eat with a spoon (there was no fork or knife). She gave me a bony drumstick and a heap of rice. There was flatbread on the table and a small plate with slices of tomato and cucumber. I ate the few morsels of meat that I managed to scrape from the bony drumstick, a little rice, and a couple of slices of tomato and cucumber. At home, I hardly ate bread, and certainly not at dinner; my meals were based on fish, dairy products, fruit, and vegetables, as I watched my weight and cholesterol level. At the Palmyra Hotel in

Amman and at the Peace Corps training site at Al al-Bayt University, we had received decent meals. Here, at my first lunch with my host family—lunch being the most important meal of the day—I felt hungry. There wasn't really much to eat other than carbs—white rice and white flatbread. I looked at my watch. It was almost 3:00 p.m. Perhaps supper would be served early. I sat quietly until everyone had finished eating and then helped Umm Omar clear the table.

I noticed that Latifa had a lot of household chores to do. If she wasn't taking care of her little sister, she was vacuuming the carpets or doing the dishes. Zahra was irritable, crying at nothing and everything, her teething gums making her cranky. Every now and then Umm Omar would pick her up and cover her with kisses, calling her *dubba* and other terms of endearment. All of a sudden, I felt very tired. The first meeting with my host family, especially the nervous tension that preceded it, exhausted me. I needed to get some rest.

I left the four kids in the sitting room and went into my room. There was a pink coverlet with a matching decorative pillow on the bed. I removed them and put them inside the wooden wardrobe, a worn out piece of furniture whose interior had a musty smell and whose doors squeaked when I opened and closed them. I rested my weary body on the bed; it was bouncy, and the metal springs poked me through the thin foam mattress. I fetched my sleeping bag, rolled it out on the mattress, and lay down on top of it. I closed my eyes and hoped to nap a little. Just then, the kids turned on the television in the sitting room and the shrieks of animated cartoons echoed in my room. I inserted earplugs into my ears, but it was to no avail. The television volume was too high and the door offered no protection from the noise on the other side of it. Then Zahra started to cry. Umm Omar called out to Latifa to take care of her sister. Latifa protested, saying that she was doing her homework. The boys started fighting with each other, their screams rising above the loud television. I sighed with despair. This would be my home for the next couple of months. Would I survive?

Around 6:00 in the evening Abu Omar returned. I heard his voice in the sitting room and smelled the cigarette smoke, which wafted into my room from under the door. I thought it would be impolite to stay in my room any longer. I tidied myself up, took a deep breath, and crossed the threshold into the sitting room. Abu Omar was sitting on the floor with Zahra in his lap, listening to his children talking all at once. There was a tray with a coffee cup and an ashtray with several cigarette butts beside him. He smiled amicably at me and invited me to join him and his children. Umm Omar came out of the master bedroom and joined us too. She was still dressed in casual clothes and looked fresh and animated. We chatted about small things for about half an hour. Then Abu Omar rose, saying that he was going to visit his parents, and left. Abu Omar's parents lived in the back of the olive grove that stretched behind his house. They had a big house, to which they had added another floor to accommodate one of their married sons with his wife and children. Abu Omar visited his parents every evening. He ate supper with them and returned home late at night, when everybody was already asleep.

Meals in Jordan don't have a fixed time. Breakfast can be as late as 11:00 a.m., lunch as late as 3:00 p.m., and supper as late as 9:00 p.m. My daily schedule started at 7:30 in the morning, when I had to go to the village girls' elementary school to observe classes until 11:00 a.m. From 11:00 a.m. to 1:00 p.m., I had to be at the Peace Corps classroom, and then I would go home to rest for two hours. From 3:00 p.m. to 6:00 p.m., I had to be back at the Peace Corps classroom. This meant that I had to have breakfast before 7:30 a.m., when I was due at the village girls' elementary school, and lunch before 3:00 p.m., when I was due at the Peace Corps classroom. As it turned out, Umm Omar paid little attention to my schedule. Sometimes I had no lunch because it wasn't ready on time, and sometimes I had no breakfast or supper because there was nothing for me to eat in the house. I anticipated that I would lose weight during the months of pre-service training, but I didn't worry. At the end of this period, I would move into my own apartment, where I would cook my own meals and regain whatever weight I had lost.

We had supper around 8:00 p.m. Again, we ate seated at the kitchen table. To my disappointment, supper was a meager meal: it consisted of two tiny bowls, one with olives and the other with yogurt, a plate with mini wedges of processed cheese, and flatbread. We tore off a piece of flatbread, dipped it in the yogurt, and ate it with an olive. The olives weren't cured long enough and tasted bitter. The kids relished the processed cheese, but I didn't touch it. I wished that I could have a whole cup of yogurt rather than a few drops clinging to a piece of flatbread. I was still hungry from lunch. I wondered why there was no zaatar and olive oil on the table—they are the staple food in every Arab home. How would I quiet my hunger? Umm Omar offered me a cup of tea, and I jumped at the idea. Tea would calm my stomach, but it had to be herbal tea, without caffeine. I explained to Umm Omar that if I drank caffeine at this late hour I wouldn't be able to sleep at night. She took a few leaves of na'na, put them in a glass, and filled it with hot water. I let the leaves infuse for a while and then drank this herbal tea, which had a cool mint flavor. Jordanians drink at lot of dark, very sweet tea all day long. I knew that sooner or later, I would have to participate in this ritual—there was no escape from it, especially at the village girls' elementary school—but right now I could excuse myself because it was nighttime.

After supper I helped Latifa do her English homework. She was a diligent student and her grades at school were high. English was her favorite subject. In fact, English is the most popular foreign language in Jordan, if not an undeclared second language. Shopkeepers, cab drivers, and people on the street love to speak English with foreigners. As soon as they figure out that you are not a local person, they switch to English, no matter how poorly they speak it. Latifa's pronunciation wasn't as good as her knowledge of grammar, a problem that most schoolchildren in Jordan have because they learn to pronounce the words the way they are spelled. I tried to get her to speak English with me, but she was too shy and self-conscious, so we spoke only in Arabic.

It was well after 9:00 p.m. when I retired to my room. The next day was Friday, the Muslim holy day, which is a day off for everyone in Jordan. I could spend the entire day with my host family and continue to bond with them. Without taking a shower, I changed into my pajamas and crept into my sleeping bag, falling asleep instantly. I had no idea how long I had been asleep when I was awakened by Zahra's crying. In the stillness of the night, her voice was shrill and piercing. I thought that Umm Omar would quickly calm her down and that we would all go back to sleep, but Zahra kept crying, and Umm Omar didn't seem to care. I waited and waited, and the crying went on and on. Perhaps Umm Omar was too tired to get up from her bed for her daughter. But where was Abu Omar? How could he sleep through this racket? After all, they shared the same room with their baby. I lay awake, feeling utterly helpless. How could I adjust to these living conditions? How could I function without sleep?

Zahra cried without interruption through the rest of the night. My earplugs and pillow and bed covers were of no use. The walls were too thin and the house too cramped to offer any privacy or refuge. I was still awake at dawn, when the muezzin's call to prayer came, transmitted over loud speakers from all five mosques in the village. Around 7:30 in the morning, Latifa and her brothers, who slept together on farshas in the sitting room, got up and immediately turned on the television. Shortly afterward, a strong smell of cigarette smoke began to creep into my room from under the door. The commotion in the sitting room grew louder still. I heard Abu Omar talking with his kids, who sounded very animated. An hour later I heard him say goodbye to them and the front door slammed shut. I rose, took my towel and toiletries bag, and, still dressed in my pajamas, opened my door. Six pairs of eyes turned toward me, staring in curiosity. I smiled faintly and said "Good morning" as I stepped into the sitting room. The sliding door that connected it with the hallway leading to the interior parts of the house was wide open. When I passed through, I quickly glanced right and left. Umm Omar and Zahra were nowhere to be seen. They were probably napping after the long restless night. I was amazed that they weren't disturbed by the loud television and the children's racket in the sitting room. I went into the bathroom and wanted to take a shower, but no hot water came out of the faucet and even the flow of cold water was very weak. I looked at the water heater tank that was installed in the upper corner of the bathroom. It was very small, barely enough for one person's use. How did it serve all six members of this family? I washed my face with cold water and stared at the squat toilet with dismay, then I reluctantly assumed the position, careful not to splatter pee on my legs. "Practice makes perfect," I told myself, as I cleaned up the mess that I had created.

Back in my room, I put on a pair of loose-fitting pants and a long sweater, and tied my hair back in a ponytail, before I ventured into the kitchen to make myself a cup of Turkish coffee, something I couldn't start my day without. It was a habit that I had acquired during the year that I had spent in Israel, teaching Arabic literature at the Hebrew University of Jerusalem. I always looked forward to this first cup of coffee, which I drank leisurely while reading the daily newspaper or one of my favorite magazines. Now I sipped my coffee while reviewing Peace Corps handouts in my room. It was well after 10:00 a.m. when I set foot in the sitting room. Zahra and Umm Omar were already up and about and the place was bustling with activities.

"How did you sleep?" Umm Omar asked me immediately, looking worried.

"Fine," I lied.

"Did you hear Zahra crying?"

"Yes."

"She was terrible last night," Umm Omar apologized. "She didn't want to sleep in her crib. She wanted to be at my breast all the time. The minute I put her in her crib, she started screaming."

So this was the reason for the continual disturbance in the middle of the night! Zahra had a temper tantrum and terrorized the entire household. Now she was all cheers and smiles, wobbling on her tiny feet from one end of the room to the other. The boys were playing a video game on the computer. She wanted to join them, but they pushed her away, saying that she would ruin the computer. She instantly started to scream. Umm Omar picked her up and gave her the breast. Zahra sucked at it avidly.

"Doesn't she bite your nipples when she sucks?" I asked, baffled. After all, this baby had eight front teeth.

"No, she's gentle." Umm Omar said, kissing her daughter. "She can't eat anything. She has allergies to all baby formulas. Breast milk is the only food she tolerates. That's why I continue to suckle her."

Umm Omar was comfortable breast-feeding her baby in front of her boys and me.

Omar came up to me, holding a little green book in his hands.

"Dalya, can you hear the voice on the loudspeaker outside?" he asked.

"Yes," I said.

"Do you know what it is?"

"It's Friday's sermon, delivered by the imam at the mosque."

His eyes lit up. He held out the book in his hands. "Do you know what this book is?"

I took the book from him and paged through it. "It's the Koran," I said.

"Can you read it?"

"Yes."

He opened the Koran on the first chapter, the Fatiha (Opening), and asked me to read it out loud for him. I actually knew it by heart. When I studied for my PhD at Georgetown University, I took a year-long course on the Koran. My professor recommended that we learn by heart a few suras (chapters) to get the flavor of the text, its diction, and rhyme. To date, I had not forgotten the Fatiha.

Omar beamed with delight. "Do you want to study the Koran with me? We can study a portion every day."

I was stung by his words. Was this ten-year-old boy proselytizing? His suggestion was utterly bizarre. Umm Omar, who was listening to the conversation, intervened.

"Omar, leave Dalya alone. She has enough to study."

I glanced at my watch. It was almost 11:30 in the morning and we hadn't eaten breakfast yet. I noticed empty bags of potato chips lying around. The kids must have snacked. When would breakfast be served? Were we waiting for Abu Omar? I didn't dare ask where he was. I assumed that he went to the mosque. Zahra finished suckling at her mother's breast and struggled to break free from her arms. Umm Omar kissed her all over, calling her *dubba* repeatedly, then let go of her.

"Now we'll have breakfast," she announced.

"Do you need any help?" I asked.

"No, thanks. Latifa will help."

I followed her into the kitchen anyway. Latifa removed the chairs from the stack and placed them around the table. Umm Omar put three mini bowls on the table: one with olives, one with yogurt, and one with slices of cucumber and tomato. Then she took flatbread and warmed it over the flame of the gas burner. The smell of burnt bread wafted in the air, whetting my appetite. The boys were called to join us, and we all sat down to eat. Once again, I tore off small pieces of flatbread, dipped them in the yogurt, and put them in my mouth. I tried the olives; they were still bitter, probably the same as yesterday's. I took a few slices of cucumber and tomato, careful not to monopolize the mini bowl. This wasn't enough. My stomach was growling. Where was the legendary Arab food hospitality? I wondered. So far I hadn't encountered it in this house. Surely, this family wasn't *that* poor. They were all well dressed and owned a car and lived in their own house. Most importantly, they were *paid* to feed me. In fact, they were paid *a fortune* to feed me—about JD200 every two weeks. Hosting a Peace Corps volunteer was a lucrative business. Perhaps they hadn't had time to do food shopping before my arrival. No, this was absolutely inconceivable. They knew in advance when I was coming. To allay my hunger, I drank several cups of hot herbal tea. Inwardly, I consoled myself, "This is only your second day here. Wait and see. It's too early to judge."

I spoke in Arabic with everyone in my host family. In the beginning, I used a lot of *fusha* words (modern standard Arabic) to express myself. Then, little by little, I began to replace *fusha* words with words in colloquial Jordanian. In fact, my difficulty wasn't so much with interference from the *fusha* in my speech as with interference from colloquial Egyptian. I had specialized in colloquial Egyptian when I was at the American University in Cairo and spoke it fluently. It differs from colloquial Jordanian in pronunciation, syntax, and vocabulary. I didn't find colloquial Jordanian to be difficult, just different. I walked around with a pen and a notebook, writing down the differences and making vocabulary lists. My oral Arabic skills, a bit rusty from lack of practice, were improving dramatically.

After the late breakfast, we had visitors. Umm Omar's sister and sister-in-law (who was also her cousin) stopped by. It was clear that they were dying to meet me. They were completely covered up when they came to the door, but as soon as they entered the house they took off their abayas, revealing outfits that consisted of bright-colored sweaters and casual pants. The sister-in-law, Fatin, had just graduated from Al al-Bayt University with a bachelor's degree in English, but felt more comfortable speaking in Arabic with me. Umm Omar's sister was married and her two little kids were with her. They started playing with their cousins and their racket drowned our voices, so Umm Omar sent them to play outside. As soon as they left, Fatin turned to me and began to pepper me with questions.

"Are you married?"

"No," I said with an amused grin.

"Why not?"

I shrugged my shoulders. *"Nasib!"*

She looked astonished. She didn't expect this answer. It's an answer that closes the subject. Who can argue with fate?

"Do you live alone?"

"Yes."

"Isn't it hard for you to live alone?"

"No. Many people, both men and women, live alone in the United States."

"Here, it's not customary to live alone."

"I know," I said. "I think it's nice to have your family around you."

I got the impression that Fatin was conflicted: on the one hand, she wanted to be independent; on the other, she was attached to her family. She lived in her parents' house, of course. The youngest of their eleven children, she had her own car and was allowed to study at the university, but living by herself was out of the question.

"Why did you come to Jordan?"

"To help Jordanians learn about American culture and society, and learn from them about Arab culture and society."

"How much are you being paid?"

"I'm not being paid at all. We're volunteers."

She curled her lip in a show of skepticism. The notion of "Americans who work for free" was as fantastic to her as a flying saucer.

Fatin asked if I could tutor her for the TOEFL exam. She needed to obtain a high score on this exam in order to be admitted to the master's program in English at Al al-Bayt University. She was weak in grammar and reading comprehension. I told her that I would be happy to help her. I would have to inform my Peace Corps supervisors about it, but I had no doubt that they would grant me permission to tutor her in my free time.

When the guests left, I went to my room to rest—I was exhausted from the constant social interaction, especially after enduring a sleepless night. I curled up on the bed and instantly dozed off, when suddenly I was startled by forceful banging on my door. What on earth was going on? I waited, hoping that the banging would stop and that whoever was at the door would go away, but it persisted. I heard Abu Omar's voice calling out my name.

"Dalya! Dalya!"

I jumped from the bed in panic and hurried to open the door.

"Yes," I said in a trembling voice, fearing that my secret had been discovered.

"I want you to meet my brother, Kamal. He's a teacher of English at the village boys' elementary school," Abu Omar turned toward a young, red-haired man by his side.

"Kamal, this is Dalya."

I muttered automatically, "Nice to meet you" and put my right arm across my chest.

The situation was awkward. My disheveled appearance revealed to them that I had been napping.

"We'll see you later," Abu Omar said apologetically.

"Yes, later," I replied in a weak voice.

I heard the front door open and slam shut. They must have left. I heaved a weary sigh, feeling physically and emotionally drained. It would be impossible for me to maintain any personal space here. I must get used to this new reality. I must be tough and hang in there. I now realized why the dropout rate among Peace Corps volunteers is the highest during the period of pre-training service.

I tried to rest while the commotion behind my door continued. An hour later, I gave up and left my room, saying to myself, "If you can't win them, join them." The sitting room was a hub of activity, what with the television and the computer and the front door. The children were constantly coming and going, bringing with them friends and cousins. Obviously, Friday afternoon was not an appropriate occasion for "alone time." I found Umm Omar in the kitchen with Zahra.

"Hello Zahra," I said. "Do you want to play with me?"

Zahra peeked at me from between her mother's legs.

"Come, let's play!"

She gave a joyful shriek and ran away from me. Umm Omar laughed.

"I'm going to prepare lunch now, Dalya. Do you want to watch me cook?"

"Sure. Can I help you?"

She pointed to a big pot of potatoes sitting on the table. "These potatoes need to be peeled and diced. Do you know how to do this?"

I nodded my head affirmatively. Of course I knew how to peel potatoes, and I showed her.

"Now cut this potato into small pieces."

I placed the potato on a flat plate, as there was no cutting board, and began to slice it along its length and breadth.

Umm Omar smiled. "Now let me show you how *we* do it."

She took the peeled potato and held it up in one hand. With the other hand, she used a knife to make close vertical cuts, about half an inch deep, into the potato. Then she made close horizontal cuts into the vertical cuts. Small potato cubes started dropping onto the plate. I looked at the knife. It was very sharp and I was accident prone. My hands had several scars from handling knives clumsily when I was cutting bread, fruit, or vegetables—and I was attempting to cut big slices at that! Now Umm Omar was asking me to dice potatoes, with a sharp knife, without using a cutting board! I was terrified. I looked at the pot on the table. There were at least ten big potatoes in it. Would I manage to accomplish this task without cutting one of my fingers off? The Peace Corps nurse told us to stay away from kitchen knives—they were the leading cause of accidents among volunteers. I was faced with a dilemma, but I couldn't back out of the situation without losing face.

"I'll try," I said in a small voice.

Umm Omar brought me a chair to sit on and placed a clean bowl before me. I took the knife and began to cut up the potato as she had shown me. I worked slowly and with the utmost care. I knew that one careless movement could cost me dearly. From time to time Umm Omar came to check on me. I breathed a sigh of relief when I finished dicing the first potato. After I had cut up two more, I laid the knife down and stopped. I didn't want to push my luck.

"My hands are tired," I said to Umm Omar.

"That's fine. I'll do the rest."

"What are you cooking?"

"*Siniyat dajaja.* It's chicken baked with diced potatoes, tomatoes, and onions. What makes it special is the aromatic combination of spices, including cinnamon, nutmeg, pepper, and cardamom, which I put in it."

I wondered why the potatoes had to be diced if they were going to be baked anyway. They would most likely turn out like mashed potatoes. Arab cuisine is based on a lot of chopping, dicing, and mincing. Dishes like tabouleh and fattoush are tasty and appealing, but quite labor intensive and time consuming because of all the fine cutting involved.

Umm Omar placed the pan with the chicken and vegetables in the oven to bake for forty-five minutes. Today, she was dressed in a velour blouse and matching pants, which revealed her full figure. Her hair shone with a rich chestnut luster imparted by henna dye. She looked pretty and vivacious. Her initial reserve toward me had vanished, and she was quite talkative. "Perhaps I've made a good impression on her sister and sister-in-law," I thought to myself. Later on, I learned that many of her relatives had objected to her hosting a Peace Corps volunteer in her house. First, the idea of a total stranger coming to live with her family was unacceptable to them. Second, they thought that her house was too small to accommodate a guest for a lengthy period of time. Indeed, Latifa had to give up her own bedroom for my sake, sleeping with her brothers on farshas in the sitting room. But after Umm Omar's relatives had seen me and spoken with me, their reservations and concerns had dissipated.

I was watching television with the kids in the sitting room, when the front door opened and Abu Omar came in. Latifa jumped from her seat and rushed to him, took his hand, and kissed it in deference. Abu Omar placed his other hand on her head, stroking it affectionately. Zahra wobbled on her tiny feet toward him and tugged at his pants. He picked her up and hugged her tenderly, planting many kisses on her face. She giggled with joy. He then sat on the floor and played with her, letting her climb over him and pull his pen out of his shirt pocket. He tickled her, called her *ayuni* (the apple of my eye) and *habibti* (sweetheart), and said repeatedly, "Daddy is crazy about you." I watched them with great interest. This pattern of father–daughter interaction was quite different from the traditional cultural model depicted in many Arabic autobiographies and social studies that I had read. Abu Omar was warm and loving toward his little daughter—not cold or stern. It was a heartwarming scene.

Lunch was ready around 3:30 p.m., and Umm Omar called us into the kitchen. I wished that we would eat in the traditional way, seated on the floor rather than at the table. It seemed so strange and unnatural to eat from an individual plate with a spoon. Umm Omar served portions of the *siniyat dajaja* on the kids' plates and mine, but she and her husband ate straight out of the tray, which was placed between the two of them. Abu Omar praised Umm Omar's cooking, saying that it was delicious, so I hastened to compliment her too, and she beamed with satisfaction. As soon as Abu Omar finished eating, he lit a cigarette, blowing a cloud of smoke in my direction. The bitter smoke filled my mouth and throat, giving me heartburn. Involuntarily, I began to cough.

"Are you sensitive to the smoke?" he asked.

"Yes," I admitted.

"I will just have this one cigarette."

His wife and kids didn't seem to mind the cigarette smoke, although Umm Omar had complained to me that she suffered from an unknown allergy that caused her constant sinus congestion and runny nose. I ate the meat that I managed to scrape from the bony drumstick on my plate and some of the minced potatoes, which, after baking, looked and tasted just like mashed potatoes, then put my spoon down, even though I was still hungry. The meal was heavily based on starch and carbs, with no fiber and little proteins. I realized that I needed to take vitamin supplements to make up for the lack nutrients in my meals. When lunch was over, Umm Omar told Latifa to do the dishes. Latifa protested that the water in the faucet was too cold, so her mother heated up a kettle of water for her.

I had spent almost the entire day indoors and felt cooped up. I wanted to take a walk outside, and Omar and Hasan volunteered to accompany me. In this village, like any other traditional Arab village, a woman is not supposed to go out for a walk by herself. She must have a male escort, even if he is a young boy. I went out, flanked by my two "bodyguards." They showed me their neighborhood—a nameless street with an unpaved dusty road and shabby-looking houses on both sides. A group of kids who were playing outside eyed me curiously. With my uncovered head, I was attracting attention. They followed us, shouted repeatedly in English, "Hello, how are you?" What's your name?" and giggled at their own words. Omar and Hasan yelled at them to go away. Brimming with pride, they took me to see their father's *doukkan* (shop). It was a small and dingy place with mostly empty shelves, except for bottled water, soft drinks, cigarettes, and assorted candy. They made me promise that I would buy bottled water only from their father's *doukkan*. After walking for about an hour, we decided to turn back.

When we arrived at the house, Abu Omar was already gone and Umm Omar was alone in the sitting room. She looked tired and lonely.

"Where's Zahra?" I asked.

"She's napping in her crib."

"Wouldn't this disrupt her sleep at night?"

"I hope not," she sighed. "She's teething and the pain makes her cranky."

I wanted Umm Omar to show me how to use the shower, but hesitated to ask. She had finally gotten a rest from Zahra and her household chores, and it would be inconsiderate to bother her now. I glanced at my watch—it was after 6:00 p.m. When would the day end? I longed to go to my room and be by myself, in complete silence. The next day, a Saturday, I was supposed to meet my group at the Peace Corps classroom. I wondered what their experiences were like. Our placement with a host family was like a lottery—we had no say in the matter. How did they fare?

At 8:30 in the evening, we had a meager supper similar to the one we had the day before: flatbread with bitter olives, yogurt dip, and a few slices of tomato and cucumber. Umm Omar asked me why I ate so little. I replied that I liked having hummus or olive oil with zaatar for supper. I knew that these foods were nutritious and very cheap. She apologized that she didn't have any in the house. Her son Omar fetched a pen and a piece of paper to make a list of items to buy for me. "What do you like to eat for supper, Dalya?" he asked. Emboldened, I said that, in addition to hummus, olive oil with zaatar, and jam, I would like to have a cup full of yogurt to eat with a teaspoon, like pudding. The local yogurt (*laban*) was lean and plain, without added flavor or sugar, and I loved it. Omar wrote everything down carefully, and gave the list to his mother. I thought it sweet of him to fuss over my food like that. I was confident that I would have all these things for breakfast and supper the next day.

I finally retired to my room. It was a long day and I desperately needed to get some sleep. It turned out to be another rough night. The boys were rowdy, the baby cried constantly, and the television was switched on even though no one was watching it. The kids didn't have school the following day, so they were allowed to go to bed as late as they wanted. I slept fitfully, jolted into wakefulness numerous times by the nonstop uproar all around me. When morning came, every muscle in my body ached from tension and exhaustion. Still, I had to meet my obligations for the new day. I dragged myself out of bed and into the kitchen to make my morning cup of coffee so as to clear my head and get my "engine" started. Then I went to the bathroom to wash up at the sink. To perform these two simple tasks, I had to change my footwear three times: I had to wear socks to walk on the rug in the sitting room, slippers to walk on the tiled floor in the kitchen, and flip-flops to go into the bathroom. In traditional Jordanian homes, you are not allowed to wear bathroom slippers anywhere else in the house because the bathroom floor is considered unclean, mainly because of the squat toilet. Jordanians leave their bathroom slippers, usually cheap ones made of plastic, outside the bathroom door and slip them on when they go into the bathroom. I kept my flip-flops in a plastic bag in my room to make sure that no one else would wear them. In our medical sessions, we were told to observe strict hygienic rules to avoid fungal infections, such as athlete's foot, which can be transmitted by sharing footwear.

I had to attend my language classes in the morning. I skipped breakfast—the idea of a few morsels of bread dipped in a tiny bit of yogurt and consumed with a couple of bitter olives didn't appeal to me. I hoped that for supper I would get hummus, zaatar, and olive oil, as I had been promised. After I had finished getting dressed, I carried my shoes in a plastic bag to the front door and put them on outside. This "ritual" surrounding the shoes was wearing me down—I couldn't leave them outside at night for fear that they would be stolen, a common occurrence in the village. Whenever I came home, I took them off by the front door, put them in a plastic bag, and carried them to my room. Whenever I left the house, I carried the bag to the front door and put my shoes on outside. I discovered quickly that wearing sneakers with shoelaces was not a good idea because it took a long time to tie and untie the shoelaces. I needed shoes that I could slip on and off easily. At the same time, sneakers were the only shoes in my possession that were sturdy enough for the rough, unpaved village roads.

Walaa came to walk me to the Peace Corps classroom. She wore a hijab, a tunic sweater, straight-leg pants, and high heels. I smiled inwardly. We were told to wear outfits that would hide the shape of our bodies, and here was my Jordanian LCF openly contradicting these cultural assumptions. Walaa was plain, short, skinny, dark-skinned, and flat-chested. Aged twenty-something, she came across as being immature, arrogant, loud-mouthed, and narrow-minded. This was her first teaching job. She had been hired for three months only, until the end of our pre-service training. Unemployment in Jordan is high, and young people, even those who are university educated, do all kinds of odd jobs to earn a bit of money.

We walked up the unpaved street and then turned left into a narrow, paved road. It was the village main street, where the post office, the girls' elementary school, and a dozen small shops were located. Although it was early in the morning, many young boys were already outside, hanging around or playing. They followed us, shouted repeatedly in English, "Hello, how are you?" "What's your name?" and then roared with laughter. We arrived at the girls' elementary school, an old and run-down building surrounded by a gated courtyard. On the façade of the building hung a big portrait of King Abdullah and his eldest son, with the slogan *Kulluna al-Urdun* (We are all Jordan). A barrel of garbage stood by the gate, emitting a nauseating smell of burnt plastic from the incinerated trash inside. We left the school behind us and continued down the road, passing an open field with three transmission towers. The Peace Corps classroom was located in Mona's host family's house, at the far end of this long road. By the time we reached our destination, we had walked from one end of the village—the eastern quarter, to the other end of it—the western quarter, and had covered the distance of about one and a half miles in forty-five minutes.

Village streets don't have names. Mona's host family's house, which looked spacious and fairly new, stood at the corner of a short and nameless street facing the field with the transmission towers.

Walaa pointed to a big house at the other corner of the street and said, "This is where Zach is staying." She pointed to a nice house across the open field and said, "This is where I'm staying." And then she added casually, "Damen and Will are roommates in a house around the corner from Zach, and Mat is in another house nearby." I listened to her in amazement, trying to process this information. There were six of us in this group. Five were placed in nice houses in close proximity to each other and to the village boys' and girls' elementary schools. One was placed in a crummy house, far away, literally at the other end of the village. I was that person. Who had made this decision and on what basis? I was puzzled.

We opened the courtyard gate of Mona's host family's house and entered. The space by the entrance was occupied by a sheep pen and right next to it was a chicken coop. A strong smell of animal dung hung in the air and the sound of sheep bleating mingled with the clucking of chickens. We walked up the stairs leading to the front door. On the left end of the stoop was a side door that opened into a room that was externally attached to the main house—this room was rented out to the Peace Corps to serve as our classroom. We would come here to have Arabic classes every day, except for Fridays, from 11:00 a.m. to 1:00 p.m., and then again from 3:00 p.m. to 6:00 p.m. From 8:00 a.m. to 11:00 a.m., we would observe or teach English classes at the village elementary schools.

My group was already inside, exchanging impressions about their host families. Mona was elated: she had a big and sunny room, the bathroom in her house was equipped with a commode, and her host father was a nonsmoker. Damen and Will had an indulgent host family who fed them all kinds of special Arab dishes and pastries. Zach had a television set and a computer in his room. And Mat was treated like a prince by his host family, who drove him around in their car and stuffed his pockets with sweets and nuts. I felt pricks of envy when I heard their stories. I thought to myself: *It's true that this village is poor, but even in a poor village there are those who have more and those who have less.* For some unknown reason, the five members of my group had been given much better accommodation. They were well fed and rested, whereas I was hungry and sleepless. They were all clustered together within a few minutes' walk from each other, from the village elementary schools, and from the Peace Corps classroom, while I was isolated at the other end of the village. I had to walk approximately six miles per day from my host family's house to the girls' elementary school and the Peace Corps classroom. They were young, in their mid- to late-twenties, while I was much older. Where was the logic in this?

Walaa started our first Arabic class, going over basic vocabulary and pronunciation. I sat there, observing her and the group in silence. Americans have difficulty in pronouncing the guttural sounds of Arabic, specifically the *'ayn, qaf, kha,* and *ḥa,* and in following the rules of Arabic grammar. Mona spoke the Palestinian dialect from home but could not read or write modern standard Arabic. Walaa asked each of us to repeat after her certain Arabic words. The four guys in the group found it hard to get their tongues round these words. When my turn came, I pronounced all the words smoothly and effortlessly. When I finished, Mona turned to me and asked in a strange tone, "Dalya, from where do you have such perfect pronunciation?" All eyes stared at me, waiting for my answer. I smiled and said, "This comes from a lifetime of learning and practice." She looked at me suspiciously and said, "Your pronunciation is flawless. There must be another reason. Do you speak Hebrew?" Her question startled me. I was afraid that she was going to expose my identity. She knew that my last name was Cohen—it appeared on the volunteers' telephone list that was given to all of us. Why ask me this question in front of Walaa? In our safety and security sessions, we were emphatically told to protect each other's sensitive personal information and abide by a code of silence. Affecting nonchalance, I said, "I speak Dutch, and Dutch has a lot of guttural sounds in it." By way of illustration, I enunciated in Dutch the number 888, which contains a series of *kh* sounds in a quick succession: *acht honderd acht en tachtig.*

It sounded funny, everybody laughed, and the tension was defused. I realized that my knowledge of Arabic was arousing envy in Mona. Perhaps I had better stay away from these classes—I was bored stiff in them anyway. I should look for something more useful to do with my time. I made a mental note to speak with Sultan and Bryan about it on our next "center day."

The class ended at noon. Mona's host mother, Umm Khaled, invited me for lunch. She cooked *maqlubeh,* a delicious casserole consisting of layers of rice, vegetables, and chicken. I was faced with a dilemma. On the one hand, I wanted to stay and have a good meal. On the other hand, I worried that my host family might be offended if I ate elsewhere. So I politely declined the invitation, saying that my host family was expecting me for lunch. Umm Khaled was only twenty-seven years old but looked much older because she was overweight and had already borne three children. A kindhearted and hospitable woman, she always served us tea during classes and allowed me (but not the guys) to use her bathroom. As I prepared to go home, Walaa offered to escort me. I saw no need for that as I already knew the way.

The sun was high in the sky when I started walking back. The village main street was full of young boys who were hanging around, bored with nothing to do. From my uncovered head, and the fact that I was walking alone, they could tell that I was a foreigner. A bunch of them began to follow me, continually shouting the same two phrases in English at me, "Hello, how are you?" "What's your name?" I ignored them and walked on. Some villagers wearing traditional Arab garb came toward me. I greeted them politely in Arabic and continued to walk briskly. I could feel dozens of eyes watching me, scrutinizing me. Women stared at me from rooftops and the windows of their houses. It was a small village and I was a new face—a stranger. I was confident that in a few days, the novelty of my arrival would wear off and no one in the street would pay any attention to me.

I was wrong. My regular walks to and from the girls' elementary school and the Peace Corps classroom became increasingly unpleasant with time. I made this walk four times a day: at 7:00 in the morning, at 1:00 in the afternoon, again at 2:30 in the afternoon, and finally at 6:00 in the evening. The afternoon walks were the most stressful. Rough boys in the street would shout obscenities at me, curse me, and throw stones at me. I became concerned for my safety.

Meanwhile, the situation with my meals and sleep showed no signs of improvement. I noticed that Umm Omar rarely left the house. It was Abu Omar who did the shopping and brought home the food. It was not unusual for the family to run out of basic provisions and to have to wait a couple of days until Abu Omar replenished them. I once opened the refrigerator to look for something to eat and it was completely empty—there was nothing on the shelves, not even old leftovers. The promise to provide hummus or olive oil and zaatar for supper remained unfulfilled. For lunch, I continued to get meals high on carbs and low on proteins, and always remained hungry. Fruit was kept hidden, although the kids knew where to find it, and I would often see peels of oranges or bananas in the kitchen. I knew that my host family was being paid a lot of money for my room and board, about JD200 every two weeks. It was an excellent source of income for them. But I was underfed. I started to lose weight and feel weak. I always looked forward to our weekly visits to the training site at Al al-Bayt University, where we would get decent meals. I learned that I wasn't the only volunteer in the J15 group who encountered this problem. A couple of girls told me that sometimes they received merely bread with a boiled egg or fried eggplant for dinner, and rarely had any fresh vegetables or fruit. But no one else experienced this problem to the extent that I did. Umm Omar and Abu Omar were certainly nice people. But where did the money that they received to feed me go?

There was no time to waste. We had come to the village to learn about traditional Arab life and elementary school education. The guys in our group did their practicum at the boys' elementary school, and Mona and I did ours at the girls' elementary school. The school's condition was a sorry sight: broken door handles, broken chairs and desks, dirty floors and walls, flaking paint and plaster, no heating in the winter, and no air conditioning in the summer. The classrooms were small and crowded and the bathrooms were unsanitary, with squat toilets that gave off a stench and broken faucets without running water.

The school day began at 7:30 in the morning, when all the teachers gathered in the improvised sitting room located in the entrance hall. Every teacher who arrived greeted those who were already present personally, going from one woman to another and shaking her hand or hugging and kissing her. Then the ritual of drinking sweet tea began: cups were filled out and passed around. If there were any last-minute changes to the schedule of classes due to a teacher's illness or absence, they were discussed and posted on the bulletin board. At 7:45 a.m., there was a fifteen-minute assembly in the school courtyard. All the students lined up in orderly rows arranged according to their classes, from the first to the eighth grades. The principal, her two assistants, and the teachers stood on a concrete platform across from the students. The assembly began with a recitation of the first chapter of the Koran, the Fatiha, in unison. Next, the national anthem was sung, and then the Jordanian flag was hoisted on the pole. Afterward, there were warm-up exercises, brief announcements, and dress code inspections (the girls had to wear uniforms and were not allowed to put nail polish on their fingernails).

As I stood there, watching the scene, my thoughts drifted to the distant past, when I was a young girl standing in the morning assembly of my elementary school, about two hundred miles from here—across the border. My school assembly was similar in structure to this one, but different in content. It began with a recitation of selected verses from the Bible by one of the students, then we sang the Jewish national anthem and proceeded to raise the Israeli flag on the pole. Next, we had warm-up exercises, followed by short speeches or announcements, and lastly inspections of our heads (for lice) and fingernails (for trimness and cleanliness) were conducted. I grew up in Lod, a mixed Arab-Jewish town 15 km southeast of Tel Aviv, which is 110 km from Amman. When I was in the fourth grade, an Arab boy named Arafat was seated next to me. He was older than the rest of the class by a couple of years. Shy and taciturn, he rarely spoke or asked for anything. On Muslim festivals, he used to bring a large bag of clementines or candy to class and treat us to it. We would have a party, eating the fruit and throwing the peels or candy wraps at each other for fun. Once, he invited the whole class to come to his house, which was located midway between the towns of Lod and Ramle. Escorted by our class teacher, we made the trip on a specially chartered bus. When we arrived, we saw a big flat-roofed house, made of Jerusalem stone, surrounded by a whitewashed wall. A vast citrus orchard stretched beyond the wall, comprising rows upon rows of orange, clementine, and lemon trees. Arafat's family, dressed in traditional Arab attire, welcomed us warmly and let us roam around freely. I remember that the place, which was secluded and serene, seemed like an enchanted realm to me, filled with mystery and wonder. And here I was, several decades later, a scholar of Arab culture and society and a Peace Corps volunteer in Jordan. Who could have imagined that my path would lead me here?

After the assembly, the students rushed all at once into the school building. There was a lot of pushing and shoving and screaming and yelling as they ran through the hallways, climbed up the stairs, and disappeared into their classrooms. On my first day of practicum, I chose to observe an English lesson in the first grade. My plan was to work my way up from the lowest grade to the highest one, so that I would get a general impression of the entire English program at the school. I was surprised to see a few boys among the girls in the first-grade class, even though it was a girls' school. I learned that in government schools, boys and girls can be mixed together up to the fourth grade, after which they are segregated: the boys go to an all-boys school and the girls to an all-girls school. It was a small class of about twenty kids, seated in pairs in two long rows. When the teacher entered, they stood up and greeted her in English in unison: "Good morning, teacher. How are you?" She replied, "I'm fine, thank you. Sit down, please." She was holding a two-year-old toddler in her arms. The toddler had a runny nose and flushed cheeks and was coughing. I assumed that the toddler's mother would soon arrive to fetch her child but no one came and the toddler remained in the classroom throughout the entire lesson. I then assumed that she must be the teacher's own child. Perhaps her babysitter had called in sick in the morning and she had no one else to help her. The affection that the teacher displayed toward the little girl, frequently kissing and caressing her, reinforced my assumption that she must be her own daughter. From time to time she put her down and let her walk around the classroom. The toddler seemed completely at ease in this setting; she didn't cry or whine, as if she was used to it. She would approach a student's desk and grab a book from it, then go to another desk and grab a pencil or a crayon, distracting the kids, who were watching what she was doing rather than paying attention to what the teacher was saying. With a gentle reprimand, the teacher asked the class to pay attention to her, then picked up the toddler and held her in her arms once again. It must have been hard for her to teach and look after the toddler at the same time, but she seemed relaxed and not the least bit irritated or uncomfortable. When the bell rang, announcing the end of the class, I asked her if the toddler was her daughter. To my surprise, she said, "No. She's the vice principal's daughter. There's no daycare center for her where they live, so she comes to school with her mother every day and we all help to keep an eye on her." Indeed, during my two-month practicum, I saw this toddler at school every day, moving between different teachers and different classrooms. Sometimes she stayed in the kitchen with the custodian, and sometimes she stayed in the teachers' room with a teacher who had a free period. No one treated her as a burden or a nuisance; on the contrary, everyone was kind to her. This was *not* because she was the vice principal's daughter, but rather because the teachers, who were all women, and most of them wives and mothers, knew how hard it is to juggle two jobs—the home and the work-place—and genuinely wanted to help. I discovered that the teaching staff was a close-knit group, like a family, with a strong sense of sol-idarity and mutual support.

I enjoyed the time that I had spent with the first-grade students. In my career as a teacher I had always worked with adults and being with such young kids was an entirely new experience. First-graders are so sweet and impressionable; they look up to the teacher with eyes full of affection and admiration. It was common for a first-grade girl to approach me with a gift of a flower or a candy and to say that she wanted to give me a kiss or a hug. As volunteers could choose the grades that they would teach at the end of the pre-service training, I began to consider seriously the idea of teaching first-graders.

Naturally, I was the center of attention in the classes that I attended. First, the teachers would introduce me to their students, saying that I was an American teacher of English who came to live and work in Jordan. Then they would ask the students to introduce themselves to me by stating their full names. I noticed that many of the students shared the same last name and learned from this that they were related and that the entire village population consisted of three large clans. In the higher grades that I observed, and later co-taught with my Jordanian counterparts, there were marked dif-ferences in the students' level of knowledge and constant issues with classroom management. Because of lack of resources, low, interme-diate, and advanced level students were placed together in the same class. This made the teacher's task extremely difficult. The advanced students would jump in their seats with their hands up, shouting *Sitt! Sitt! Sitt!* (Miss! Miss! Miss!) so that the teacher would call on them, while the weak students would stare blankly at the blackboard or engage in disruptive activities. Throughout the lesson there were constant interruptions from outside: students would knock on the door and come in asking to borrow a textbook, a piece of chalk, the cassette recorder, or the portable heater. Many classroom doors had a broken latch or no handles and couldn't be closed. The teacher would place a chair or a plank against the door to keep it shut, and every time someone came knocking, she had to remove it to open the door and position it back there again. It was a time-consuming nuisance.

A day in the village girls' elementary school consisted of six to seven periods, each forty-five minutes long, with two fifteen-minute breaks. At the end of the sixth or seventh period, all the students and teachers went home. If I happened to walk home, many students— whether they knew me or not—would tag along with me. They would cluster closely around me, tug at my jacket or my sleeves or pull my arms to get my attention, repeating the same set of questions in English over and over again, "What's your name?" "How are you?" "Where do you live?" They had no sense of personal space. Surrounded by a throng of schoolchildren, I would feel besieged, almost smothered, with barely enough room to move my legs and step forward. After experiencing the hassle of walking home during dismissal time, I started to leave a little earlier or later in order to avoid this situation.

The school had about four hundred and fifty students from the first to the eighth grades. Each grade was divided into two or more classes, with up to thirty students per class. There were about twenty-eight teachers, ranging in age from mid-twenties to early fifties. The administration included the principal (*mudira*), a vice principal, a secretary, and a custodian (*adhina*). We were advised to make friends with the principal and the custodian because they could give us access to the classrooms after school hours in order to carry out extra-curricular activities with the students.

I had never worked in a girls' school before and had no idea that they could be extremely rowdy and unruly. Some of the classes that I observed were so noisy that the teachers had to yell repeatedly at the girls. On one occasion, the teacher punished a troublesome girl by telling her to stand in a corner of the classroom with her face toward the wall for twenty minutes. On another occasion, the teacher angrily slapped a girl across the face. From my male colleagues in the village, I learned that corporal punishment was swifter and harsher in the boys' elementary school, where some male teachers used a stick or a ruler to discipline boys who misbehaved. I could tell from the girls' clothes and outward appearance that many of them were very poor. Everybody sat in the classroom with their coats and hats on; it was early November and quite chilly indoors, especially in the mornings. The school provided the students with textbooks free of charge, but they had to supply their own pencils, crayons, erasers, etc., and it was *aadi* (normal) to see students without any writing implements.

The school curriculum included history, geography, math, science, computer studies, religion, Arabic, English, home economics, and physical education. Because I became exempt from attending the Peace Corps classroom, I could stay at school the entire day and spend my time observing classes on any subject that interested me. It was a privilege for me, as a scholar of Arab culture and society, to sit among Jordanian schoolchildren and learn with them history, geography, science, and so on. I could observe the methods of instruction, the teacher–student modes of interaction, and the learning materials provided for the students. I was struck by the relaxed and informal atmosphere in the classrooms. The teachers were kind to the students and patient with them, making sure that everybody understood the lesson in progress. They were flattered that I wanted to attend their classes and surprised that I could follow them in Arabic. When they learned that I had a doctorate in Arabic, they were impressed and treated me with great respect and appreciation. They began to address me as "Daktora Dalya" (Dr. Dalya) and deferred to me on various matters, educational as well as personal.

A teacher's salary at the village girls' elementary school ranged between JD240 and JD280 per month, depending on her degree and years of experience. A *mudira*'s salary ranged between JD260 and JD290 per month. Despite the low salary, (an income of JD400 or less per month is considered below the poverty line), teaching is regarded as a great job for a woman because of the short workdays, the many paid vacations, and the fringe benefits. For example, during the summer break and half-year break, a teacher continues to get a full salary, and after giving birth, a teacher gets three months of paid maternity leave. In addition, a teacher gets health insurance and social security benefits. Given the difficult economic condition in the Kingdom, Jordanian men prefer to marry girls who have jobs or are employable. But getting a teaching job at a school has become exceedingly difficult in recent years because all the positions are already filled.

English, a priority in the country's foreign languages, was a popular subject among the students. The teachers of English were all native-born Jordanians with little exposure to spoken English and little opportunity for practice. (After all, who could they speak English with in the village?) They made mistakes in pronunciation and grammar, which they transmitted to their students. One of the most common mistakes was the pronunciation of the word "clothes," which they tended to pronounce as "closes" (as in "she *closes* the door"). The discrepancy between the spelling of English words and their actual pronunciation, the occurrence of silent letters as in "knee" and "autumn," and the enunciation of the consonant *p,* which doesn't exist in the Arabic alphabet, were major difficulties. The English textbooks selected by the Jordanian Ministry of Education for use in elementary schools were a British series titled *Action Pack,* which covers the first through eighth grades and is a rich source of classroom materials and activities, including flash cards and cassette tapes. However, there was only one cassette recorder in the entire school and sharing it meant that it was not always available when needed. More often than not, there would be a knock on the door in the middle of a classroom drill, and a student would enter and say that teacher so-and-so needed the cassette recorder. The teacher would stop the drill at once and hand the cassette recorder to the student. The shortage of teaching aids, whether auditory or visual, was a big problem at this school.

Most of the teachers were married and had children. There were only four single women, among them the principal, who was in her early fifties. Although the teachers shared close ties with each other (and some of them were also related by blood or by marriage), they were not a homogenous group. For one thing, they differed in their degree of religiosity, which was manifested in their views and style of clothing. Some were veiled and wore black abayas, others wore the traditional Arab *thoob* or dress, but the majority wore Western-style clothing. Everyone, without exception, covered her head with a hijab. A few of the young teachers smoked cigarettes, but they did it discretely in the kitchen, where they wouldn't be seen. In the village, smoking was considered shameful for young women but permissible for elderly women. Some teachers expressed liberal views about marriage and male-female relationships and others expressed conservative views. They were eager to learn from me about dating, sexual mores, family values, and women's interests and concerns in the United States. Whatever they knew about American culture and society was derived from watching movies on television, and these movies gave them a distorted image of a society characterized by violence, crime, corruption, drugs, promiscuous sex, gay couples, and single mothers with children born out of wedlock. And here I was, an American woman, debunking these stereotypes and misconceptions with firsthand accounts.

Of course, they wanted to know if I was married and if I was a Christian or a Muslim. The idea that I could be anything else—a Buddhist or a Hindu or an agnostic or an atheist—never crossed their minds. When I said that I was a Christian, one of the veiled teachers began preaching to me that Islam was superior to all other religions. She was openly proselytizing while the other teachers looked on in silence. When she finished, I said calmly, "We are all God's children

and we all believe in God, who has different names, according to our
different cultural traditions." Then, to put an end to this unpleasant conversation, I got up and left the teachers' room. I went to the
kitchen and stayed there until the bell announced the beginning of
the next period. The following day, when I met with my Jordanian
counterpart to prepare an English lesson for her class, she said that
she wanted to apologize to me for yesterday's incident in the teachers'
room. She thought that her colleague's lecture on the superiority of
Islam over other religions was inappropriate and that it might have
hurt my feelings. She wanted to assure me that the rest of the teachers respected my religious beliefs and had no intention of converting
me to Islam. I was touched by her sincere and sensitive words. We
hugged and kissed each other in a show of reconciliation and then she
treated me to homemade cookies and, yes, sweet tea. The subject of
religion was never brought up again.

The ritual of drinking sweet tea was inviolable. Before classes,
between classes, and after classes, tea was consumed in large quanti-
ties. I would take small sips from my cup so as not to finish it quickly
because then I would immediately be offered another cup. I generally
preferred Turkish coffee to tea because it was served in a small *finjan*
(coffee cup) and contained less sugar. We would sit around the petro-
leum heater, steam rising from our drinks, and chat about this and
that. The married teachers loved to tell me the stories of how they
got married. I was amazed to hear that even among the older generation there were women who defied the custom of arranged marriage and refused the prospective husbands selected by their parents.
Some were married to their cousins, others to men from the same
clan or village, and still others to fellow students they had met at the
university. All of them came across as being confident and assertive.
Education and employment have done a great deal to boost their
self-image and self-esteem. They were always dressed nicely, taking
care to change their hijabs and outfits on a daily basis. I had no idea
that hijabs came in such a wide variety of colors, sizes, and manners

of tying, which allowed them to express their sense of style. As for beauty products, they loved to apply makeup. Their eyes were always beautifully enhanced with kohl, their lips painted with lip gloss or lipstick, and their cheeks rubbed with rose water or touched with rouge. In a society where a woman's hair and body must be covered in public, whatever remains uncovered is accorded special attention. They were astonished that I wore no makeup. Their greatest ambition was to get me to entrust my face to their trained hands so that they could make me up. I would look irresistible, they promised. Perhaps I would even find a husband ...

The daily routine at school was now and then interrupted by a celebration. One festive occasion was when the principal had returned from her pilgrimage (*hajj*) to Mecca and treated all her staff to a dish of *mansaf* during lunch break. A teacher's birthday was another cause for celebration and we would be treated to pastries and sweets or to a lavish breakfast or lunch. Once in a while, a female vendor would come to the school with a suitcase full of scarves, socks, gloves, and jars of olives and jam. She would hang around the teachers' room the whole morning and the teachers would look through her merchandise, bargain, and buy some items. To an American, the idea that a vendor could enter the school building when classes are in session to sell merchandise to the teachers is inconceivable. But in the village, this was considered *aadi*, that is, normal. It reminded me of a poignant short story titled "God's World" by the Egyptian Nobel Prize Laureate Naguib Mahfouz. In this story, a tie and perfume vendor comes to a government office in Cairo at the beginning of each month (which is when the employees receive their salaries) and goes around the clerks' desks, selling his wares. I laughed when I had read this story, thinking how unacceptable this practice would be in an American setting. Years later, I took up a job as a language instructor at the Foreign Service Institute in Rosslyn, Virginia. I discovered that it was customary among my colleagues to shop online or browse through consumer's catalogues when they were sitting at their desks. I recalled Mahfouz's story, and the similarity between the two scenarios made me laugh once again.

The teachers' main complaint about village life was the lack of entertainment—there was no place to go to and nothing to do. No park, no community center, no movie theater, no gym or sports club. The only source of entertainment was the television. What the men in their families, and by their accounts all the men in the village, liked watching the most was horror movies. I was intrigued. Why were these men attracted to movies filled with torture and violence? Did this fascination have any special significance? I decided to explore the topic but this was not a simple undertaking. In the segregated society of my village, I couldn't approach strange men on the street and ask them to explain their fascination with horror movies. The few men accessible to me, such as Abu Omar and his brothers, would not necessarily give me candid answers. So when we went back to our training site at Al al-Bayt University, I researched the topic online. I found some articles that shed light on the "horror paradox" in my village. According to Glenn Sparks, a professor of communication at Purdue University, scary movies may be one of the last vestiges of the tribal rite of passage, where the entrance to manhood was associated with mastering threatening situations. "We've lost that in modern society, and we may have found ways to replace it in our entertainment preferences. In this context, the gorier the movie, the more justified the young man feels in boasting that he endured it." Given the fact that the men in my village were Bedouins, this "initiation rite substitute" was a plausible explanation. As for the effects of horror movies on viewers' behavior, some psychologists believe that horror movies "act as a sort of safety valve for our cruel or aggressive impulses," in the sense that watching violence prevents the need to act it out. But others argue that "consuming violent media is more likely to make people feel more hostile, to view the world that way, and to be haunted by violent ideas and images."[3] I was so intrigued by this topic that I decided to delve deeper into it when other means of investigation would become available to me.

The first time we returned to the Peace Corps training site for "center days" was at the end of October. I was happy to find out that I had been moved to a room on the second floor of the women's dorm, away from the courtyard. To my astonishment, Lora had been moved with me, even though the noise on the first floor didn't bother her and there were many spare rooms in the dorm. The new room was as shabby as the previous one, but it was quiet. At the very least, I would be able to get enough sleep and food on our weekly visits to the training site. I wondered why Rifaat, the homestay coordinator, insisted that I should wait so many days for the new room to be "cleaned." It was quite obvious that the room hadn't been cleaned in a long time. How could a women's dorm on an acclaimed university campus be so dirty and neglected? My experience of living at the women's dorm of the American University in Cairo was entirely different: the rooms and bathrooms there were swept, mopped, and scrubbed thoroughly every day. As soon as we arrived at our dorm, we rushed to take a shower and do our laundry. The bathrooms were gross, but we had no choice. The drains in the showers were clogged, and despite wearing flip-flops, the slime and soap scum that accumulated on the floor would rise with the water and cover my feet. Before long I contracted athlete's foot. I had never had such fungal infection before and didn't recognize the symptoms. When I finally realized that something was wrong, it had spread to both of my feet.

The days we spent at the training site were long and crammed with technical sessions. I approached Bryan and asked him if he had found a suitable language class for me. He said that he had no resources to accommodate my level separately. All he could offer me was a few private sessions with an LCF now and then. I loved those one-on-one sessions. I would read aloud an article from an Arabic daily newspaper and then translate the written standard Arabic into colloquial Jordanian. This allowed me to see how words and grammatical structures changed from one form of the language to another. Regrettably, these sessions were very few and far between. I had to rely on my interaction with members of my host family and teachers at the village girls' elementary school to advance my Arabic skills.

We had connection to the Internet on campus. Everybody looked forward to the opportunity to log onto their email accounts and read letters from their friends and families. I was probably the only volunteer who approached her email account with trepidation in her heart. Would there be bad news about my brother? I had not received any message about his condition since my arrival in Jordan and this silence worried me. I saw little of Lora. She was in the special education sector, so she followed a different program. The only sessions we shared were on medical and safety topics. We chatted a little during our breaks and meal times. In the evenings she stayed out late studying her Arabic vocabulary with girls from her class. She told me that her host family was a young couple with a baby and that she was well fed and looked after. She had told them that she was widowed instead of divorced. In a traditional Arab milieu such as a village, divorced women carry a stigma and invite endless speculations, but widowed women elicit sympathy and respect.

When my TEFL group got together for the first time after arriving from our villages, we were asked to share our impressions of our host families. The Peace Corps supervisor asked Natalie to begin. She surprised us by saying that she preferred to be the last person to recount her experiences. The supervisor obliged her and called on other volunteers to speak out. Everybody praised the warm hospitality of their host families and their attention to their physical comfort, food, and meals. I felt uneasy as I listened to their stories, thinking that it would sound strange if my story contradicted theirs and I complained about insufficient food and sleep. So when my turn came, I praised my host family for welcoming me into their home and gently remarked that their irregular meal times and heavy reliance on bread and carbs required getting used to on my part. Finally Natalie's turn came. Plainly, and without mincing her words, she said that she wasn't well received by her host family: they didn't pay attention to her and didn't give her enough food to eat. She was ignored most of the time and left to her own devices. She said that listening to other volunteers' stories made her realize all the more how differently she was treated. I felt embarrassed when I heard her speak out so frankly, without trying to conceal or embellish anything. Here I was, afraid to tell the truth and tiptoeing around like an acrobat. But was I really in a position to speak out as Natalie did? I was *Jewish* and my host family was *Arab*. Everybody around me knew this. My criticism might be construed as biased and tainted by ulterior motives. I had to be careful. The supervisor advised Natalie to give her host family a little more time to adjust to her presence in their household. This was precisely what I had told myself before we had even begun this discussion.

After two days of intensive training on campus, we returned to our villages. It was early November, and we looked forward to an important event: our placement interviews with Lana, the education program manager. Lana was in charge of assigning the TEFL volunteers to their permanent sites by matching their skills with the needs of particular schools throughout the Kingdom. A pleasant, soft-spoken Jordanian in her mid-forties, she was my favorite Peace Corps staff member. When she arrived in my village to conduct interviews with members of my group, I had no expectations whatsoever. Mona, on the other hand, was well prepared with a list of requests and preferences. She wanted to be placed in a village close to Amman, claiming that whenever her father would have a business trip to Yemen, she would be able to meet with him at the airport. In fact, everybody wanted to be close to Amman because it is the hub of all the action, from arts and culture to shopping and dining to entertainment and night life, and everybody dreaded the idea of ending up isolated in a remote village, far away from any urban center. Mona was the first to go for the interview with Lana, and it took quite a while before she returned, grinning with delight.

It was then my turn. After greeting each other and exchanging pleasantries, Lana asked me what my preferences were. I replied briefly, "I love the kids in the first grade and would be happy teaching first grade, but I would be equally happy teaching another grade." She smiled and said, "Actually, I have other plans for you." I looked at her questioningly. "With your PhD and teaching experience, I think you're suitable to teach at a Jordanian university. I've sent your resume to the dean of an acclaimed university and he responded positively. The only issue he raised is your last name, *Cohen*. He was concerned that it might be problematic." Intrigued by this information, I responded cautiously, "Alex and Bryan advised me to use an alias here, and I chose the name Seymore. I would be known to the students and staff members as Dalya Seymore. Would this work for the dean?" Lana nodded in approval. "Yes, I think it would." I felt a sudden rush of excitement sweeping through me. Even in my wildest dreams, I didn't imagine that I would be teaching at a Jordanian university. This would be the climax of my academic career, no doubt about it.

I didn't share the good news with my group, fearing that it might cause envy, and kept a low profile. As it turned out, of all the thirty-eight J15 volunteers, only three were selected to teach at institutes of higher education including myself.

Contrary to this positive development, my situation with my host family showed no improvement. One Friday, Abu Omar hosted members of his brotherhood for lunch. Eight or ten bearded men, dressed in traditional Arab garb, arrived and were led straightaway into the formal reception room, where they were served coffee and other refreshments. The rest of the family remained inside the main house. Umm Omar worked all morning to prepare a lavish lunch. I saw a big tray of roasted chicken with steamed rice, a tray of *malfufa* (cabbage leaves stuffed with rice), and several dishes of salad on the kitchen table. The sight and smell of the cooked food made me salivate. I thought that Umm Omar was going to serve each of us a portion, as she always did, on individual plates. But Abu Omar came to the kitchen and carried away all the trays of food one by one to his guests in the reception room. It was after 3:00 in the afternoon and I had hunger cramps. I didn't understand when or what the rest of us were going to eat. Umm Omar looked at me apologetically and said, "Do you like eating hot food? I prefer to wait until it has cooled down." I had no idea what she was talking about. Was there more cooked food that had to cool down before we ate it? Forty-five minutes later, Abu Omar came back to the kitchen, carrying trays with some leftovers. There was no chicken left, just some rice, *malfufa*, and salad. And that was what we—Umm Omar, her children, and I—ate for lunch. Cold leftovers. I felt a deep sense of resentment. The men eat first, and then the women and children get the scant remains! This family was being *paid* to feed me. Where did the money go? To feed their guests? If the guests had to be honored first, then I was a guest too. Although several other volunteers in the J15 group had similar complaints, no one experienced this problem as badly as I did. Theresa once confided in me that she had been getting a boiled egg with bread for dinner for three days in a row. Her host father had undergone an operation the week before. "Where did the money they get to feed me go?" she asked. "To pay for his operation?" While we understood that the villagers were poor, and sympathized with them, we had to make sure that we got enough food to nourish our bodies and stay healthy.

The next day Fatin, my host father's sister, came over to see me. I told her that I had received the Peace Corps approval to tutor her for the TOEFL exam, and she was very pleased. We chatted a little in the sitting room and then went into my room so that we could have some privacy. Fatin was in her early twenties and still single. She said that her parents allowed her to put off marriage until she finished her master's degree. She was fair-skinned, like Umm Omar, with light brown hair and brown eyes. She wore a velour sweat suit that emphasized her full figure, but she always covered herself in an abaya when she stepped outside. Her English vocabulary was limited and her knowledge of grammar weak. She had multiple choice questions on a TOFEL practice test that she didn't know how to answer. We agreed to meet in her house to go over these questions. I showed her an article that I had to translate from modern standard Arabic into colloquial Jordanian. Published in the daily newspaper *al-Raa'i*, it dealt with the problems surrounding the discipline of psychology in Arab culture in general and in Jordan in particular. These problems include the stigma of being "crazy" that is attached to a person who goes to see a psychologist, the stigma of being a "weirdo" that is attached to a person who studies psychology, and the slim prospects of finding employment with a degree in psychology in an Arab society. Fatin gave me an interesting insight into the topic. She said that the stigmas attached to the field of psychology are closely related to a concept popularly known as "the culture of shame" (*thaqafat al-eeb*) in Jordan. According to this concept, certain occupations, among them cleaning, waitressing, and construction, are considered "shameful" to do. Jordanians avoid doing them and bring foreign workers, many of them Asians, to do them instead. For example, Filipinos, Pakistanis, and Indonesians are employed as domestic help (*khuddam*) in the houses of the rich; Egyptians do construction work and also serve as cleaners and waiters in hotels and restaurants. Jordanians look down on these foreign workers and treat them with contempt. This situation is a constant source of aggravation for Asian American Peace Corps volunteers, who are often mistaken for domestic help when they go shopping or ride in a bus and are subjected to derogatory remarks and rude treatment. From firsthand accounts of J14 Asian American Peace Corps volunteers, we learned that it was stressful for them to cope with these disparaging attitudes. Lupe, a Mexican American, told us that whenever she rode in a bus with a blonde fellow volunteer, the driver and passengers automatically assumed that she was her maid. Janine, an Asian American volunteer, acknowledged that the local people's attitudes to her ethnicity frustrated and depressed her.

There are two major religious festivals in Jordan: Eid al-Fitr, the Feast of Breaking the Fast, which marks the end of the fasting month of Ramadan, and Eid al-Adha, the Feast of Sacrifice, which marks the end of the pilgrimage to Mecca (*hajj*). The Feast of Sacrifice commemorates the "binding" of Ishmael (whom Muslim tradition substitutes for the Biblical Isaac) by Abraham, when God sent a ram from heaven to be sacrificed to him in his stead. Every Muslim who has the means is enjoined to sacrifice an animal. As reported in the news media, in November 2011 Jordanians spent 24 million dinars on the slaughter of animals for this feast. The price of an animal varies: a sheep costs JD150–JD300, a goat JD70–JD100, a cow JD500; and a camel JD1000–JD1500. It is meritorious to give part of the meat to the poor as charity. During the Eid, which lasts three to four days, people wear new clothes, visit their relatives, and bestow presents on each other. Most families also visit the tombs of their relatives on this occasion, and the women bring food to distribute to the poor who throng the cemeteries.

Abu Omar's father had bought two sheep to slaughter for the entire extended family, which had gathered at his house from far and near to celebrate the Eid. My host family asked me if I wanted to attend the slaughter ritual. I knew what to expect: the Muslim slaughter ritual and dietary laws are similar to the Jewish ritual and laws. "No, thank you," I said. "I can't stand the sight of blood and animals squealing in pain." They laughed. The kids said that they loved to watch the sheep being led to the slaughter and even to hold them fast while the knife was being brought down on their necks. Omar wore his new khaki pants to the ritual and they were stained by drops of blood from the slaughtered sheep. He was worried that the blood spots might not come out in the wash and would ruin his pants.

The children's excitement over the slaughter ritual brought back old memories to my mind, when I was a little girl preparing for Yom Kippur or Day of Atonement in my hometown of Lod. My parents used to buy three chickens to offer as sacrifice for their three children. My brother, who was my closest companion and playmate throughout my childhood, and I were thrilled to grab the struggling chickens by their legs and carry them to the ritual slaughterer (*shokhet*). He would slit their throats with a sharp knife in one swift stroke and then throw them on the ground to bleed to death. We would watch, spellbound, as the chickens convulsed and jumped in the air, until the blood drained out of them and they lay still. Then we would grab them by the legs again and bring them back to our mother, who would pluck their feathers, clean them thoroughly, and cook them for the festive meals before and after the fast. In those days, I didn't think about animal cruelty and the sight of blood didn't sicken me. For the Jewish High Holidays, my siblings and I would get new clothes and shoes, candy, and pocket money, much like what my host family's kids got for the Eid.

Umm Omar asked me if I wanted to help her make *ma'mul tamr* (cookies filled with ground dates) for the Eid. I was glad to give her a hand and learn a new recipe. Making the dough was easy; shaping it into dainty cookies filled with ground dates was difficult. It was done by hand while crouching on the floor. We would flatten a small amount of dough on the palms of our hands, put some ground dates in the center of it, roll it into a ball, and then insert it into a wooden cookie mold. To remove it we had to bang the mold, upside down, hard on the floor. It was a time consuming and labor-intensive activity. Umm Omar checked my cookies from time to time, instructing me to make them smaller and thinner. After one hour my back started to hurt and my bottom felt numb. There were half a dozen large trays waiting to be filled with cookies so that Umm Omar would have enough to distribute among her entire extended family. Latifa helped us a little but then Zahra started to whine and she had to take care of her little sister. By 9:00 p.m., we had filled only two trays. I decided to call it a night and retired to my room. I heard Umm Omar still banging the wooden mold on the floor until well after midnight.

The morning of the first day of the Eid began for me like any other morning—without breakfast. Abu Omar was gone, visiting his parents' house, where all his siblings had gathered. The kids put on their new clothes and went outside to play. Umm Omar, in terry-cloth pants and a sleeveless blouse that revealed her white forearms, was giving the house a thorough cleaning all by herself—Latifa was exempt from doing household chores on this day. She mopped the kitchen floor, vacuumed the carpets, scrubbed the bathroom, and washed the window panes. I didn't want to stand in her way so I made myself scarce. I went outside and stood by the gate in the front yard, trying to place a call to my brother to inquire about his health. I dialed his cell phone number, then his home number, and then his wife's cell phone number, only to get the same recorded message, "The number you dialed is not in service. Please check the number and dial again." I was in disbelief. The numbers I dialed were the exact same numbers I had been dialing for months. What on earth was going on? Could it be that Peace Corps cell phones were monitored and certain lines blocked by the Jordanian authorities? But there was a peace treaty between Jordan and Israel and businessmen on both sides of the border called each other daily! I dialed more than a dozen times, feeling more anxious with every failed attempt. Finally I gave up. With no access to the Internet and no phone connection, I had no way of getting in touch with my brother.

As a last resort, I called my friend Miri in the United States. The call went through immediately and she picked up on the first ring. This confirmed my suspicion that the numbers I had tried to call in Israel were deliberately blocked. Before I had left for Jordan, I had agreed with Miri that we would speak only in English on the phone and avoid using words that would reveal my identity. "Hi Miri," I said quickly. "I can't get in touch with my brother. There's something wrong with the phone line. As you know, he is in the hospital. Can you please call my sister-in-law on my behalf and ask her how he's doing, and then call me back to let me know?" "Yes," she replied without hesitation. I gave her the telephone number, worrying that whoever was eavesdropping on the line would recognize from the area code that it was located in Tel Aviv. Then I hung up and waited. Within ten minutes she called me back, saying, "Dalya, I spoke with your sister-in-law. Your brother's condition hasn't changed. He's still in the hospital, and the doctors are doing whatever they can for him." My heart sank at this discouraging news. I thanked my good friend, who was always ready to help me, and hung up. These international calls cost a fortune.

When I went back to the house, Umm Omar rushed toward me in panic. "Dalya! Dalya! Where have you been?" she asked hysterically. Astonished, I replied, "Outside, in the front yard of the house." "Please tell me where you go when you leave the house," she said in a reproachful tone. "All of a sudden you disappeared and I didn't know what happened to you!" Her reaction puzzled me. Couldn't she see me from her kitchen window or the sitting room window standing in the front yard? If she was really concerned about me, why didn't she offer me breakfast? Did she think I lived on air? I said nothing, trying to look nonchalant. Just then, Zahra wobbled into the room, all dolled up. In her new red shoes and a red-hooded poncho, she looked like Little Red Riding Hood. I smiled at her and we played hide and seek. The house looked clean and tidy and the air smelled of freshly baked cookies. From time to time, there was a knock on the front door. Children came by to ask for candy for the Eid. Umm Omar brought out a bowl of candy and gave each of them a piece. This custom, which is part of the Eid's traditions, reminded me of the Halloween tradition of Trick or Treat, except that the village children didn't wear costumes and didn't threaten anyone with a trick.

Around noon, Umm Omar's brothers and sisters, along with their spouses and children, came by. I was introduced to the guests, and we exchanged greetings and pleasantries. Umm Omar served them coffee and *ma'mul tamr*, still dressed in the same clothes, her bare forearms gleaming in the bright sunlight that penetrated through the window. I was astonished, as I expected that she would change from her sleeveless blouse and terrycloth pants into her Eid clothes. Before long, the men started lighting up and the air in the small sitting room became suffocating from cigarette smoke. The children ran around, creating a commotion, so the men gave them their money gifts for the Eid and sent them to play outside. I noticed that Omar's uncle gave him one dinar and told him to share it with his two siblings, Hasan and Latifa. I recalled that our LCF Walaa said that we should give each child in our host family three dinars as a gift. I was flabbergasted. How did she come up with this figure? Did she think that Peace Corps volunteers were loaded? We lived on a meager allowance and had to subsidize our expenses out of our own pockets. Our host families were blessed with five to ten children. Offering three dinars to each child would amount to a sum of JD15–JD30, which was quite a fortune, by local standards. I pondered for a moment, then took three dinars out of my purse and gave each of the older children in my host family one dinar for the Eid. They initially refused the gift, as required by etiquette, then, after I insisted, as required by etiquette too, they accepted the gift with gratitude.

Before the Eid, Mona had told me that a rumor was circulating in the village that I was rich. The rumor was fueled by the fact that I had a doctoral degree. It was automatically assumed that the high degree brought with it a high salary. In addition, I had made a trip with Abu Omar and his wife to the town of Mafraq, where I had changed a fifty-dollar bill to Jordanian dinars so I could buy phone cards for my cell phone. The news about my trip to town immediately spread among the village people, and it was concluded that I must be rich. This perception made me feel uneasy because it could compromise my safety and security.

The guests didn't stay long—they had other visits to make. Shortly after they had left, Umm Omar changed into her holiday outfit and put on her jewelry. She wore a thick gold ring, a heavy gold bracelet, and a heavy gold watch—no doubt her wedding gifts. Her new robe and ankle-length coat looked quite expensive. I smiled under my nose, thinking to myself, "This is probably where the Peace Corps money that they had received to feed me went." Her head was covered with a hijab and her face was heavily made up. She looked pretty and beamed with satisfaction when I complimented her on her appearance. She said that we were going to her in-laws' house, where Abu Omar and her children were waiting for us. She filled a plate with *ma'mul tamr* for her in-laws and gave it to me to carry, then she lifted Zahra into her arms and we set off on the short walk to their house.

When we got there, the house was teeming with guests. Fatin, Abu Omar's youngest sister, welcomed us at the door and led us to the formal reception room, where we found Abu Omar sitting with his parents. His father, in his early eighties, was dressed in a traditional robe, and his mother, in her early seventies, wore a robe and a headscarf. They both had a stern and conservative mien about them. I was first introduced to Abu Omar's father. I laid my right arm across my chest, as custom dictates when strangers of the opposite sex are introduced to each other, and uttered the traditional Arab greeting. Then I was introduced to Abu Omar's mother. I spontaneously held out my hand to shake hers, as is expected between women, but she quickly laid her arm across her chest. This gesture meant that she didn't want to touch my hand. I was taken aback, feeling unwelcome and rejected, and immediately started worrying that perhaps she suspected something about me. Later on, I learned that Abu Omar's mother had strongly objected to her son's decision to host a Peace Corps volunteer in his house, first because his house was too small and cramped for this purpose, and second because I was an *ajnabiya* (a foreigner) and a *masihiya* (Christian).

We sat on farshas on the floor and Abu Omar's mother served us Turkish coffee and chocolates. I was ill at ease and my empty stomach was making growling noises from hunger, which embarrassed me. I wished that the visit would end quickly. Fatin rescued me. She took me to the kitchen to introduce me to her sisters-in-law, who were busy preparing lunch. Two of them had come all the way from Saudi Arabia to celebrate the Eid with the extended family. Unlike Umm Omar, they were all dressed in simple robes, had no jewelry on, and wore very little makeup, but their heads were covered with hijabs, *even* in the house, *even* among close relatives. Fatin reached toward a fruit bowl on the kitchen counter, took a banana, and gave it to me. I accepted it with gratitude—it was the first thing I had gotten to eat all day.

All that Turkish coffee was hard on my bladder, and soon I had to go to the bathroom. Gathering the edges of my long skirt in one hand, I pushed the bathroom door open with the other, and lo and behold! There was a commode and a squat toilet side by side! This modern convenience was clearly not a luxury but a necessity: both Fatin's father and mother were elderly and corpulent, and squatting was probably hard on their knees. I peed in perfect comfort, scrutinizing the tiles on the floor and the fixtures on the walls, and when I finished I automatically pushed on the valve to flush the toilet. To my alarm, it didn't work. I instantly checked the water tank: it was empty. I panicked. Perhaps the commode was out of order and I wasn't supposed to use it! What should I do? I went to the kitchen looking for Fatin, but she wasn't there. I timidly approached one of her sisters-in-law and whispered in her ear that the mechanism for flushing the toilet didn't work. She walked with me back to the bathroom, pointed to a plastic pitcher by the sink, then to the faucet, and explained that I had to fill the pitcher with water and pour it into the toilet bowl. This was how it worked. The commode wasn't connected to a water supply; there was only partial plumbing. I thanked her, locked the bathroom door behind me, and burst into hysterical laughter.

Around 3:00 in the afternoon, we sat on the floor of the sitting room to eat lunch. They served the liver, lungs, and kidneys of the sheep that had been slaughtered earlier in the day. Despite my hunger, I couldn't bring myself to eat from these dishes. I dipped pieces of flatbread in labaneh (yogurt cheese) and ate them with some salad—that was all I had. I was content to sit quietly, without being the focus of attention, amid this large gathering, and listen to the lively conversation that flowed around me. The guests talked about their work, homes, pastimes, and travels. From their stories, I got the distinct impression that Abu Omar's siblings were quite well off and that he was the poorest member of his family.

After lunch, we headed for Umm Omar's parental home. Her father, like her father-in-law (who was also her uncle), was a teacher who had lived and worked for many years in Saudi Arabia. Her mother, like her mother-in-law, was illiterate. This puzzled me. How could educated men, who, of all professions, were teachers, marry women who couldn't read or write? And why, after so many years of marriage, had they not taught their wives to read and write? Umm Omar's parental home was as big and spacious as that of Abu Omar's. Her elderly parents lived on the ground floor, and two of her married brothers occupied the second- and third-floor apartments. When we arrived, the mother was alone in her quarters. Unlike Abu Omar's mother, she hugged me when we were introduced and kissed me three times, once on the right cheek, and then twice on the left cheek, a gesture that made me feel welcome and put me at ease. My sense of ease turned out to be fleeting. After rebuking her daughter for not bringing her a plate of *ma'mul tamr* for the Eid, as she had done for her mother-in-law, the mother started to pepper me with questions. She wasn't so much interested in getting information about my personal life as in criticizing American policies in the Middle East.

"Why is America waging wars against Muslims? Why are American troops killing Arabs?" I answered evasively that I had no understanding of politics and couldn't opine on this subject. But she went on and on with her criticism. "Why does America support Israel? Why does America allow Israel to occupy Palestine?" I recalled that Umm Omar had told me that her family was Syrian in origin. Syrians are known for their intransigent position on Israel. While both Egypt and Jordan had signed peace treaties with Israel, Syria had refused to do so. The mother seemed quite agitated. I began to dread these one-on-one conversations. It was far better to be "lost" in a large gathering, where no one paid attention to me. But where were Umm Omar's father, sisters, and brothers? I had no idea.

After a short visit with her mother, Umm Omar took me to the third-floor apartment to call on her brother. In contrast to the downstairs quarters, which were furnished in a traditional style with farshas and pillows on the floor, the upstairs apartment was furnished in a modern style with a sofa set and a coffee table in the living room, and an oak dining set in the dining room. In addition, there was a Western-style bathroom with full plumbing, and an up-to-date kitchen, complete with a dishwasher, a microwave oven, a cooking stove, a Caesar stone countertop, and matching wood cabinets on the walls. It was a far cry from Umm Omar's shabby kitchen, where a tattered curtain hid the pots and pans from sight while the hideous buta gas cylinders were in full view. I wondered whether Umm Omar envied her sister-in-law. It must be hard to be poor when all your close relatives are well off. The sister-in-law was dressed casually in a blouse and a short skirt, and her hair was uncovered. She was in her late twenties and heavily pregnant with her second child. Her toddler daughter was the same age as Zahra. She beamed with pride as she showed us around her beautiful apartment. I understood from her comments that it had been recently renovated and that Umm Omar was seeing it all done for the first time.

We settled on the comfortable sofa and began to chat. The sister-in-law was eager to tell me that both she and her husband were university educated and that their marriage was not an arranged union. They had met while studying at the university and fallen in love, but postponed their marriage until they had both graduated and he had found a job. Now she was a stay-at-home wife and mother. Her husband had worked as a flight attendant for several years but the growing safety risks connected with flying made him quit. With a degree in liberal arts, he remained unemployed for a couple of years, until he landed a job with a government agency for public safety and security. As we were chatting, Umm Omar's mother came in and joined us in the living room. She kissed her two granddaughters, who were playing with each other. Suddenly, Zahra snatched her cousin's toy. The little girl began to cry. When Umm Omar scolded her daughter, Zahra threw the worst temper tantrum I had ever seen. She screamed at the top of her voice, threw everything within her grasp on the floor, kicked her feet, and sobbed bitterly. The sister-in-law looked on in disapproval but said nothing. Her daughter, who was quiet and well behaved, looked frightened. My ears started to hurt from Zahra's piercing screams, when suddenly the door opened and Umm Omar's brother walked in. His appearance had a magical effect on Zahra, who shut up as abruptly as she had exploded. Umm Omar immediately gave her the breast and rocked her in her arms to lull her to sleep.

We were introduced. The brother, a tall, fair-skinned guy in his mid-thirties, seemed disappointed when he heard me speak Arabic fluently. I sensed that he wanted to practice his English with me. Jordanians don't miss an opportunity to speak English. But I insisted on speaking Arabic in order to allow everyone to participate in the conversation and at the same time escape being the focus of attention. My strategy failed. As soon as the brother settled in his chair, he began to pepper me with questions. "Daly, are you married?" *Wow! He cut straight to the chase!* This was the first time that a Jordanian *man* had asked me such a personal question. "No," I said, wondering why he was calling me "Daly." "Why not?" he continued. "*Nasib*," I replied with a shrug. He gave a half-smile, his eyes acknowledging that this was an unassailable answer. Then the next question came. "Tell me, how much money do you make as a teacher?" I was evasive, saying that it depended on the teacher's degree, years of experience, number of classes per week, etc. He insisted that I give him a figure. I refused. In our technical sessions, we were warned that appearing to be rich could jeopardize our safety. Instead, I said that in general teachers earn little money in the United States, while doctors and lawyers make a lot of money. He was satisfied with this answer and remarked that the same situation existed in Jordan with respect to these professions. Then he talked about the differences between the two countries, expressing an extremely negative view of American society: "People in the United States have no values, no moral under-pinnings. The society is 'fragmented' (*al-mujtama' mufakkak*) and 'disintegrated' (*munhall*) from crime, violence, corruption, drugs, promiscuous sex, and materialism. Family ties are weak and people don't care about each other. As soon as the children grow up they leave their parents' homes and go to live in faraway places." I asked him if he had ever been to the United States. "No," he admitted. He gained his knowledge about American society from watching movies on television. "But movies give a superficial and often distorted view of American society," I argued. "They tend to focus on the fringes of society rather than on mainstream society, and to highlight the negative aspects of life rather than the positive ones. Most Americans love their families, work hard, serve their communities, and believe in God." He listened to me with a skeptical expression and continued to call me "Daly" instead of Dalya.

I was exhausted from this conversation. I got the distinct impression that while publicly the brother castigated American society, secretly he admired its enormous achievements—the high level of progress and prosperity, the availability of opportunity and social mobility, the democratic institutions and civil liberties, the great economic and military might. I had encountered this kind of "ambivalence" on the part of many Jordanians who, on the one hand, rejected the United States and what it stood for, and on the other hand wished that they could live there. The American dream had a universal appeal, even among Arabs in the Middle East.

We concluded our visit and returned to the ground floor, where Umm Omar's extended family had already gathered: brothers, sisters, spouses, and their children. I felt that I was being paraded around like a trophy. Umm Omar seemed proud of me and at the same time weary of me. I just wanted to get something to eat and have a rest. The intense social interaction drained me, perhaps because I was constantly under scrutiny. The men of the family smoked heavily and the cigarette smoke gave me heartburn. Umm Omar stood out among the simply dressed women in her gold jewelry and expensive new robe and coat. I noticed several young women who were dressed in jeans and sweaters. I approached them and chatted with them. I learned that they were full-time students majoring in computer science, engineering, and communication at Al al-Bayt University. They seemed self-assured, goal-oriented, and well-informed. I looked at Umm Omar's mother, the matriarch. Here she was, an illiterate traditional village woman, and there they were, university-educated modern women. The generational gap between the grandmother and her granddaughters was huge, the progress from ignorance to knowledge dramatic. Arab women were undeniably coming out of the shadows.

It was late in the evening when we ate dinner. We were served *mansaf*. Three large trays with long-grained white rice topped with pieces of chicken were placed on a sheet of plastic on the carpeted floor. I was slightly disappointed that there was no lamb—perhaps Umm Omar's parents had not slaughtered sheep for the Eid. Everybody was invited to dig in with their right hands. I was about to dig in myself when Umm Omar appeared out of nowhere and handed me a plate with a bony drumstick and a heap of rice. I froze in embarrassment. I wanted to eat from the communal tray, just like everyone else. The assumption that I needed to eat from a plate with a spoon like an inept child annoyed me. And why was she always giving me a drumstick? Couldn't she at least ask me if I liked it? I struggled to hide my displeasure. If I turned down the plate it might offend her and the entire family. The most important thing for me was to conduct myself with respect and dignity. I forced a smile on my lips and accepted the plate, but my appetite had vanished. I ate a few morsels and put the plate down. "Dalya doesn't eat much," I heard Umm Omar say to the woman sitting beside her, and I bit my lower lip in frustration.

After dinner, I went to the bathroom to wash my face and hands. My hair, skin, and clothes reeked of cigarette smoke. I had a throbbing headache and terrible stomach cramps. I looked for Latifa and asked her to take me home. She rushed to tell her mother, who said that she would take me home herself. Although Zahra was tired and throwing another temper tantrum, Umm Omar was in no hurry to leave. Why wouldn't she let me go home by myself or with Latifa? All the other volunteers in my group received the *house key* from their host families and could come and go *at will*. But I had to be escorted home by none other than Umm Omar herself, who, like a babysitter, would also stay at home with me. I felt like a prisoner.

After a lot of procrastination, Umm Omar finally got up to leave. We said goodbye to everyone and walked the short distance home. It was after 10:00 p.m. and the night was cold and breezy. I breathed in gulps of clean fresh air, thinking about the huge amount of secondary smoke that I had inhaled all day. We spoke little. When we got home, Abu Omar wasn't there. I assumed that he was still at his own parents' house. I went to the bathroom to brush my teeth when suddenly the light in the ceiling fixture flickered and went out, leaving me standing in the dark. I groped my way to the door anxiously. What would I do if I needed to pee in the middle of the night? I told myself not to worry. Umm Omar would surely notice the burnt light bulb and tell her husband to replace it promptly.

As I lay in bed I contemplated the events of the first day of the Eid. I was impressed by the centrality of the Arab family in all aspects of life. The family is really the "alpha and omega of the whole system," the "indissoluble atom of society."[4] A remarkably cohesive unit, the Arab family provides its members with a strong sense of identity and belonging, as well as security and support, both economic and emotional. All activities revolve around the family. This distinctive feature of Arab life contrasts sharply with American life, where the *individual* is the nucleus of society, and the role of the family has been considerably reduced by the state and other agencies. Yet, even in this traditional Jordanian village, where family life and family ties come first and foremost, young people go wherever they can to find jobs, often migrating to urban centers both within and outside their home country. Several of Abu Omar's and Umm Omar's siblings had relocated to Saudi Arabia, where they could make a better living. They kept in touch with their families by coming home on major religious festivals and celebrations of life passages, just as Americans do on similar occasions. On the one hand, it is hard to imagine that a member of an Arab family would ever feel lonely; on the other hand, it is hard to be a part of such intense social interaction.

I closed my eyes and slept soundly until Zahra's cries woke me up. This happened repeatedly throughout the night. Her shrill screams would startle me out of my sleep and unnerve me, so much so that I imagined hearing her screaming even when she wasn't. I had been with my host family for just two weeks. How would I survive two whole months like this? I told myself that I wasn't a quitter. I came to Jordan for a two-year Peace Corps service and I was going to make it by hook or by crook.

When I opened my bedroom door in the morning, the children were at play in the sitting room, Abu Omar was already gone, and Umm

Omar was alone in the kitchen. I greeted everyone cordially and went to the bathroom. I tried to switch on the light. It didn't work. Umm Omar must have forgotten to tell Abu Omar about the burnt light bulb. Some dim light penetrated through a small, opaque glass window fixed close to the ceiling. I strained my eyes to see in the dark, careful not to trip over objects and fall as I used the squat toilet and washed up. After I had gotten dressed, I joined Umm Omar in the kitchen. "The light bulb in the bathroom isn't working," I said. "If you have a new light bulb, I can replace it." She shook her head. "Sorry, I don't. I'll tell Abu Omar to bring one today. In the meantime, leave the door open when you go into the bathroom, so you will not be in the dark." Her casual attitude astonished me, but I refrained from commenting on her suggestion. I made myself a cup of coffee and sat at the kitchen table to drink it, thinking that I must try to forge closer bonds with her. "I enjoyed meeting your family yesterday," I said. "They are all very nice people. It's great that you live so close to them." Her face lit up and she began to tell me her family's history, some parts of which I had already heard before. Originally from Syria, they had intermarried with Jordanians and had lived for many years in Saudi Arabia, where she was raised. Abu Omar was her cousin (*ibn amm*) on her father's side, and as such he had "a right to her" and chose to marry her. She and Abu Omar had moved to the village two years earlier. Before that, they had lived in rented apartments in Mafraq for several years, until Abu Omar had saved enough money to build this house on a piece of land that belonged to his father, whose own house stood in the back of the olive grove. Although Abu Omar's house was small and simple compared to those of his siblings, Umm Omar was very proud that they owned it and no longer had to deal with a landlord.

Zahra had soiled her diaper and Umm Omar attended to her. I fetched my notebook and sat with Latifa to write the new words that I had learned in colloquial Jordanian. I used a mechanical pencil that I had brought from the United States, and Latifa was taken with it. She had never seen a pencil like this before, and asked if I could give her one. I had another one in my dorm room at the training site and promised to bring it for her at the earliest opportunity. She was delighted. I knew that she would show it to all her friends at school and impress them with this little gift from her American guest.

Latifa loved to teach me Arabic and scolded me if I wrote a word sloppily. She would erase the word and tell me to rewrite it neatly, or she would write it in her own beautiful handwriting and ask me to copy it precisely. We would often tease each other and have a good laugh. She was a lovely girl—bright, modest, and dutiful. On the last school day before the Eid, I had happened to go to the bathroom at the crack of dawn when I saw her sitting by the window and studying for a history test in the dim light, while her two brothers lay sound asleep beside her. Once, I asked her what she wanted to be when she grew up. She said that she didn't know yet. Her mother was married off at the age of seventeen and could not complete high school. But Abu Omar's youngest sister was university educated and several other young women on both sides of her family were university students. So Latifa had plenty of female role models to emulate. Whenever Umm Omar ordered her to drop everything, even her homework, to take care of Zahra, she obeyed her, although sometimes under bitter protests. She would pick up her screaming sister and mutter in exasperation, "I hate little children," but a moment later she would cover her face with kisses and hug her affectionately. She was like a second mother to Zahra, who was an extremely spoiled and difficult child.

On the second day of the Eid, Latifa told me excitedly that her father promised to take us on an excursion in his car. Going on a short pleasure trip is another custom connected with the Eid. I was thrilled at the news, longing to get out of the confines of the house and the village and see another place, perhaps with green meadows and gardens instead of this arid and barren terrain. The desert was starting to have a depressing effect on me.

I went to the kitchen to get some yogurt for breakfast. Before the Eid, I had bought Quaker's oatmeal at the *mu'assasa*, a government grocery store that operated in the village, and was planning to sprinkle it on the yogurt. Umm Omar knew what Quaker's oatmeal was. She used it to make . . . soup. I had never heard of putting oatmeal in soup before, but she said it was delicious. She showed me a small tin can of Quaker's oatmeal that Abu Omar had bought for her in Mafraq, emphasizing that it was very expensive. I thought it would be inappropriate of me to consume her expensive oatmeal and had bought a packet for myself at the *mu'assasa*, where it was quite cheap. Umm Omar couldn't believe that I had paid so little for such a big packet. She didn't even know that the *mu'assasa* sold Quaker's oatmeal. The reason for this was that she never did the food shopping herself; Abu Omar did it for her. And here I was, a total outsider, telling her where she could get this staple food at a cheap price.

I prepared my breakfast of yogurt and oatmeal and took the bowl to my room to eat. The concoction that I had made was cold and not particularly tasty, but at least it was nutritious and filling. As I sat on the edge of the bed, eating while reviewing some Peace Corps handouts, the door of my room was suddenly flung open and Umm Omar burst in. Her face was flushed and she looked furious. "What happened?" I stammered, almost choking on the yogurt. She stared at the bowl in my hands and at the packet of oatmeal on the small plastic stand by the bed, and started to apologize. "I'm so sorry, I'm so sorry. I forgot that you're using this room now. I'm used to entering without knocking." And she turned around and left as abruptly as she had burst in. I was stunned. It was such a lame excuse. I had been here for two weeks now. Even her children never came into my room without knocking first. What was her true motive? Did she suspect that I had taken something without permission from the kitchen? Had she come to check on me, perhaps even confront me? I couldn't understand her behavior. An oppressive feeling of uneasiness washed over me.

The morning passed without any visitors. Abu Omar didn't return from his parents' house and we ate lunch without him. It was the same measly lunch as always, Eid or no Eid. I wondered where the meat from the slaughtered sheep had gone. In my mind, I imagined feasting on all kinds of special dishes for the Eid, with lavish amounts of sweets and nuts and pastries. I had seen none of these things, just the *ma'mul tamr* (cookies filled with ground dates) that I had helped Umm Omar to make. Even if Umm Omar hadn't kept them hidden, I wouldn't have eaten any of them because of their high butter content. I knew from my phone conversations with Mona and other fellow volunteers that they were being fed *ad nauseam* all kinds of special holiday treats.

When the afternoon came and Abu Omar had still not returned, I realized that the promised excursion was canceled. Disappointed, I tried to rationalize the situation: his car was too small to accommodate all of us, four kids and three adults; or perhaps he wanted to spend more time with his siblings, who had come all the way from Saudi Araba for the Eid. My thoughts shifted to the other members of my group. Mona had gone off with her host family to Irbid. The four guys had taken a cab in the morning to tour the north of the country. I wasn't allowed to socialize with them in the village or to be seen riding with them in a car, as this would violate the strict sexual code of this segregated society. I felt cooped up.

The only bright spot of the day was when Fatin dropped by in the evening. Her company cheered me up and dispelled my ennui. For supper, Umm Omar prepared a pot of lentil soup and the three of us sat at the kitchen table to eat. Fatin looked at the soup, grinned widely, and said to me, "In Arabic we call lentil soup *lahm al-fuqara*—'the poor people's meat'—because poor people, who can't afford to buy meat, eat lentil soup instead, because it is rich in proteins." How appropriate, I thought to myself, and glanced in Umm Omar's direction. Was she offended? She didn't seem to care or to get the sting in Fatin's remark. I relished the lentil soup—it was hot, filling, and soothing to my stomach, which suffered constant hunger cramps in this house. Fatin asked if I could come to her house the next day to tutor her for the TOEFL exam. I was all too happy to oblige. We chatted about clothes and fashion, and they gossiped a little about their relatives. Shortly after supper, Fatin put on her head covering and abaya and left.

Much to my dismay, I discovered that the burnt light bulb in the bathroom had still not been replaced. If I closed the bathroom door behind me, it was pitch-dark and I couldn't see a thing. If I left it open, the squat toilet would be in full view of anyone in the sitting room. I didn't have a flashlight and neither did the kids. Once again, I mentioned this problem to Umm Omar, who didn't seem to be the least bit concerned. "Leave the door ajar," she said. "No one will enter. Don't worry." I protested that I might fall and fracture an arm or a leg. Could she perhaps replace the light bulb herself? No, she said, only Abu Omar knew how to do this, and he wasn't at home.

I retired for the night, consumed with doubts about my ability to stay in this household. Umm Omar's nonchalance about the absence of light in the bathroom infuriated me. My powers of endurance had eroded from lack of proper sleep and proper nutrition. My walks to the girls' elementary school had become unbearable as boys along the way continued to harass me and throw stones at me. What if a stone hit me in the eye or the head? I couldn't help but conclude that my placement with this host family had been inappropriate. It was absurd that Walaa, the twenty-something language instructor of my group, had been placed in a host family whose house was merely a few minutes' walk from the girls' elementary school and the Peace Corps classroom, while I was placed a mile and a half away and had to walk this distance four times a day. Moreover, all the members of my group had good accommodation—except me. I wasn't looking for any conveniences—I had renounced all the comforts of home when I had volunteered for Peace Corps service. I just wanted to ensure my health and safety.

After another restless night in which Zahra terrorized the entire household, I decided to confide in Mona about my predicament. I went over to her house and was warmly received by her host mother, Umm Khaled, who immediately invited me to stay for lunch. We drank tea in the sitting room and they told me about their excursion to Irbid the day before. When Mona and I retreated to her room, I told her about the problems that I was facing: my host family's house was far away; the *shabab* were throwing stones at me when I walked to school every day; and Zahra was throwing terrible temper tantrums every night. I said nothing about not getting enough food. If word of this got out, it would bring a great shame to my host family. Mona was sympathetic. She said that my host family was paid a lot of money for my accommodation and that a period of two weeks was long enough to know whether this was a good fit or not. She advised me to approach Sultan, our program manager, and Rifaat, the homestay coordinator, and inform them about my situation. In the meantime, she invited me to stay with her, saying that she was used to having a roommate from her days in college. Umm Khaled herself had already suggested this because she took pity on me for being so far away and isolated from my group. Umm Khaled had also told her that she didn't mind hosting two female volunteers together. She had even taken the liberty of proposing this to Rifaat when he had come by to give her the bimonthly payment.

I thanked Mona and Umm Khaled for their support, feeling reassured and composed. Suddenly, the prospect of my moving to another host family seemed neither unreasonable nor unfeasible, but rather unavoidable. I wanted to survive the period of pre-service training so that I could move on to the next stage, the service itself. The pre-service training is the hardest part of the Peace Corps mission, with a high dropout rate, no doubt because volunteers are at the mercy of their host families. I felt I was near my breaking point.

On my way home I called Walaa and asked her to inform Sultan that I wished to be moved to another host family. I wanted him to have the opportunity to process the information before I spoke with him. A few minutes later, he called me on my cell phone and asked for the reasons for my request. I had decided in advance to focus only on the issues of distance and safety. I told him that I had to walk four times a day along a street where rough boys were hurling stones and verbal abuse at me; that the distance I had to cover on foot—four to six miles per day—was too much; and that the days were getting shorter and walking alone in the street in the dark was dangerous. He sounded sympathetic over the phone. His main concern was that the news about my moving to another host family would spread like wildfire in the village and might tarnish the reputation of Abu Omar's family. I said that I would make it clear to everyone that I had to move solely because of distance and safety considerations. I emphasized that I liked Abu Omar's family and that I would stay in touch with them and visit them as often as possible. This would show everyone that there was no quarrel between us, and there would be no gossip. Sultan was satisfied with my answer and promised to get back in touch with me after the Eid. As soon as I hung up, Laurene, the Peace Corps nurse, called. She was unsympathetic and oppositional. She said that she had checked the distance from Abu Omar's house to the girls' elementary school before I had been placed there and had found that it was within Peace Corps parameters. I was dying to say, "Then why didn't you put Walaa there instead of me? She is in her early twenties; she can make the walk much more easily than me, and no one in the street would bother her." But I didn't. Instead, I explained that I was concerned for my safety and that I wanted to remove myself from harm's way. This was one of the most important rules that we were taught in our safety and security sessions. We had to be *alert* to danger and take the necessary steps to *avert* it. Laurene sounded pissed off. I wondered why it was so hard for her to acknowledge that she was wrong.

In the evening, I visited Fatin to tutor her for the TOEFL exam. When her mother saw me, she spontaneously held out her hand to shake mine. I was quite pleased, as this implied acceptance. Her warming up to me was undoubtedly linked to my willingness to help her daughter. But this was precisely the reason for my being here as a Peace Corps volunteer: to share my skills and knowledge with members of my host community and thus promote friendly ties and cross-cultural understanding. On subsequent visits, Fatin's mother would hug and kiss me three times, once on the right cheek, and twice on the left cheek. We would chat over a cup of coffee in the sitting room, where Fatin's father would also be present, and then Fatin and I would retreat to her room to practice TOEFL exams. When she got tired or bored, we would put the exercise book aside and talk about various topics. "I love watching horror movies," she told me with a big grin on her face. She had a television set in her room and watched movies until late at night. "I love makeup," she confessed, and pointed to dozens of cosmetic articles on her dressing table. She even had a variety of colored contact lenses—blue, green, black, and purple. Her own eyes were brown. She was fair-skinned and a bit plump. At twenty-one, she still hadn't figured out what she wanted to do. All she knew was that she wasn't ready for marriage yet and the only way to postpone it was to continue her studies at the university. We also talked about men and dating. She wanted to know how men dated women in the United States. Was it possible for an American man and woman to have a platonic relationship, or were sexual relations the norm? How would an American woman deal with a jealous and possessive boyfriend? My age and life experience put me in a position where she trusted me and felt comfortable discussing such intimate topics.

That evening, I returned to my host family's house well after dark. As always, I took off my shoes outside the door, put them in a plastic bag, and walked inside in my socks. Umm Omar and the kids were at home but Abu Omar was nowhere to be seen. I wondered if he had replaced the light bulb in the bathroom. I flipped the switch and discovered that he had not. Umm Omar apologized that she had

forgotten to tell him. I shook my head in disbelief. This was the third
night in a row that I had to grope my way in the dark when I used the
bathroom. Didn't it bother her at all to use a pitch-dark bathroom?
Her indifference was beyond my comprehension.

As usual, supper was a skimpy meal. Umm Omar made a thin
omelet, perhaps from one or two eggs, which the six of us shared. On
the table was a mini bowl with what she claimed was olive oil, but
I had seen a container labeled "canola oil" under the kitchen counter
when the curtain was open and suspected that the oil came from
there. She said that olive oil was cheap if you made it but expensive if
you had to buy it. The olive trees in the back of the house belonged to
Abu Omar's father. Perhaps the harvest of olives this year was small
and couldn't meet the needs of the entire extended family. The promise of providing jam and hummus for supper, made to me two weeks
earlier, was never fulfilled. I knew that these items were very cheap
from my visits to the village *mu'assasa*. I looked at the four children,
who were all skinny. Better to be underweight than overweight, I
told myself, thinking of the problem of child obesity in the United
States. As on previous nights, I drank two cups of hot herbal tea to
soothe my empty stomach.

After supper, Latifa and I sat together at the computer. She had
an English–Arabic dictionary program that she loved to play with
me. I would say a word in English, which she would type in the designated box, and if she spelled it correctly, the translation into Arabic
would appear on the screen. In this way, she learned new words in
English and I learned new words in Arabic. Zahra tried to grab the
mouse and press the keys on the keyboard, but Latifa pushed her
firmly away. "She will ruin the computer," she said. Of course, Zahra
instantly threw a temper tantrum, forcing Umm Omar to take her
into her bedroom, where she had another, much bigger television, to
watch cartoons together.

That night I felt nervous as I lay in bed thinking about the next
day. I knew that my request to be placed with another host family

in proximity to my group, the Peace Corps classroom, and the girls' elementary school would be granted. But would the new host family be a better fit this time? I thought of the saying, "Better the devil you know than the devil you don't." Then I reminded myself that if I wanted to make it through the period of pre-service training, I had no choice but to stand up for myself. "Well-behaved women rarely make history,"[5] I whispered, as I closed my eyes.

We had language classes in the morning, although it was still Eid. Filled with anticipation, I walked briskly to the Peace Corps classroom. Walaa stood outside, waiting for me. "You have a new host family," she announced. "As soon as Rifaat gets here, we'll go to meet them." "Do you know who they are?" I asked. "No," she said, averting my eyes. She was clearly lying, perhaps to keep me in suspense. A few minutes later, Rifaat arrived and we climbed into his car. He drove to the end of the street, which was very short, turned left onto a dirt road, and pulled up in front of a shabby house flanked by a brand new house on one side and a house under construction on the other side. "This is your new home," he said to me, pointing to the shabby house. "I live across the road from you," Walaa remarked, and pointed to a nice house on the opposite side. The empty field with the three transmission towers stretched from the back of her house to the street where Mona lived, offering a full view of it. I could see Mona's house at one corner of the street and Zach's house at the other corner. My new home was within a five-minute walk from them. Not bad, I thought to myself.

"What's the name of my new host father?" I asked Rifaat. "Abu Ali," he said. "And of my new host mother?" I clumsily continued. "Umm Ali," he said, and burst into laughter. "That's not what I meant," I quickly corrected myself, my cheeks hot with embarrassment. "I meant what are their first and last names?" "Mustafa and Nadia al-Ikhlassi," he replied. We walked toward the house, careful not to stumble over iron rods, building blocks, wooden beams, piles of gravel, and other construction materials that lay on the ground. "Their second son is getting married in the summer, and they're building a house for him," Rifaat explained. "How many children do they have?" I instantly asked. "Ten," he said, grinning from ear to ear. My heart fell to my shoes. *Oh my God! Ten children! I have gone from the frying pan to the fire!* We reached the front door and Rifaat knocked on it forcefully. A woman wearing *isharb* (a scarf that covers the head, chest, and shoulders, unlike the hijab, which covers the head and neck only) opened it. We exchanged greetings, took our shoes off, and went inside.

Umm Ali was a dark-skinned, middle-aged woman of a medium build. Her face was stern and her demeanor composed. I noticed immediately that she spoke a different dialect in which all the feminine endings were pronounced as *itch* rather than as the standard *ik*. After the introductions were completed, she gave us the tour. The house was old but surprisingly spacious. It was laid out in a T shape: the kitchen and bathroom were in the front part of the house; a long and wide hallway ran through the middle of the house all the way to the rear, ending in a back door that opened onto a large, sunny balcony. There were two big bedrooms on each side of the hallway, which was furnished as a sitting room in a traditional style. My bedroom was in the back of the house, overlooking the balcony and the olive grove that stretched behind the house. The room had farshas and pillows on the carpeted floor and curtains on the windows—that was all. No bed, wardrobe, table, or chair. The plaster in the center of the ceiling was missing, probably broken off in the process of installing an exhaust pipe for a heating stove, and the mortar and iron rods that supported the roof were exposed. The door latch and handles were broken. Rifaat told Umm Ali to install a privacy lock on the door and to give me a key. I noticed a television set in the corner of the room. "Is this going to stay here?" I asked, full of hope. "No," Umm Ali said. "This is the only television we have. We'll move it to another room." Next, we inspected the bathroom. It had no lock on the door.

I was mystified. How did a household comprising twelve members use this one and only bathroom without a lock? Did one whistle a tune or sing a song to warn the others that someone else was inside? Again, Rifaat told Umm Ali to install a lock on the bathroom door for privacy. The sink faucet handle was broken and a terrible stench of urine wafted from the squat toilet. Umm Ali apologized that it was still early in the morning and her daughters had not cleaned it yet. I didn't see any of her children; perhaps they were not at home. I took a peek at the kitchen—it was smaller and shabbier than Umm Omar's, and it looked very bare. Back in the entrance hallway, our tour around the house ended. We thanked Umm Ali, wished her *eid sa'id* ("happy holiday"), and left.

"Well, Dalya. This is your new home," Rifaat said. "I'll come tomorrow morning to help you move your things here."

"How did you find this place so fast?" I couldn't resist asking.

"They served as a host family last year. Their eldest son wasn't married yet and the new house that they had built for him was vacant, so we rented it for the duration of the pre-service training of the J14 group. We placed a male volunteer with a male LCF there and also used it as the Peace Corps classroom. Now their son is married and lives in that house with his wife."

His answer puzzled me. If the Peace Corps knew this family and had used their services before, why hadn't they placed me with them at the very beginning? Why did they choose to separate me from my group and put me in an isolated and remote part of the village?

Rifaat drove off and I walked with Walaa back to the Peace Corps classroom, where my group had already gathered for their Arabic classes. They congratulated me on moving to a new host family in proximity to them, acknowledged that it made much more sense, and wondered aloud why it hadn't been arranged this way right from the start. I smiled and said simply, "All's well that ends well."

The day seemed to drag on. I was bored stiff in the Arabic classes and wanted to go home to pack my things. At the same time,

I dreaded the confrontation with Abu Omar and Umm Omar. No doubt they had already been informed that I was moving out and were upset by the news: first, on account of the loss of income; second, on account of potential gossip and damage to their reputation. I would have to explain to them why I was leaving and assure them that it had nothing to do with their hospitality.

I stayed at Mona's house for lunch. Umm Khaled was pleased to hear that I was moving in with Abu Ali's family. She knew them well—they were not only neighbors but also distant relatives—and assured me that I would be happy there.

When I made my way back home for the day, it was already dark and the street was deserted. I rehearsed my speech to Abu Omar and Umm Omar, hoping that they wouldn't be angry. But when I arrived at the house, they weren't there. Only Latifa and the boys were at home. Their parents, they told me, had gone to Mafraq with Zahra. "They decided to avoid me," I thought to myself. "Never mind, I have work to do." I started packing my things. I removed my clothes from the wardrobe and put them in my suitcase. I collected all my papers, notebooks, and books and put them in my carry-on bag. I cleaned the room and threw the trash into the garbage can in the kitchen. When I opened the refrigerator to get a bit of yogurt for supper, I saw that it was completely empty—there was nothing on the shelves, not even scraps of food. I went to the bathroom and flipped the switch. Still no light. "This is absurd," I said to myself. "What a relief that I'm leaving this place." I went to my room and stayed there until I heard the front door open and the voices of Abu Omar and Umm Omar echoed in the house. I took a deep breath, opened my door, and crossed the threshold into the sitting room.

Abu Omar was sitting on the farsha, talking with the boys. I greeted him and sat down opposite him. His face was crestfallen and he didn't look at me. I waited until he finished talking with the boys, and then said, "Abu Omar, the Peace Corps decided to move me closer to my group. I'm leaving tomorrow morning." He lit a cigarette, took a drag, and blew out the smoke directly at me, filling my mouth with a bitter taste. "Why did they place you with us in the first place?" he asked tersely. "They didn't know that the *shabab* would start throwing stones at me," I replied. "Now they are concerned for my safety. I will come to visit Umm Omar and the kids. I love your family and will stay in touch." He looked angry but said nothing. A few minutes later he rose to his feet and left the house. I heard the loud rumble of his car's engine springing to life and then he drove off.

My conversation with Umm Omar wasn't any easier. She wanted to know if I was unhappy in her home. I assured her that I was happy and comfortable, but that the Peace Corps wanted to ensure my safety. I promised to visit and stay in touch. Then I mentioned the burnt out light bulb in the bathroom. She said apologetically that she would remind Abu Omar about it again. "Is there anything to eat for supper?" I asked. She said that they had bought some fried chicken and French fries in Mafraq for the kids. Would I like some? I looked at the time; it was after 9:00 p.m. At this late hour, I couldn't stomach fried food, which is loaded with fat and salt and contains astronomic levels of calories and cholesterol. I politely declined. "Is there anything else, perhaps fruit or vegetables?" I inquired. After all, they had just been to Mafraq, which is famous for its fresh produce market. "Not really," she said. "We haven't done any food shopping yet." I wished her good night and went to bed without supper.

The next morning I arose with the first rays of light. I rolled up my sleeping bag, took the pink coverlet and decorative pillow from the wardrobe, and put them on the bed. When I went to the bathroom to wash my face, I discovered that Abu Omar had finally replaced the light bulb. "It's too little, too late," I muttered to myself. I went to the kitchen for a cup of coffee, and sat waiting for Rifaat in my room. Even before he arrived, Latifa had started moving her things back into the room. She was happy to get her own space back. Having to sleep on farshas in the sitting room with her two younger

brothers for the past couple of weeks had been no fun for her. Abu
Omar was long gone by the time Rifaat had arrived. I helped him
load my bags into his car, hugged and kissed Umm Omar and the
kids, and said goodbye.

It was the last day of the Eid when I moved into my new host family's
house. Umm Ali waited by the door, looking solemn and serene. Six
of her children were at home and I was introduced to each of them.
Fuad, aged twenty-three, was a computer science major at Zarqa
University; Nawal, aged twenty, was a psychology major there; Rana
was in the third year of high school; Ziyad in the eighth grade of
elementary school; Adil in the fifth grade; and Huda, aged four, was
the youngest child. I learned that the two older daughters, Amal
and Mayy, were married to two brothers and lived next to each other
in one of the villages nearby. Ali, the eldest son, worked as a prison
guard, and Usama, who followed him in the birth order, was an army
officer in a military base in the area; they both came home once every
two weeks.

Abu Ali came and shook my hand enthusiastically. Tall, dark-
skinned, and mustached, he wore the traditional Arab garb, with a
checkered headdress of red and white. To my utter surprise, he said
that he had already met me once before when I was walking in the
village with Mona. He said that I had greeted him courteously with
assalamu alaykum (peace be upon you), but that Mona had turned her
head away and had not greeted him. I immediately recalled the incident. Mona and I were on the way to the *mu'assasa* to buy some snacks
and he was standing at the corner of the street, dressed exactly as he
was now. His erect figure, projecting authority, pride, and honor,
had caught my attention. I said to Mona, "Look at this impressive
Bedouin!" But she said, "Dalya, don't look at him and don't talk
to him. It's *eeb* (shame)!" But I did anyway. As an older woman, I
enjoyed more freedom than her and could bend the rules of public
conduct slightly. When we passed by him, I looked straight at him

and said respectfully, *assalamu alaykum*, to which he cordially replied, *wa-alyakum assalam wa-rahmat Allah wa-barakatu* (peace be upon you and God's mercy and his blessing). Now, this selfsame Bedouin was my host father, and I had come to live under his roof and protection. How inscrutable are the twists of fate!

Abu Ali wanted to know if I was really a "daktora" (had a doctorate). He was delighted to hear that I held the highest academic degree and my esteem rose even higher in his eyes. He worked as a security guard at Zarqa University and this entitled his children to study there free of charge. This was why both Fuad and Nawal were students there, although it was much farther from the village (about a ninety-minute bus ride) than Al al-Bayt University.

After the introductions were completed, they helped me carry my bags to my room. Umm Ali brought two blankets and placed them by the farsha that would serve as my bed. I rolled out my sleeping bag on top of the farsha, as everyone watched me with interest. I explained to them that I slept in the sleeping bag and that it kept me warm at night. I showed them how I zipped it open and closed. I got the impression that they had never seen a sleeping bag before. They looked bemused: the expression on their faces said, *Oh, those Americans and their strange habits!* There was no dresser or wardrobe in the room, and no table or nightstand, so I had nothing to unpack.

The parents and the boys left my room but the girls, Nawal, Rana, and Huda, remained. We sat on the farshas and began to chat. Before long, Fatima, the young wife of their eldest brother, Ali, joined us. She was three months pregnant and spent most of her free time with her in-laws, who looked after her and kept her company when her husband was away. Fatima was a teacher of English at an elementary school in a village nearby. She was eager to speak English with me, saying that she had no opportunity to practice at all. At her university, the emphasis was on grammar, not on communication skills, and most of her fellow students had a limited vocabulary and problems with pronunciation. Rana, who was two years away from her *tawjihi* (matriculation exams), had the same complaint. Fatima pronounced the word "Corps" in Peace Corps as "corpse." I told her that the letters p and s were silent and that if she pronounced them she would alter the meaning of the word: *corps* means "a group of people who work together to do a particular job," whereas *corpse* means "a dead body." They were mystified by this peculiar feature of the English language, which has no parallel in Arabic.

Fatima had a bag of sunflower seeds, which she shared with us. The seeds were very small and thus difficult to crack. Nawal and Rana started to giggle, saying that these were *bizr al-mutallaqat,* which literally means "divorced women's sunflower seeds." They explained to me that small sunflower seeds are popularly known by this name because only divorced women have the patience to crack them; the activity distracts their minds from their troubles and allays their worries. By contrast, big sunflower seeds, which are easy to crack, are popularly known as *bizr al-ara'is*, that is, "brides' sunflower seeds."

Naturally, they were curious to know with which family I had lived before. When I told them it was Abu Omar's family, they laughed and said that Abu Omar's family was *fellaheen* (peasants), whereas they were *baduw* (Bedouins). I was astonished. I didn't know that such a distinction existed among the population of this village. They told me that the *fellaheen* were generally fair-skinned whereas the Bedouins were dark-skinned, a characteristic that was borne out by Abu Omar's fair-skinned relatives and Abu Ali's dark-skinned family members. The color of one's skin not only revealed the origins of one's family but also played a role in a girl's marriage prospects. Fair-skinned girls were considered more desirable than dark-skinned girls and fetched a higher *mahr* or brideprice. The two different population groups were also distinguished by their dialects: the *fellaheen* spoke a colloquial Arabic that was similar to the Palestinian dialect while the *baduw* spoke a Bedouin dialect. I had already noticed that Umm Ali pronounced the feminine suffix *ik* as *itch* in phrases like *keef haalitch?* (How are you?), *shuu bidditch* (What do you want?), and *aamil litch shay?* (Shall I make you tea?). The Bedouins looked down on the *fellaheen,* regarding agricultural work as an inferior occupation. Because of the Bedouins' disdain for agriculture, attempts in several Arab countries to sedentarize them had been unsuccessful. Although no one worked in agriculture in the desert village of Hamadiyya, the distinction between *fellaheen* and *baduw* persisted.

Our pleasant chat was interrupted when Umm Ali called her daughters to do their household chores. Every day, Nawal and Rana cleaned the house and did the cooking. On days when they had classes in the morning, they did their chores as soon as they came home: they mopped the linoleum floor in the hallway, did the dishes in the kitchen, cleaned the bathroom, washed the laundry, and cooked lunch. All meals were served in the traditional way—on a sheet of plastic that was laid out on the carpeted floor in the master bedroom, which doubled as the family room.

For my first lunch in my new home, we had *mansaf.* Umm Ali thought it would be easier for me to prop my back against the wall while eating rather than to crouch with them on the floor, so she gave me a small tray with a bowl of finely chopped salad and a plate with rice topped with a chicken hindquarter. I was amazed at this lavish meal. No longer would I need to drink cups of hot tea to soothe my empty stomach! My gaze traveled around the people in the room. Abu Ali and Umm Ali were dressed in traditional Arab clothes but the children were dressed in Western-style clothes. Nawal and Ranaa removed their headscarves in the house but Umm Ali kept hers on. I listened to the casual conversation that flowed around me and felt completely at ease.

The best part was yet to come. "I don't smoke," Abu Ali said to me. "Neither does Fuad. Only Ali and Usama smoke when they come home for a visit."

In the evening, many visitors came to pay their respects to the family on the last day of the Eid. Abu Ali and Umm Ali were proud to introduce me to their relatives and everyone was amazed that I could speak Arabic. Of course, I had to endure the same barrage of questions: How old are you? Are you married? Why aren't you married? Do you have children? Are you a Muslim? and so on. I shook many hands, smiled until my facial muscles felt sore, and sipped sweet coffee with cardamom. Finally, exhausted from being the center of attention, I politely excused myself and retired to my room.

That night, I slept like a log. I didn't wake up even once during the entire night. There was no baby crying and no television blasting away. The house was quiet and peaceful. My room was in the back of the house, far from the front door, the kitchen, and the bathroom, and thus far from any source of noise or disturbance. I had had little expectations when I first came to this house, but now I was well fed, rested, and in the bosom of a caring family.

6. A CLOUD ON THE HORIZON

THERE IS SOMETHING ABOUT THE 13TH DAY OF THE MONTH THAT makes me dread its arrival. It is a day of bad luck. I know that this is a superstition which is completely alien to my Jewish background, but it has taken root in my psyche ever since I was exposed to it through my travels abroad. Whenever the 13th arrives, I refrain from doing anything important. I avoid using a sharp knife in the kitchen for fear that I might cut off a finger and prefer not to drive lest I get into an accident. I know that this is absolutely irrational. In Semitic cultures, uneven numbers like 1, 5, 7, and 9 are regarded as sacred and blessed. In Judaism, the number 13 is especially meritorious: it represents the age at which a boy becomes bar-mitzvah, which is a festive rite of passage marking his transition from boyhood to manhood. There is really no rationale for my fear of the 13th, partic-ularly when it falls on a Friday, except that it reflects a deep sense of insecurity in me. And when bad things happen to me on such a day, my fear is validated.

On the 13th of November, I came with my group from the village to the training site at Al al-Bayt University. Like everyone else, I rushed to take my laptop out of storage and logged onto my email account to check my messages. After spending ten consecutive days in the village in connection with the Feast of Sacrifice, I was concerned that there might be urgent messages awaiting me about my family. Indeed, when I checked my inbox, I found a letter about my brother from my sister in Australia. She wrote that his condition had become critical: the stem cells that had been transplanted into his body had begun to attack his internal organs. He had been in the hospital for four weeks now, with no improvement. She also wrote that our mother's condition had deteriorated; she experienced fainting spells and her doctor diagnosed a weak heart valve. My spirits sank at this news. Neither the complication in my brother's bone marrow transplant nor my mother's fainting spells bode well. Here I was, so close to them, yet so far away! All my assumptions proved wrong. I couldn't even place a direct phone call to them!

As I was replying to my sister's letter, Sultan's assistant approached me to say that Alex Boston, the country director, had sent me an email and requested that I answer it immediately. This was highly unusual. I hastened to check my inbox again, and indeed, there was a message from him with a forwarded letter from another Peace Corps officer. The letter read:

Dear Dalya,

My name is Amy Coltart and I am the Chief of Operations of the Office of Volunteer Recruitment and Selection. The preliminary results of your National Agency Check background investigation were returned to our Suitability and Security Specialist and we need additional information to further assess your eligibility for Peace Corps service. Please read the attached form in detail, complete it, and return it to me as soon as possible.

Best Regards,

Amy Coltart

The attached form that I was asked to complete stated at the top:

The results of your background investigation disclosed a possible connection between your background and the intelligence community. Peace Corps policy makes it necessary to review your eligibility for volunteer service, as it relates to our intelligence policy. This policy requires total separation of the Peace Corps from intelligence activities, both in reality and appearance. Any semblance of a connection will compromise the Peace Corps ability to maintain trust and confidence in our host countries.

This policy applies to any applicant who has engaged in intelligence activities or related work, who has been employed by or connected with such activity, or has an immediate family member who has been so employed. The results of the review may find you fully eligible for service, may bar you from service for a specific time period, or limit your service to certain parts of the world. If doubts exist about an applicant's association with intelligence activity, the issue will be resolved in favor of exclusion from service.

To continue processing your application, we will need to review your answers to the following questions.

I scanned rapidly through the list of questions. In twelve detailed queries, I was asked to describe the intelligence activity that I was involved with, the agency involved, the regularity of contact with the agency, the duration of the connection, the location where the activity was performed, whether contact with foreign nationals was involved, the specific training involved, the duties performed, whether the activity entailed the clandestine collection of information or the analysis of such information, whether the activity was known by the public, whether other family members were connected with the intelligence community, and whether I had any additional information to disclose.

I was in a state of shock as I read Amy's letter and the form. I immediately connected the phone calls that I had tried to place to my brother in Israel with this letter. They must have caught the attention of the Jordanian authorities who were monitoring the volunteers' communications and made them suspect that I was involved in intelligence activities. What a mishap! To think that I was involved in intelligence activities was such an absurdity! I grabbed my laptop and rushed to Sultan's office. He knew my true identity and I felt that I could confide in him. I told him about my brother's hospitalization in Israel, how the week before I had tried to call him on my cell phone and failed, and how now I had received this disturbing email. Sultan seemed totally unaware of this development and quite concerned about it. He called Alex on his phone for me and left the room so I could speak with him in private. I repeated the whole story to Alex, emphasizing that, unless I had been doing something in my sleep that I was unaware of, I had never had anything to do with intelligence activities. Alex replied that he had nothing to do with the actions or decisions of Peace Corps Headquarters in Washington, DC. He asked if I had completed such a form before. I answered that, to the best of my recollection, I had never been asked to fill out such a form before. He advised me to answer all the questions on the form and email it back with an explanation about my phone calls to my brother in Israel. "But I have no idea how to answer these questions," I said. "They are not applicable to me!" He insisted that I must answer the questions. "I don't care what you write. You can write 'none' next to each question, but you must write something."

Reluctantly, I followed his instructions. I wrote "none" next to each question and emailed the completed form back to Amy with a letter in which I stated that I had never been involved in any intelligence activities and that my brother's grave condition was the reason for my repeated attempts to place telephone calls to Israel.

A couple of hours later, Amy responded.

Thank you, Dalya, for your reply. My very best goes to you and your brother. I'm so sorry to hear of his illness. My request is not related to your phone calls. It is in regard to the background check that is conducted upon invitation to serve and the results of that check.

Again, my best to you and your brother and thank you for completing this form.

Amy

Amy's reply was even more disturbing than her first letter. The results of the background check called my eligibility to serve in the Peace Corps into question? The background check was supposed to be conducted *before* extending to me the invitation to serve and *before* sending me overseas! All their pamphlets state that this is the order of the stages in the application process, which I had completed back in April. Now, *after* they had already sent me to Jordan, and *after* I had been in the grueling pre-service training for almost a month, then they bothered to inform me that I may not actually qualify for service! I had been in the application process for almost a whole year, and had waited another six months for my departure date. During this long period, they had plenty of time to conduct my background check. They could have, *should have*, informed me, while I was still in the United States, that there was a problem with my background check. I, an ordinary woman, a spy? What a joke! They imagined my mundane life to be much more adventurous than it really was! But this was no laughing matter. The Peace Corps service meant so much to me—I had put my heart and soul into this undertaking. To be disqualified from service at this juncture, when I had already come so far, would be a terrible blow to me. I ran to my dorm room, flung myself down on the bed, and broke into tears.

My roommate Lora came into the room and saw my red nose and puffy eyes. "What's the matter, Dalya?" she asked, puzzled. "I've got a bad cold," I said, wiping my face with a tissue. "Do you need anything?" she inquired. I shook my head. "No, thanks. I'll lie down for a while and then return to class." She took her book bag and left. I remained curled up on the bed, struggling to regain my composure. A few minutes later, I grabbed my laptop and wrote Miri a frantic letter.

Hi Miri,

You're not going to believe what happened today. I received an email from Peace Corps Headquarters in Washington, DC, informing me that the results of my background check call my eligibility to serve in the Peace Corps into question. I'm in shock! We were ten days in the village, without access to the Internet. I tried to call my brother on my cell phone but the line was blocked. When we returned to our training site at Al al-Bayt University, I rushed to check my emails. There was a worrisome message from my sister about my brother's grave condition and my mother's failing health. My small family is falling apart! Then there was this bizarre email from Peace Corps Headquarters in Washington, DC. I couldn't believe my eyes! I had been in the application process for almost a year and waited another half year for my departure! I answered every questionnaire they had given me and passed all their interviews and requirements. Now, after all these efforts, coming to Jordan and being in training for a whole month, they tell me that I may be disqualified from Peace Corps service because I am allegedly involved in some sort of "intelligence activities"! I don't know who or what they're talking about! I have no idea where I will find myself tomorrow.

Dalya

Within a few minutes, I received her reply.

Hi Dalya,

I'm so sad to read about the condition of your brother and mother. There's nothing you can do about it, except pray with all your heart. I am praying with you . . . and I'm praying for you to be strong.

Reading about the Peace Corps, I'm absolutely shocked. After the wringer that they have put you through . . . to come up with this kind of stupidity! It's absolutely NUTS.

You have to take it one day at a time. Hopefully they will sort things out.

Please take care of yourself.

Miri

Somberly, I began to consider what I would do if the worst came to the worst and I was disqualified from Peace Corps service. I consoled myself that I wouldn't go home immediately. I would first travel around Jordan and see the beautiful sights of the Kingdom. Petra. Yes, Petra first of all. Those red rocks about which I had heard so many legends in my childhood would be my number one destination. Then I would visit the biblical sites of Lot's Cave, Mt. Nebo, and the Springs of Moses. After that, I would go to Madaba, Wadi Rum, and Aqaba. I had already been to the Dead Sea, but it would be interesting to see it from the Jordanian side ...

I was calm and collected when I picked up my cell phone to call Alex. "May I return tomorrow to my village with my group?" I asked in a dispassionate tone of voice. "Yes, of course," he said. "Until we hear otherwise, you will continue your training program like everyone else."

I returned to my village and the home of my new host family, who received me with open arms. "We missed you," Umm Ali said, hugging me warmly and kissing me four times, once on the right cheek and thrice on the left cheek. It was the olive harvest season and there was a lot of work to do in the small olive grove that surrounded their house. I was glad to give them a helping hand. Harvesting olives was a collective effort in which every member of the family participated. First, Ziyad and Adil spread a large sheet of plastic under an olive tree, then gently shook the branches with their hands or with a stick or a rake to make the ripe olives fall off. The girls, Nawal, Rana, and Huda, collected the olives from the ground, filling small cans and buckets that they emptied into a heap on the balcony floor. Abu Ali and Umm Ali picked up the olives from the high branches that Ziyad and Ali couldn't reach or the olives that remained stuck on the branches even after vigorous shaking. When they finished with one tree, they moved on to the next one. Sometimes Adil had to climb up a tree to reach the highest branches. Once, in his rush to get to the treetop, he broke off a big branch. I expected that Abu Ali would yell at his son angrily for being careless. Olive trees are a vital source of livelihood in Arab villages and their owners cherish them and treat them with great care. But Abu Ali looked kindly at his son and didn't admonish him. The harvesting effort lasted for about ten days, and, by the time it ended, the heap of olives on the balcony floor had grown into a little mountain. Then all the olives, which were small and of mixed green and black colors, were placed in big canvas sacks and carried to the village oil press. The quantity of oil that the family got from their olives would meet all their needs throughout the year, until the next olive harvest season. Nothing was wasted—the mixture of crushed olive pits and flesh that was left over after extracting the oil was shaped into cakes and dried in the sun so as to serve as fuel to heat up the house in the winter. A certain quantity of green olives was kept aside for curing and pickling.

The picking of olives brought back fond memories to my mind. I had lived most of my childhood in a neighborhood called the "Olive Grove" in the town of Lod. It got its name from being nestled among olive trees, which were old and graceful, with thick trunks and big branches. My little friends and I used to play hide-and-seek among these trees, compete in climbing to their tops, and look for bird nests on their branches. During the harvest season, the branches would be weighed down with an abundance of fruit. My brother and I would pick the plumpest olives and sort them out by color: black olives went into one can and green olives into another. Then we would go from door-to-door to sell them to our neighbors and earn some pocket money. My brother was timid but I was bold, never too shy to knock on a stranger's door and display our luscious olives. What we couldn't sell we gave to our mother, who would wash the olives, cut three slits in each of them, and put them in jars filled with salt water to cure and pickle them. The years went by and I grew up, and my family moved out of that neighborhood to the city of Bat Yam by the sea. I was in my mid-thirties when I went back to visit the setting of my childhood. I didn't recognize the place. All the olive trees were gone and high-rise apartment buildings stood in their place. A sense of grief and loss gripped me at the sight of this transformed land-scape, which was bereft of its former charm and beauty.

I asked Abu Ali for permission to take pictures of his family picking olives. He agreed, smiling broadly at the camera, with his sons and daughters by his side. Umm Ali also allowed me to snap a picture of her as she carried a big tray of food into the family room for all of us to eat. In these pictures, I saw the faces of simple, hardwork-ing, and decent people. Abu Ali, in his checkered kaffiyeh and black robe, was the figure of authority. Umm Ali, in her burgundy *isharb* (head covering) and matching robe, was the source of nurturance. Abu Ali would get up at 5:00 a.m. five days a week to go to work as a security guard at Zarqa University, a commute that took an hour and a half each way by bus. I never heard him raise his voice to his wife or children. Umm Ali had borne him ten children, five sons and five daughters. She loved to test my memory by asking me to name all her children according to their birth order. I would recite in one breath: Ali, Usama, Amal, Mayy, Fuad, Nawal, Rana, Ziyad, Adil, and Huda and she would grin with delight.

Umm Ali thought that I was younger than her. "I'm approximately forty-eight years of age," she told me. "You must be a little younger than me." "No," I said, "I'm actually older than you." She was astonished. "But you don't have any gray hair!" she exclaimed in disbelief. "I dye my hair," I confessed. She pulled back her *isharb* and showed me her hair. "I dye my hair too, with henna. But it doesn't cover the gray roots," she said ruefully. She wanted to know if I still had my own teeth or if I was wearing dentures. "No false teeth," I said, laughing. "These are my real teeth." She was impressed and eager to know how I took care of them. She had seen me carrying a bottle of green liquid (Listerine mouthwash) with my toothbrush and toothpaste on my way to the bathroom and wanted to know what it was for. "It's a rinse that kills the germs in my mouth during my sleep at night," I explained to her. Surprisingly, Listerine mouthwash was available at the *mu'assasa* in the village, but it was extremely expensive. The Peace Corps medical officer advised us to do without it because we wouldn't be able to afford it on our modest monthly allowance. I told Umm Ali that using a mouthwash wasn't a must. Brushing her teeth regularly with toothpaste was good enough.

The teachers at the girls' elementary school told me that the village's very first primary school had been opened in Umm Ali's parental home when she was a little child. Yet Umm Ali was illiterate. "Why didn't you learn to read and write when the primary school was held in your parents' house"? I asked. She replied that, at that time, all the teachers were male and a girl was forbidden to attend classes taught by male teachers. It was considered *eeb* (shameful). "What about now?" I continued. "All your children know how to read and write. Don't you want to learn now?" She gave me an embarrassed smile and said, "Now my brain is rusty" (*mukhkhi msakkar*). I was dying to say to her, "It's never too late. If you want, I can help you learn to read and write." But I kept my mouth shut. There was a certain status quo in the household and I had no right to disrupt it or to meddle in their private affairs.

There were striking differences between the personalities and lifestyles of my first and second host mothers. Unlike Umm Omar, who was confined to her house and helplessly dependent on her husband to do everything for her, including food shopping, Umm Ali was an independent and resourceful woman who did everything by herself, from running the household to shopping for food and supervising the construction workers who were building a house on the family plot for her son. Once a week, she took the bus to Mafraq to buy groceries, vegetables, and poultry for the family. She would come to me and ask if I needed anything, and I always gave her the same answer: Turkish coffee and pita bread. I preferred pita bread, which is light and fluffy, to flatbread, which is doughy and chewy. I never saw Umm Ali put on makeup or wear jewelry or fancy robes and coats. She didn't have a vain bone in her body. I often recalled how, during the Feast of Sacrifice, Umm Omar stood out among her relatives in her gold jewelry and new, expensive clothes.

"Heaven lies at the feet of mothers," states a famous saying by the Prophet Muhammad. Umm Ali's children cherished her, obeyed her, and treated her with great respect and affection. The only "luxury" that Umm Ali enjoyed was having her daughters, Nawal and Rana, do the household chores for her, from cooking to cleaning to washing the laundry. This gave her a fair amount of free time. I often wondered how she spent this time. Where did she go? What did she do? I learned that she liked to socialize and would visit female neighbors and relatives. Once, we even happened to meet by chance at the same social gathering in one of her neighbors' houses.

I liked Umm Ali's children and got on well with all of them, except for Usama. Unlike his siblings, he was edgy, restless, and quick-tempered. He served on a military base near Mafraq and came home once every fortnight for the weekend. He was engaged to the sister of his brother's wife and was building a house opposite theirs on the family plot. In the village, it was customary for two brothers from one family to marry two sisters from another family and vice versa. For the brides, who normally have to leave their parents' homes and join their husbands' households, this custom has the benefit of reducing their feelings of homesickness by providing them with the comfort of each other's company. For the grooms, this custom has the advantage of reinforcing family ties and interests and preserving family property within the clan. Abu Ali's two older daughters, Amal and Mayy, had married two brothers and lived in apartments next door to each other in a neighboring village. All the financial resources of Abu Ali's family, including the Peace Corps payment for my room and board, went into building the house for Usama. There were days when I had merely a boiled egg with bread for dinner, and I would say to myself, "Today, Peace Corps money went to pay the construction workers."

Usama regarded me with disapproval. I assumed that he was uncomfortable with the fact that, as a woman, I was better educated than him and held the highest academic degree. What was a well-educated woman like me doing in this forsaken village? Why was a single woman my age traveling alone? The idea of volunteering to "promote world peace and friendship" and working "for free" to train Jordanians in various work areas was an utter absurdity to him, as it was to most of the local people I had met. He ascribed ulterior motives to my being in the village and looked at me with distrust and suspicion, as if I was . . . an American spy. Bryan Butki, our programming and training officer, recounted a similar experience from his own career. In introductory remarks about himself, he told us that from 1999 to 2002 he had served as a Peace Corps volunteer in Guatemala, where he had met and fallen in love with a local girl whose brother regarded him as an American spy; and even after he had married the girl and was now her husband of many years, the brother continued to regard him as a spy. So here I was in an incredulous situation: Usama suspected that I was an American spy, while Peace Corps Headquarters suspected that I was . . . an Israeli spy?

I was so intimidated by Usama's demeanor toward me that I started locking my suitcase whenever he came home for a visit. I had several Peace Corps papers in my suitcase bearing the name Dalya Cohen. What if he sneaked into my room in my absence and searched my suitcase? Should he find out that my last name is Cohen, all hell would break loose.

Once, when Usama was at home, I was preparing to wash my hair in the bathroom. As a precaution, I clicked the small padlock on my suitcase shut before leaving my room, unaware that I had left the key to unlock it inside the suitcase. I went to the bathroom, washed my hair and showered, and when I returned to my room, I discovered my mistake. What should I do now? I tried to pry the padlock open. No luck. The only option was to break the zipper. This would ruin the suitcase and I wouldn't be able to use it again. What a pity! I went to Umm Ali and, blushing with embarrassment, told her about my problem. "Don't worry, Dalya," she said reassuringly. "Abu Ali knows how to pick a lock. When he was a soldier in the army, he always lost the key to his trunk, so he had to learn how to pick a lock and is an expert at it. He will open your suitcase in no time after he returns from work in the evening." I thanked Umm Ali and anxiously awaited Abu Ali's return. But how would I explain to him *why* I had locked my suitcase?

When Abu Ali came home, he applied himself to the task of unlocking my suitcase without asking any questions. The entire family gathered around to watch him in action. First, he took a thin paper clip, straightened the metal, and shaped one end into a tiny hook. Then he inserted it into the keyhole and wriggled it right and left several times. No luck. The lock was strong and resistant to prying, and the paper clip broke. I sighed in resignation, certain that I would have to break the zipper. But Abu Ali wasn't ready to give up yet. He looked at my hair and asked me to give him one of my bobby pins. He unbent the bobby pin until the two sides were at a right angle, then, with the help of a pair of pliers, he twisted one end into a slight hook. Next, he probed this makeshift pick into the keyhole and turned it ever so gently inside the lock. Suddenly we heard a click and the lock opened. I was beside myself with joy and thanked Abu Ali profusely. Smiling kindly, he said, "Dalya, you don't need to lock your suitcase in my house. Trust in God. We all put our safety, and the safety of our valuables, in God's protection (*fi aman Allah*)." I felt terribly ashamed. How could I tell him why I had locked my suitcase? How could I explain to him that the *only valuable* item in my suitcase was my *true name and identity,* which I had to keep hidden from him at all times?

This incident heightened the sense of injustice that haunted me in regard to my host family. Here I was, living in their household and enjoying their hospitality under false pretenses. I wasn't a Christian and my name wasn't Seymore, as I was instructed to tell them. I was Jewish, and my name was Cohen, and I was born and raised in Israel. Didn't they deserve to know who the guest they were feeding and sheltering under their roof was? Didn't they have the right to decide who to welcome into the privacy and sanctity of their home? I had no right to deceive these good people. I was a liar and an impostor. Why did the Peace Corps place me in Jordan? Of the many countries— more than seventy-five—in which the Peace Corps is active, only *one* country is hostile to Jewish volunteers: Jordan. Why was I sent to Jordan and not elsewhere? China, for example, welcomes Jewish volunteers, feeling an instinctive affinity for the Jewish people on account of their longevity and ancient history. Jordan, on the other hand, has a large Palestinian population that has been fighting off and on with the Jews of Israel for a hundred years. Why put me in a place where my safety and efficacy as a Peace Corps volunteer could be compromised, then ask me to conceal my identity and pretend to be someone else? Perhaps I should approach Alex to tell him about my moral dilemma and my reluctance to keep lying to these decent people, even if the lies were well-intentioned and for a good cause. Perhaps I should resign from the Peace Corps altogether—it would be an honorable way of departing, rather than being disqualified on the absurd grounds of espionage. But then again, perhaps I should wait a few more weeks to see how this drama would play out, before taking any action.

I kept my promise to stay in touch with Abu Omar's family. Shortly after I had moved out of their house, I returned to visit them. It was a Friday morning and everyone was at home except for Abu Omar, who, by Umm Omar's account, was at the mosque. Umm Omar seemed lonely and depressed when I arrived. She was excited to see me and eager to hear about my new host family. Was their house bigger than hers? Yes. Did I have a bed and a wardrobe in my room? No. What food did they cook for me? *Mansaf, maqlubeh, mulukhiyya, shorbat adas* .... Was their cooking better? No. I tried to be as tactful as possible, affirming to her repeatedly that if it were not for the big distance from their house to the girls' elementary school, I would not have moved out.

We sat in the family room to drink coffee. The television was on and the news anchor was discussing Obama's threat to veto Palestinian national aspirations at the United Nations. Many people in the Arab world considered it a betrayal of the speech he had made in Cairo at the beginning of his administration. Amr Musa, a former secretary-general of the Arab League, was quoted as saying, "We are very, very disappointed." Suddenly, Umm Omar turned her face from the news anchor toward me and said, "I think Obama is an Israeli." I was so stunned by her words that I almost spilled the coffee in my cup. "Why?" I asked, trying to appear nonchalant. "Because his name is Barack, just like the name of the Israeli Defense Minister, Ehud Barak." I needed a few moments to compose myself. Go figure! Americans suspect Obama of being a secret Muslim, while Arabs suspect Obama of being a secret Israeli. How ironic! Slowly, and with a detached tone of voice, I explained to Umm Omar that Barack Obama was born to a Muslim father from Kenya, and that his first name is derived from the Arabic word *baraka,* which means "a blessing." It has nothing to do with the last name of the Israeli Defense Minister, which comes from Hebrew and means "a flash of lightning." Imagine me having to explain this to Umm Omar! On the one hand, I wanted to debunk her misconception; on the other hand, I was afraid that I was revealing too much knowledge and that this might cast suspicions over my own head. After all, how was it that I knew that "barak" means "a flash of lightning" in Hebrew? To be on the safe side, I emphasized that I had researched the similarity in these two names out of intellectual curiosity. Umm Omar listened to my explanation with interest, but the expression on her face indicated that she wasn't the least bit convinced.

Umm Omar switched to the topic of physical exercise and talked about how much she wanted to get back into shape. She had gained weight after giving birth to Zahra and wanted to lose those extra pounds. She said that she used to follow a fitness program on television but it had been taken off the air. Could I get her a workout DVD to do at home? I was astonished by her request. How was I to get her something like this? Her husband had a car and often drove to Mafraq and Amman. Couldn't he get her a workout DVD from one of the shops there? Still, I politely replied that I would ask my fellow volunteers about it. Her daughter Latifa reminded me that I had promised to bring her a mechanical pencil, and I assured her that I hadn't forgotten. She showed me her room: her bed was neatly made with the pink coverlet and matching decorative pillow, and there was a buta gas heater in one corner. She opened the wardrobe and showed me how she had arranged her clothes in it. Her face lit up when I complimented her on her neatness. Umm Omar invited me to stay for lunch, saying that she planned to cook fish. I thanked her but declined the invitation. I didn't want to impose on her and it was certainly not her task to feed me anymore. We kissed and hugged, and I left. As I was walking back toward Umm Ali's house, my cell phone rang. It was Abu Omar. He was very pleased to hear that I had visited his wife and kids and apologized for having missed me. "If I had known you were at the mosque, I would have come a little later," I told him. To my surprise, he replied that he wasn't at the mosque. We exchanged pleasantries and I promised to visit again soon. I took a roundabout way to Umm Ali's house so as not to run into the *shabab* who used to harass me, walking from one end of the village, the eastern quarter, to the other end, the western quarter. During the long walk, I thought about Umm Omar and how different her lifestyle, concerns, and interests were from those of Umm Ali. Then I thought about Abu Omar. He was away from home a lot. I wondered if he was seeing another woman.

Umm Ali appreciated the fact that I had visited Umm Omar. It demonstrated to her that I cared about Umm Omar's feelings and reputation. After all, this was a small village and the news that I had moved out had provoked a lot of speculation. Umm Ali anticipated that I would not eat at Umm Omar's and saved me a plate of food from their lunch. I could tell that she took her duty to feed me seriously. There was always yogurt, tomatoes, cucumbers, eggs, zaatar, olive oil, and olives in the kitchen. Occasionally, she would buy oranges or bananas, or Abu Ali would bring with him pastries, hummus, and teheena on his way home from work. For lunch, I usually ate chicken and rice cooked as *mansaf* or *maqlubeh*. On days when they were low on provisions, I would get lentil soup (*lahm al-fuqara*—the poor people's meat) or a boiled egg. There wasn't a great variety of food but there was *enough* for everyone. I was never hungry and never needed to drink cups of hot tea to calm my growling stomach. I also slept well at Umm Ali's house—there was no baby screaming in the middle of the night and no television going at full blast. It was incredible that, in this large and busy household, which at times comprised fifteen members, I had managed to find peace and quiet.

There wasn't a single table in Umm Ali's house. Everything was done on the floor, from cooking food to eating meals to doing homework. In the evenings, we would gather in the family room, which was also the master bedroom. Nawal would study for her classes at the university and I would help Rana with her English homework. Once, she asked me to write an English composition for her, which I firmly refused. Peace Corps rules forbade us to perform such favors for the children of our host families; we were allowed to help them with homework but not to complete it on their behalf. Rana tried to put pressure on me through her mother, who pleaded with me that her daughter badly needed this composition. Gently, I explained that I was bound by Peace Corps rules and had to comply with them. They were disappointed but never broached the subject again. Fuad was shy and usually kept to himself in his room, which he shared with Ziyad and Adil. Little Huda played with her siblings or by herself. She was loved and pampered by everyone in the family. I often brought her pieces of candy from my visits to the *mu'assasa* or my trips to the training site at Al al-Bayt University.

I hadn't seen any works of Arabic literature in the house and hadn't seen Nawal or Rana read novels or collections of short stories. When I asked them about contemporary Jordanian writers, they had no names or books to mention to me. Arabic literature is the domain of the intellectuals, the wealthy, and the educated. The overwhelming majority of Arab people are poor and illiterate, and even when they are able to read and write, the daily battle for survival leaves them no time or resources to devote to literature.

Abu Ali told me that he had been an expert sharpshooter in the Jordanian army. He proudly showed me a photograph of the then-Prince, Abdullah, now the King, handing him a certificate of excellence as a sharpshooter. Now his two older sons as well as his two sons-in-law worked for the army. The army is the biggest employer in the region and in the country as a whole. Arab etiquette dictated that I should not be alone in a room with my host father, but since the household had so many members, this rarely happened. In addition, little Huda always followed me around. Abu Ali came home from work around 7:00 in the evening, and then the entire family would gather in the master bedroom. It was the center of family interaction and the only warm place in the whole house, as it had a wood-burning heating stove.

The bathroom was very old and in a state of disrepair. The handles of the sink faucet and shower faucet were both broken and I had to insert a fingernail in the groove of the screw to turn them on or off. There was no ventilation and the smell of urine wafted constantly from the squat toilet. The water heater tank was very small; I had to shower fast or else the water would turn cold. When I did my laundry—by hand, of course—I had to use water sparingly because each family received a certain amount of water, calculated according to their size. The first time I did my laundry, which included a couple of bras and underwear, I hung it to dry on the clothesline on the rooftop. It was enclosed by a three-foot-high wall and no one went up there except to hang out the wash or take it back into the house. Within minutes, Umm Ali came to me and asked that I remove my bras and underwear from the clothesline because people walking in the street could see them and it was *eeb* (shameful). She said that there was another clothesline on the rooftop, specifically designed for such intimate items. It was stretched very low, almost touching the concrete floor, so that people passing in the street would not be able to see it. I hurriedly complied with her instructions and assured her that this mistake would not happen again.

Umm Ali's two married daughters, Amal and Mayy, came for an extended visit. Both of them were pregnant, Amal for the second time. Her little daughter, Suad, was Huda's best friend. With these guests and Umm Ali's daughter-in-law, Fatima, the house was teeming with people—fifteen members, including me. It was impressive to see how close-knit the family was. Fatima, who was confined to bed during the first months of her pregnancy, received enormous support from her family-in-law. They cooked for her, cleaned her house, did her laundry, and kept her company on nights when her husband was away. These family members surely felt secure and protected, knowing that they could count on each other in times of need. It was an admirable aspect of Arab family life.

For a while, my days in the village revolved around a pleasant routine. In the mornings, I went to the girls' elementary school, where I did my practicum and attended classes on subjects that interested me. In the afternoons, if I felt like it, I joined my group in the Peace Corps classroom. If I didn't feel like it, I stayed at home with my host family. This happened more often than not, as my relationship with Walaa, the language and culture facilitator, became increasingly tense. An immature, inexperienced, and opinionated Jordanian of Palestinian origin, she knew my true identity. She had seen my last name on the list of volunteers that was provided to the teaching staff and also displayed on the bulletin board at the training site. She had also seen my last name posted above the door of my room in the women's dorm. We both had rooms on the second floor, hers at the beginning of the hallway and mine at the end of it, close to the bathrooms. Every time she went to the bathroom, she passed by my room. That her hostility toward me stemmed from ethnic and religious intolerance was borne out by several incidents. On one occasion, I was sitting in the classroom when one of the guys in my group asked her for the Arabic word for "stingy." As she was about to reply, Mona jumped in and said, "In my family, we use the word *Yahudi* (that is, a Jew) for stingy." Walaa nodded in agreement and the two of them burst out laughing. I gave them a long, hard look, and said,

"This is a racist remark that doesn't befit the Peace Corps mission." They immediately wiped the smiles off their faces and pretended that it was a joke. A very *revealing* joke, I should say.

I sensed that my education was also a factor in Walaa's hostility toward me. I heard her make false statements about controversial aspects of traditional Jordanian culture (for example, that honor crimes and female circumcision are nonexistent in Jordan). Although I never corrected her in class, she was well aware of my academic background and my ability to detect her mistakes. Her demeanor toward me as an older woman was at times condescending, at other times patronizing, and generally discourteous.

I had no idea how hostile Walaa had become until I saw her written assessment of my language training. It was so negative that it smacked of pure prejudice. I could read and speak Arabic fluently; I interacted effectively with my host family, village people, and teachers at the girls' elementary school; I completed all my assignments and submitted them on time. And here was this fatuous girl finding fault with all my work. I told Walaa to her face that her report was biased and that I would dispute it in my upcoming meeting with Bryan Butki, our programming and training officer. In a lengthy conversation that I had with him, I openly expressed my concerns about Walaa's overt animosity toward me. I pointed out to him that my last name *wasn't protected* by the Peace Corps office and that, although they had asked me to assume a different last name, I continued to appear as Cohen and *not* as Seymore on all the lists of the J15 group and subgroups that were posted on the bulletin board and above classroom doors. He was astonished to hear this and said that he would alert the office about it. I also pointed out to him that Walaa's Arabic classes were ridiculously below my level and that she failed to engage me in any meaningful activity. Her conduct was unprofessional and inconsistent with the Peace Corps core principle of tolerance and respect for other people's differences. Bryan was visibly unhappy about all this. He said that he would have a talk with Walaa and then follow up with me. I left the meeting doubting that anything productive would come out of it. The Peace Corps office hires a lot of HCNs (host country nationals) as auxiliary staff. Complaining against one of these employees is a very sensitive and complicated matter, which has to be handled extremely delicately so as not to offend the host community.

The conflict with Walaa reminded me of what had happened to my aunt Alice, my mother's youngest sister. Alice was a bright student at the government school that she had attended during the 1940s in Baghdad, the city where she was born and raised. Her Arab Muslim teacher hated her because she was Jewish and constantly abused her verbally and physically. One day she hit her hard on the head—corporal punishment in the classroom was a common practice in those days—and since then Alice could not talk or walk properly again. She must have suffered brain damage from the severity of the blow that she sustained. In 1952, when all the Jews were expelled from Iraq following the establishment of the State of Israel, Alice came with her family to Israel. She had spent a few years in the hospital but never recovered. As a little girl, I had seen her a few times before she passed away and asked my mother what was wrong with her. My mother would always break into tears when she recounted her sister's tragedy.

Now, I was getting a taste of this blind hatred. Walaa was not my first encounter with this form of bigotry. I had a similar experience in Egypt in 1999, when I was awarded a summer fellowship at the Arabic Language Institute of the American University in Cairo. One of the staff members there was an elderly female instructor of colloquial Egyptian who made my life miserable. With a name like Cohen, it is as if I'm wearing the Star of David on my forehead. It doesn't matter that there are peace treaties between Egypt and Israel and between Jordan and Israel. Those who want to hate the Other will always find a justification for their hatred.

A couple of weeks had passed since I received that disturbing email from Peace Corps Headquarters, and there was still no news. Although my training continued as usual, I had lost a lot of my motivation and enthusiasm. On the one hand, I walked around like a doomed person whose time was running out. On the other hand, knowing that my stay in Jordan might soon be terminated made me savor every minute. As part of our pre-service training we were scheduled to go on a two-day site visit to a Peace Corps volunteer in active service. When I found out that my destination was the village of Taybeh in the southern part of Jordan, just a fifteen-minute drive from the sacred mountains of Petra, I was beside myself with joy.

7 . ROCKS TO DIE FOR

ANY SABRA WHO GREW UP IN ISRAEL IN THE LATE 1950s WOULD
have heard the haunting song *"Ha-Sela Ha-Adom"* (The Red Rock),
which sings of Petra. Recorded by the popular Israeli singer Arik
Lavie in 1958, it was forbidden to be played on the radio for fear that
young Israelis might be tempted to cross the border into Jordan to
see Petra and put their lives in danger. Several groups of Israeli hikers who tried to reach Petra between 1953 and 1957 were shot dead
by Jordanian troops. In Israel's early history, Petra came to symbolize
the most daring, dangerous, and heroic adventure. Hiking to Petra
became the ultimate dream of the Sabra, serving as a test of courage,
perhaps even a rite of passage. Only few realized this dream, and very
few were able to return home safely. Their stories became the stuff
of legends, celebrated in songs, plays, documentaries, movies, books,
and numerous newspaper articles. Despite the danger—or perhaps
because of it—the myth of Petra continued to spark the imagination
of Israeli youths and remained the ultimate destination for Israeli
hikers until the Six-Day War in 1967, when vast new territories for

exploration were opened to them, foremost among them the Sinai Peninsula. The tradition of hiking to Petra continued into the early 1990s, and Israeli daredevils caught by Jordanian troops were usually shot dead and occasionally arrested, interrogated, and returned to Israel. With the signing of the peace treaty between Israel and Jordan on October 26, 1994, Petra became accessible to Israeli tourists, who arrived in droves to see it. Petra is still the foremost attraction for Israeli visitors to Jordan.

These thoughts flashed across my mind as I sat on the bus heading for the town of Wadi Musa—the gateway to Petra—where I was to meet Sharon, a J13 Peace Corps volunteer serving in the neighboring village of Taybeh. Sharon told me over the phone that she had a fabulous view of the rocky mountains of Petra from every window in her house. I was thrilled. I had never seen Petra. Every time I tried to join an organized trip from Israel to Petra, all the tours were booked full. Now I was going to have a front-row view of this mythological place, chosen in 2007 as one of the new Seven Wonders of the World.

The objective of our site visit was to learn from the experiences of our host Peace Corps volunteers both at work and living in their communities to get their advice on how to make our transition to Peace Corps service a smooth one and to hear about the challenges and obstacles they had faced. What coping mechanisms and strategies of resilience had they developed? What successes were they able to achieve and how? The specific site visit chosen for a volunteer in training was not necessarily his or her permanent site.

The trip to Wadi Musa was long and multi-legged. First I boarded the bus from Al al-Bayt University to Mafraq, then I got on another bus from Mafraq to Amman. In Amman I took a taxi to get from Raghadan bus station, which is located downtown, to Wahadat bus station, from where the bus to Wadi Musa departed. Buses in Jordan don't have a fixed schedule. They leave the station when all the seats are occupied, so people have to wait on the bus until it fills out. Sometimes the wait is just ten minutes; sometimes it is an hour or even longer, depending on the destination and time of the day. The bus ride from Mafraq to Amman took about one hour, and from Amman to Wadi Musa it took about three hours, with a short stop midway. Four other girls traveled with me: two were visiting the youth development Peace Corps volunteer in Wadi Musa, and two were visiting the youth development Peace Corps volunteer in Taybeh. They were a little nervous—it was the first time for them to venture out on their own into Jordanian society and rely on whatever communication skills in Arabic they had acquired. I, on the other hand, felt completely at ease and in my element.

I negotiated with the taxi driver the price for the ride from Raghadan bus station to Wahadat bus station and sat next to him in the front while the other four girls squeezed together in the back seat. The driver and I spoke in Arabic. When he heard my companions speak in English he asked me who we were. I told him that we were American Peace Corps volunteers. As soon as he heard the word *American,* he launched into a tirade against the United States. "Why does America kill Arabs in the Middle East? What right does America have to interfere in the Arab countries' internal affairs? Why is America always on Israel's side?" I answered evasively that we were Peace Corps volunteers, and as such we had no political affiliation or sentiments. He dismissed my answer out of hand, regarding me with skeptical eyes. The girls in the back seat fell silent. The expressions on their faces indicated that they had no idea what the driver was so angry about. "How is it that you agree to work for free?" he asked me suspiciously, laughing at the idea that we had come to Jordan to promote world peace and friendship. "America *makes wars* in the Middle East, not peace," he said accusingly. He was a Palestinian who had lived in Kuwait for many years, until he was expelled in the wake of Saddam Hussein's invasion of Kuwait in 1990. Still, he was loyal to the Iraqi dictator. "Saddam Hussein was good to us. He gave Jordan free oil. He gave money to the families of martyrs. Now that he is gone, is the Middle East better off? Iraq is destroyed and there

is no Arab leader who can stand up to Iran. It's all America's fault!"
he stated bitterly. His angry words, which echoed the criticism made
by Umm Omar's mother and brother, revealed to me how badly tar-
nished America's image was in the minds of ordinary Jordanians.

When we boarded the bus to Wadi Musa, we had to wait forty-five minutes until all the empty seats were filled. I sat in one of the
front rows by the window, watching the colorful procession of people
in the street and those who got on the bus. A young English couple
arrived, looking distinctly like tourists. The driver charged each of
them twice the fare (JD5) that he charged us (JD2.65), and when
he saw me looking at him with a smile on my face, he asked me in
Arabic not to say anything to them. They settled in their seats across
the aisle from me and then the girl wrapped her arm around her boyfriend's neck and drew him close to her. I wondered whether she was
unaware of the rules of public conduct in this conservative society or
whether she was aware of them and simply didn't care. A Bedouin
dressed in shabby clothes and carrying two large plastic bags filled
with plump green olives wanted to get on the bus. The driver refused
him, saying that oil might leak out of the bags and make the bus
floor slippery. The Bedouin pleaded with him, swearing that the bags
were made of sturdy plastic that wouldn't leak. After a long wait,
the driver relented and let the Bedouin fill the last empty seat. Then
we set off on our journey through the stony, bleak desert. There was
nothing green in sight—no trees or vegetation, just sandy hills and
rocks. Steel transmission towers carrying power lines and telecommunication cables crisscrossed the desolate terrain, bringing electric-
ity, telephone, and television services to small villages scattered here
and there. The monotonous view coupled with the motion of the bus
lulled me to sleep.

I was aroused from my slumber by a lively conversation on the
bus radio. A talk show host was asking Jordanian men and women to
weigh in on the topic of exercise and physical fitness. I was amazed
by the large number of English words that the radio host and her

guests mixed into their spoken Arabic. The conversation was both entertaining and informative, as it revealed the interests and concerns of the local people. In contrast to the old Arab ideal of feminine beauty, which endorsed corpulence, the men on the radio said that they wanted to see their wives watch their weight and stay in shape. Likewise, women expressed a desire to see their husbands exercise regularly and take care of their physiques. The radio host moved on to the topic of personal relationships, taking calls from listeners. A guy called in, complaining about an obnoxious male relative who was treating him badly, and asked how he should respond. "If you want to kill a man, ignore him," the radio host advised. I burst into resounding laughter. Here I was, on a bus in the middle of the desert, getting a valuable lesson on how to deal with a bully. Why had no one back home ever given me this precious piece of advice? In the home of my host family in the village, I had no radio. Realizing now what I had been missing, I decided to buy one at the earliest opportunity.

We had a short break in a resting area exotically called the Oasis of Dreams (*Rahat al-Ahlam*). All the passengers got off the bus to stretch their legs and get something to eat. The women lined up in front of the toilets—Turkish-style, of course, but surprisingly clean. I bought some snacks at the convenience store. I spotted the English guy from the bus sitting with three traditionally dressed Bedouins at a café table, sharing their meal. He seemed very hungry. Couldn't he afford to buy his own meal? His girlfriend stood at a distance, impatiently waiting for him. She had taken off her sweater and was wearing merely a tank top, her bare white skin gleaming in the sunlight. The local people were staring at both of them. They seemed completely out of place and out of touch with the values of traditional Arab culture.

After the break, we continued on our way. We had started our journey at 7:30 in the morning and arrived in Wadi Musa at 1:30 in the afternoon. As the bus approached the small town, spectacular views of the rocky mountains of Petra began to unfold before our eyes. The unique rosy color and the swirl of the rocks, wrapped up in the glow of the sun, were breathtaking. All the legends that I had heard about Petra in my childhood came flooding back to me. I couldn't take my eyes off this spellbinding sight. I wished that we could forget the objective of our site visit and just go sightseeing!

Our hosts, Sharon, Jane, and Barbie, were waiting for us at the final bus stop in Wadi Musa. I had met Sharon briefly during the "culture night" at the training site at Al al-Bayt University the month before. It was impossible to forget Sharon once you had met her. A petite and elegant lady in her golden years, she was perhaps the oldest Peace Corps volunteer serving in Jordan. I immediately understood why we were paired together: it was on the basis of age. Although I was considerably younger than Sharon, I was also considerably older than my fellow volunteers, who were in their early twenties to early thirties, the same age as Jane and Barbie.

Hungry after our long trip, we agreed unanimously to have lunch first. Jane took us to a restaurant that served local food. Choices on the menu were limited and the prices high, but Jane knew the owner and negotiated a discount. I listened to her as she spoke Arabic with him. Not bad, I thought. Some volunteers become fluent in Arabic after two years of service; others give up on Arabic and rely on English to communicate with the locals. Given the Jordanians' eagerness to speak English, this is an easy way out for them. Jane, like Sharon, was a J13 volunteer at the end of her Peace Corps service. Barbie was a J14 volunteer, with one more year to serve. After lunch, we split into three groups and went our separate ways. Jane took her two guests to her home in Wadi Musa, Barbie and her two guests boarded the bus to Taybeh, and Sharon took me to the souk in Wadi Musa to buy fruit and vegetables before heading home.

The souk was small and crammed with stalls displaying a variety of fresh produce. I had been to the souk in Mafraq before and was impressed by the abundance of local fruit and vegetables, which were sold at cheap prices. Sharon bought bananas, tomatoes, and cucumbers, and I bought a few apples and oranges, and then we went to the bus station to wait for the next bus to Taybeh.

Taybeh is the second largest village after Wadi Musa in the Petra area. Located about 10 km southeast of Petra, it is a short fifteen-minute drive from the entrance to the ancient city. While Wadi Musa is a town of hotels, restaurants, and shops that sprung up around Petra, Taybeh is a traditional village perched on top of high hills with panoramic views of the rocky mountain range around Petra. It is most famous for its unique Taybet Zaman Hotel and Resort, created using old village houses that were converted into hotel rooms furnished in the Bedouin style. The attractive resort includes stone alleys, a Turkish bath, a museum, a piazza, a bazaar where pottery, weaving, and other crafts are produced on site, a traditional Arab bakery, and a restaurant.

As usual, we had to wait until all seats were filled before the bus left the station. I had drunk a lot of water at lunch and felt a little pressure on my bladder. The bus ride was supposed to be twenty minutes long and I estimated that I could hold my pee in provided the bus filled out and left quickly. It didn't. When the driver finally set off, I badly needed to pee. I tried to distract my mind from my pressing problem by looking at the stunning view. In my heart, I prayed that there would be no stops or delays along the way. But after just a few minutes the driver veered off the main road and the bus came to a standstill. What happened? I looked in alarm out the window, fearing that we had a flat tire. I saw that we were parked at a gas station and that the driver was preparing to pump fuel into the bus tank. I wondered why he hadn't done this before picking the passengers up at the station. After a long interval during which the driver unhurriedly fueled the bus and chatted animatedly with the gas station attendant, we resumed the ride. I was growing increasingly nervous and closed my eyes, afraid that any bump on the road or sudden jolt would cause me to lose control and pee in my pants. No sooner were we back in motion than the driver abruptly pulled over, opened the door, and jumped out. What was it now? Was the engine overheated? I looked in panic out the window. I saw a produce vendor standing with a horse-drawn cart on the other side of the road. The driver was loudly haggling with him over the price of potatoes as he picked them one by one from a wooden crate and put them in a plastic bag. I gasped in disbelief. The driver was running errands while on duty! Where was he going to stop next? At the barber's shop to get a shave and a haircut? I looked anxiously around me, imagining that at any moment one of the passengers might bring out a chicken from a bag under the seat and light a portable primus to cook dinner, accidently setting the bus on fire, as had happened in India. The passengers sat quietly, their faces expressionless, as if the driver's behavior was completely *aadi* (normal)! Suddenly it hit me that I was in the Middle East, where the sun is hot, the desert vast, and time infinite. I began to laugh at myself. For the remainder of the ride, I sat stoically in my seat, praying that I would not embarrass myself. Luckily, the driver had no more errands. After a forty-five-minute ride that seemed like an eternity, he dropped us off in front of Sharon's house. I rushed into her bathroom to relieve myself and found a pleasant surprise: a Western-style toilet.

Sharon's house was modest but quiet and private. She was right about the fabulous views of the rocky mountains of Petra from her windows. I watched the sun set over the rocks in the distance, turning their rosy-red color into a dazzling spectacle of glowing red as it slowly disappeared behind the mountains. I drank in this spellbinding sight, justly named by the BBC as "one of the forty places you have to see before you die." As if in a daydream, melodies and lyrics in Hebrew began to steal into my ears. I closed my eyes and abandoned myself to these familiar sounds from my childhood, expecting them to vanish momentarily. Surely, this was just my imagination. But no, there was no mistake. These were Hebrew words and songs. *"Kan Galei Tzahal"* (This is the I.D.F. radio station), I heard a voice announce. Galei Tzahal is a leading Israeli radio network, operated by Israel Defense Forces. I jumped from my place by the window and rushed to Sharon, who was preparing supper in the kitchen. "What am I hearing?" I asked, hardly able to conceal my excitement. "Oh, this is my favorite radio station," she replied. "It's broadcast from Israel. We're so close to the border that I can easily tune in to it. I don't understand a word of what they're saying, but they have great music and I love listening to it." I was speechless for a moment. "But what if your neighbors find out that you're listening to an Israeli radio station?" I asked when I finally found my tongue. She shrugged her shoulders indifferently. "They can't hear it and I listen to it only when I'm by myself." I wanted so much to tell her right there and then that I was a Sabra, that I spoke Hebrew, and that I understood every word they were saying on the radio, but I didn't. A secret is no longer a secret once you divulge it, even to a single soul. All this time I had been guarding this secret with my life, so why make an exception now? I had to be consistent.

Sharon was a widow from Tucson, Arizona. She held a PhD in educational psychology from the University of Arizona and had taught for twenty years at the University of Phoenix, Tucson campus. The mother of two married children and the grandmother of several grandchildren, she looked for something meaningful to do after her husband's passing. As she recounted to me, she was sitting in a contemplative mood on her porch and staring at the horizon when suddenly the words "Peace Corps" appeared before her eyes. She applied, passed all the medical tests and other requirements, and was sent to Jordan as a teacher of English. A petite, soft-spoken lady, with minimal Arabic language skills, she adapted successfully to village life in Taybeh and was loved and respected by her students and colleagues at the girls' secondary school.

Sharon told me that a year into her Peace Corps service, her elderly father had fallen very ill and the Peace Corps had given her permission to travel to the United States to nurse him and had even paid for her flight. I thought immediately about visiting my brother.

Earlier, when I had checked my emails on her computer, there was a distressing message from his wife about his condition. The doctors were losing hope, she wrote. If I wanted to see him, now was the time and I must hurry up. I resolved to fly to Tel Aviv as soon as I returned from Taybeh to the training site at Al al-Bayt University. Our site visit was meant to last only a couple of days. Upon our return, we would have a site visit debrief, followed by a ceremony in which our site assignments would be announced. Both Alex and Bryan would be at the ceremony, which would give me the opportunity to approach them with my request.

The next day I was expected to accompany Sharon to her school. She told me that she usually got up at 5:30 in the morning to prepare for school. I assumed that she got up so early to do her lesson planning for the day, but I was in for a big surprise. I woke up when her alarm clock rang and observed her morning routine. She got up so early . . . to do her hair and makeup! She sat in front of the television with an iron curler in one hand and a cup of coffee in the other, styling her hair as she watched David Letterman's late night show and sipped coffee. She had the same hair color and hairdo as Nancy Reagan's; not one strand of hair stood out of place. After she finished styling her hair, she applied her makeup: green eye shadow for her light-colored eyes, black mascara, and pink lipstick. When she was done, she looked like she had just stepped out of a beauty parlor. I couldn't help but admire her attitude and stamina. Alone and isolated in a remote village, Sharon structured her days around fixed rituals that helped her cope with her new living reality and also made her feel good about herself.

We left for school at 7:30 in the morning. The sun was low in the sky and the air was chilly. We climbed up a steep, unpaved road strewn with stones, where one wrong step could result in a fall and perhaps a twisted or broken ankle. Sharon walked with remarkable agility, her steps cautious but steady. By the time we reached the top of the hill, I was out of breath. I paused to rest and took a look around.

Ahead of us was a small park that overlooked the valley and the mountain range in the distance. The park was lovely, with pathways winding between green shrubs and leafy trees, and wooden benches to sit on. It was a rare sight to behold in this desert area. A little further ahead was the girls' secondary school, an imposing building that looked spacious and well maintained, and was equipped with a gym, a library, and even a daycare facility for the staff's children. It was a far cry from the small and shabby girls' elementary school in my village and my eyes were wide with amazement. Sharon was quick to point out to me that the school was well kept thanks to being a member of the Community School Project of the British Council. This membership entailed a cultural exchange program between five British schools and five Jordanian schools, for which the participating schools received generous funding. She proudly showed me several improvements that she had implemented in the school with the help of funding from US Aid: water filters in the kitchen, drinking fountains in the hallways, portable heaters for the classrooms, and colorful curtains for the classrooms windows.

I was introduced to the principal and teaching staff. They were curious to know who was older, Sharon or I? With a deadpan expression, Sharon told them that she was "the oldest person in the world"; she didn't know her exact age because she had stopped counting after one hundred! I couldn't suppress my laughter. Her witty reply embarrassed the teachers and they refrained from asking us any more personal questions.

Sharon took me to meet her students and see their classrooms. The girls were quiet and polite, their desks neatly organized, and their classrooms clean and tidy. The walls were decorated with portraits of King Abdullah with his wife and children, sometimes placed side by side with portraits of King Hussein and Queen Noor. The Jordanians love their royal family and show great respect for them.

We left the school around noon and went to meet Sharon's landlady, Nabila, who was the *mudira* (principal) of the girls' elementary school in the village. Nabila had asked the Peace Corps office to assign a volunteer to her school and, because I was sent to visit Sharon, she assumed that I was her replacement. It was very hard to disabuse her of this assumption. She insisted on showing me the apartment where I would be living, the furniture that I would be getting, the shops I would be buying food from, and, of course, her school.

The first thing I noticed when I entered the courtyard of Nabila's school was a large map of Jordan and its neighboring countries, which was drawn on the outer wall of the building, facing the square of the morning assembly. Lebanon, Syria, Saudi Arabia, Iraq, and Egypt were there. But Israel *wasn't* there. Instead, all the territories west of the Jordan River up to the Mediterranean Sea, then north of the Sea of Galilee up to the border with Syria, and then south of the Dead Sea up to the border with Egypt were marked as Palestine. The Jewish state was wiped off the map! My heart sank and my stomach was in knots. The peace treaty between Jordan and Israel was signed seventeen years ago. Why was Israel erased from the map? Was this what was inculcated in the minds of the young children who came to this school every day? That Israel does not exist? That she has no right to exist? A sense of disillusionment washed over me. Wherever I turned to look in this country, the never-ending Arab-Israeli conflict stared me in the face.

The poor condition of the school reminded me of the girls' elementary school in my village: small and crowded classrooms, old and broken desks and chairs, dirty walls and floors. Obviously, not every Jordanian school has the good fortune of belonging to the Community School Project of the British Council. The teachers looked at me with resentment, as if I had come to steal the job from one of them. The young students looked at me in wonder, as if I was a strange creature from another planet. There was no heating in the classrooms, so they sat on their wooden benches wearing their hats, scarfs, mittens, and coats. I greeted everyone cordially and smiled until my facial muscles felt sore. When the bell rang, announcing the end of the school day, I felt relieved. I was tired and Petra was on my mind. I wanted to go there and see it immediately—it was just a fifteen-minute taxi ride away—but the principal, Nabila, had invited us for lunch at her house and would be offended if we turned down her invitation. "What's the hurry, Dalya?" Sharon asked. "You will have plenty of opportunities to see Petra after you finish your pre-service training." I couldn't tell her about the dark cloud hanging over my head—it would be dangerous. Unable to come up with any compelling excuse, I reluctantly agreed.

Nabila was a middle-aged wife and mother. At the end of her workday she went home to cook and do her household chores. She looked very tired when we arrived and I wondered why she had invited us in the first place. Her eldest daughter, aged fourteen, helped her prepare the meal and also took care of her four-year-old sister. I had observed this pattern in both the homes of my first and second host families. Especially when the household consists of a nuclear family rather than an extended family, the eldest daughter becomes her mother's main domestic help. While this traditional pattern of Arab family life was borne out by my personal observations, others were not. For example, in contrast to the image of a stern and cold father, depicted in many Arabic autobiographies and social studies, Abu Omar and Abu Ali were warm and affectionate with their little daughters, Zahra and Huda, who were also pampered by both their mothers and siblings.

We had *mansaf* with chicken for lunch. We sat on farshas on the floor to eat and chat. The conversation was mostly in English because Sharon couldn't speak Arabic. Nabila's house was brand new—they had moved in the year before. It was spacious and furnished in a traditional style, but the guest bathroom was equipped with a commode and had full plumbing. When I requested permission to use it, Nabila sent her eldest daughter to check if there was toilet paper. In traditional Jordanian homes and public bathrooms there is no toilet paper, only a water hose for washing. The house was very cold, much colder than outside, because the concrete roof and walls had trapped in the cold air. We huddled around the *sobba* (buta gas heater) and covered our feet with blankets to keep warm. I felt drowsy from the carbon monoxide emitted by the heater. I glanced at the *mudira* and saw that she could barely keep her eyes open. I signaled to Sharon that we should leave. We rose to our feet, thanked Nabila for her hospitality, and left. The fresh air outside invigorated us and we walked briskly to the bus station. It must have been siesta time because the street was completely deserted.

Back at Sharon's house, I climbed to the rooftop to take one last look at the magnificent rocks that were the fodder of so many legends in my childhood. The grandeur of the rocks, highlighted by the glow of the setting sun, was hypnotic. I found myself humming softly, *oh ha-sela ha-adom,*[6] the refrain from the forbidden song of Arik Lavie. It felt surreal to have come so close to Petra, yet not to set foot in the ancient city and only to be able to view it from a distance. The Biblical story of Moses sprang to my mind. He had wandered with the Israelites in the desert for forty years—but he wasn't destined to enter the Promised Land; his only solace was to see it from afar. What a heartbreaking disappointment it must have been for him.

The following day was Thursday, November 24. Not only was it Thanksgiving, but also the day when our site assignments would be announced. I promised Sharon that I would let her know where I was assigned as soon as I found out. She had a lot of stuff to give away to the volunteer who would replace her: a bed, a dinette set, a television set, a refrigerator, a buta gas heater, a cooking top, a microwave oven, pots, plates, cups, and silverware. It was extremely generous of her not to ask for money for her stuff. I knew of other departing volunteers who charged those who came to replace them a pretty penny for every item. The volunteer assigned to teach at the girls' elementary school in Taybeh would be very lucky because it would be easy for her to settle into her new apartment with all this stuff. I loved the location of Taybeh and would have been perfectly happy to serve there myself, but deep down I knew that my chances were slim. For one thing, volunteers were rarely assigned to the same site that they were sent to visit. For another, I hadn't forgotten for a minute the dark cloud that was hanging over my head.

I got up at sunrise that morning, thanked Sharon for her hospitality, and set off on the long trip back to Mafraq. I met up with the other four Peace Corps volunteers at the bus station in Wadi Musa and together we boarded the bus to Amman. We were all very pleased with our site visits, which broke the monotony of our training in the village and at Al al-Bayt University. Our only complaint was that the site visit was too short. How we wished that we had another day to relax and enjoy it!

As the bus sped through the desert, I pondered over my obligations. My first priority was to see my brother. The fact that Sharon had been allowed to travel to Arizona to see her ailing father made it easier for me to ask for permission to fly to Tel Aviv. I thought it more appropriate that I should wait until after the site assignments announcement before I approached Bryan and Alex. I gazed at my fellow volunteers, who looked relaxed and without a care in the world, and I envied them. I had left the United States thinking that all my problems were behind me; yet here I was, weighed down with constant worries.

We arrived back at Al al-Bayt University tired and hungry but eager to complete the site visit debrief and anxious about the site assignments announcement. The square in front of the Peace Corps buildings had been prepared in advance for the ceremony: the lines of the map of Jordan were drawn on the asphalt and the names of various villages and towns from Irbid in the north to Aqba in the south were written in big letters on pieces of cardboard and placed in their appropriate location on the map. Bryan conducted the ceremony. He would announce a volunteer's name and site assignment and hand him or her a manila envelope that contained a certificate with a description of their specific task, information about their new community, and photos of the site. The volunteer would take the envelope, find the location of his or her village or town on the map, and stand there. When my name was announced, along with the words Karak/Mu'ta, I had no idea where the region or the town was. I located it on the map in west-central Jordan, about 24 km east of the Dead Sea. I assumed my position and glanced around to see which volunteers, if any, had been assigned to sites in proximity to me. I then took my certificate out of the manila envelope and began to read: "Congratulations! Dalya Cohen. Your University's Name: Mu'ta University." I stared at the words in amazement. I had been assigned to teach at the English department of one of Jordan's acclaimed universities! The three photos of the university that were enclosed with the certificate showed a beautiful campus with modern architecture and aesthetic landscaping. A wave of excitement swept through me. For a moment, all my worries vanished and I felt like the happiest and luckiest person in the group.

After the ceremony, we mingled and exchanged information. When I told other volunteers that I had been assigned to teach at the university level, I saw a bit of envy in their eyes. As it turned out, only three people in the entire J15 group had been assigned to teach at institutes of higher education: Mark, who had a JD degree, Danny, who had a master's degree, and me. But there was a major difference between their assignments and mine: Mark, who was assigned to Al al-Bayt University, and Danny, who was assigned to the Technical Institute in Tafila, would teach *noncredit* English language classes, whereas I would teach *credit* courses in English literature, which meant that I would have the authority to grade the students at the end of each semester. I felt extremely proud and self-assured. I took this to mean that the dark cloud hanging over my head—the suspicion that I was involved in intelligence activities—had cleared and that everything was okay. Otherwise, they wouldn't have given me such an important assignment, would they?

As I mixed with the rest of the group, I learned that Claire had been assigned to Taybeh. I immediately sent Sharon a text message to inform her, as promised. I told Claire that she would love the site, which is so close to Petra, and that she would have an easy time settling into her new apartment with all the stuff that Sharon was leaving for her, free of charge. But Claire was worried about being so isolated and far away from the others. Then Angela, who had been to Mu'ta University on her site visit, informed me that the couple who had hosted her had a fully-furnished apartment, including central heating. I was overjoyed to hear it—central heating in a desert climate is the ultimate in luxury. Theresa, the pretty Hispanic girl, had been assigned to Aqaba, the southernmost town in Jordan. "They told me that I've impressed them as being a tough girl. I wish that I hadn't appeared so tough," she said morosely. Consoling her, I pointed out that she had a unique advantage: she could practically walk over to "Disneyland"—the code name for Israel among Peace Corps volunteers in Jordan. Eilat, the Israeli southernmost city, a busy port and a popular resort, is just 7 km west of the port town of Aqaba. As I continued to mingle, a couple named Anne and Dave came up to me and introduced themselves. They said that they had served one year as SE (special education) and YD (youth development) volunteers in the village of Tafila, about 60 km south of Karak, and had just been relocated to the campus of Mu'ta University. It struck me as odd that they had been transferred mid-service from one site assignment to another but I didn't inquire about the reasons for it. I was glad to learn that I wouldn't be alone at my new site and we exchanged phone numbers.

When the wave of excitement subsided, I looked for Alex but didn't find him, so I approached Bryan instead. I told him about my brother's grave condition and requested permission to visit him. I offered to pay for the plane ticket myself, but emphasized that

I needed my passport, which was being kept at the Peace Corps office in Amman. Bryan replied that he didn't anticipate any problems, and that he would get in touch with Alex and let me know the next day. I breathed a sigh of relief.

That same evening I returned to my village. My host family received me warmly and inquired about my trip to Taybeh and my site assignment. They were delighted to hear that the volunteer they were hosting had been selected to teach at Mu'ta University, and their esteem for me grew even higher. I knew that the news about the assignment of "Daktora Dalya" to Mu'ta University would soon travel to their friends, neighbors, and relatives. As I was reserved and modest by nature, I said little about it, but deep down I felt as proud as a peacock.

As I lay down on the farsha in my room, I pondered about my trip to Tel Aviv. I didn't know how long I would be allowed to stay there or even when I would depart. The following day was a Friday and the Peace Corps office in Amman would be closed. How would I be able to organize my flight without access to the Internet and with a flimsy cell phone that had very little credit left on it? Who would retrieve my passport and give it to me so I could fly? I was worried. Perhaps Bryan would know. He had said that he would call me in the morning.

The events of the day had exhausted me and I slowly crawled into my sleeping bag. In the background, I heard the muffled voices of Abu Ali, Umm Ali, and their children. The sounds of their speech and laughter were soothing and reassuring to my ears. I had grown fond of my host family and appreciated them. They were decent folk whose lives revolved around simple joys, hard work, and modest dreams. "Al-bayt al-Arabi al-sa'id,"[7] I muttered softly to myself, as I drifted into sleep.

When I awoke the next morning the room was already flooded with sunlight. I glanced at my watch—it was almost 8:00 a.m. I quickly crawled out of my sleeping bag and changed from my pajamas into a pair of pants and a sweater, then hurried to the kitchen to make myself a cup of coffee. I wanted to be ready for Bryan's call; perhaps he would tell me to leave immediately. As I sipped my coffee in my room, I waited for Bryan's call. I waited and waited, but no call came. At 11:00 a.m., I finally called him myself and was relieved when he answered the phone. "Good morning, Bryan," I said. "Did you have a chance to speak with Alex?" "Yes," he replied. "Alex approved your trip. But you have to organize it yourself. The Peace Corps office is closed for the weekend." This was just what I had feared. "It's a bit of a problem," I said. "I have no access to the Internet in my village, and I need my passport." He was short and aloof. "If you manage to book a flight, call Mat. He will meet you at the Peace Corps office in Amman on your way to the airport and give you your passport." Mat Schwenk was the new management and operations officer at the Peace Corps office. I was disappointed. First, Bryan had wasted my entire morning by not calling me as he said he would. Second, he had not offered to help me. Perhaps he didn't grasp how urgent the situation was, or perhaps he wanted to see how resourceful I was. I had to find a way to book a flight myself or wait another two days until after the weekend. But who could I ask to help me? All the members of my J15 group were stuck, like me, in villages without access to the Internet. I needed a Peace Corps volunteer from a different group, a J14 or J13. Suddenly it hit me: Sharon!

Once again, our paths crossed. I called Sharon immediately and explained my situation. I needed to book a seat on the next flight from Amman to Tel Aviv in order to visit my sick brother. Could she do it for me on her computer? She was very responsive and discreet. Without asking me any prying questions, she searched for flights from Amman to Tel Aviv. I was certain that El Al Airline operated between the two countries, but it turned out that only Royal Jordanian offered direct daily flights from Amman to Tel Aviv, once in the morning and once in the evening. Using my credit card and personal details, she booked me on the next early flight, leaving the following day, which was a Saturday, and returning on Tuesday the following week. I thanked Sharon from the bottom of my heart. In the background, I could hear her favorite radio station, Galei Tzahal, playing music. I laughed to myself. Now she knew my secret, but I was certain that it was completely safe with her.

Next, I had to organize a ride from the village to the airport. I called Ahmad, the language and cross-cultural coordinator, to ask for his help. He was an open-minded Jordanian who knew that I was a Sabra and had once told me about an offer that he had received to study and work at Ben Gurion University in the Negev. Ahmad said that he would send Anwar, one of the Peace Corps drivers, to take me from my village to the airport. Anwar would arrive at 6:00 a.m. to pick me up and Mat would be waiting for me at 7:30 a.m. at the Peace Corps office in Amman to give me my passport. I would stay half an hour at the office to print out my itinerary and fill out some forms. The car ride from Amman to the airport was approximately one hour long. If there were no delays and traffic was normal, I should arrive at the airport around 9:00 a.m., two hours before my 11:00 a.m. flight, as required. This sounded good to me. Ahmad wanted to know how I was going to explain my absence to my host family and the teachers at the girls' elementary school. I had to use a consistent cover story that would not arouse their suspicions. I suggested telling them that I was going to the Peace Corps office in Amman for a few days of training in connection with my assignment to teach at Mu'ta University, and he was satisfied with this cover story. When I got off the phone I felt exhausted but relieved. I had managed to organize the most important details of my trip. Where I would stay once I arrived in Israel was something to worry about later.

I found Umm Ali in the kitchen, preparing a tray of food for her daughter-in-law, Fatima, who was confined to bed on account of her difficult first pregnancy. It was admirable how Umm Ali took care of her, making sure that she was well fed and never lonesome. Casually, I informed her that I was going to "Amman" for a few days of training. When she asked who else was going with me, I replied that I was the only one from my village group who had been assigned to teach at a university and needed this training. She wanted to know how I would get to Amman, and I told her that Anwar, whom she knew and trusted, would drive me there and back. It was Umm Ali's responsibility to ensure my safety and to know my whereabouts at all times, and she took her job seriously. When I had moved in with them, I was supposed to give Abu Ali an emergency card with the names and telephone numbers of Peace Corps officers so that he would know who to contact if something happened to me. Knowing that Umm Ali was illiterate, I wanted to give the card to Abu Ali in person. But when she heard what the card was about, she insisted that I give it to her. From the expression on her face, I knew that she was going to keep it in a very safe place. She was a serious, no-nonsense woman.

I lay awake a long time that night, thinking about my brother. I had a blind faith in his recovery, a faith that seemed untenable in the face of reality. About fifteen years earlier, he had undergone a risky open heart surgery to fix a rare heart valve problem, which was ultimately successful. I naively assumed that he would recover this time too. The blood match between him and my younger sister was very promising. Would luck smile on him again? *"Ha-kol bi-yedei shamayim khutz me-yir'at shamayim,"*[8] I muttered softly to myself.

The following day, Anwar arrived at 6:00 a.m. and we set off on the long drive to Amman. I closed my eyes and withdrew into myself. I didn't feel like looking out at the scenery drifting past the window. I was not in the mood and the desert started to have a depressing effect on me. All I wanted was to get to the airport. Anwar was very polite and considerate. He didn't smoke and didn't turn the radio on at full blast. It was early in the morning and we drove quickly through the empty roads. I had never been to the Peace Corps office in Amman before and was a bit curious to see it. Located near the Fourth Circle on Jebel Amman, it meant that we had to go into the city, but since it was a Saturday morning, we would still be able to avoid the heavy traffic. Jebel Amman is an affluent area, home to embassies, luxury hotels, and elegant restaurants. The clean and spacious streets were lined with leafy trees and imposing edifices. Anwar pulled up in the back of a building called Mujama Abu Hasan al-Tijari, which housed the Peace Corps office on the second floor. We rode the elevator up together and stepped out directly in front of the Peace Corps office door, only to discover that it was locked and Mat was nowhere to be seen.

I glanced at my watch. It was 7:30 a.m. "Perhaps Mat is on his way here right now," I thought to myself. Anwar suggested that we should wait fifteen minutes before we started making calls this early on Saturday morning. When it was 8:00 a.m. and there was still no sign of Mat, I decided to call him myself. He answered the phone in a drowsy voice—I must have woken him up. He was surprised to hear that I was already waiting at the Peace Corps office building and said that he would be there shortly. It took him another thirty minutes to arrive. Unhurriedly and aloofly, he asked for my itinerary and my brother's home and hospital addresses in Israel. He then explained slowly that I was entitled to ask the Peace Corps to pay for my plane ticket but first I had to fill out several forms and get my brother's wife in Israel to sign a certain form and fax it back to him. I listened nervously. I was already running late because he had not been on time. Now, he was wasting my time with all this paperwork. I told him that I was traveling on my own dime. I didn't want to bother my sister-in-law with trivialities in her hour of crisis or to create the impression that I wouldn't have come if I hadn't been reimbursed for my expenses. I logged onto my email account on Mat's computer to print out my e-ticket and itinerary, and then quickly wrote my brother's home and hospital addresses on a piece of paper. When I had finished, I discovered that Mat had disappeared. Frantically, I called out his name, trying to find my way out of the heavily secured office maze. I was close to panic when I heard his voice answering from behind the bathroom door. I waited anxiously, looking repeatedly at the time. Finally, he emerged from the bathroom, apologized that he had an upset stomach, and let me out of the fortified office. I rushed to Anwar's car and we set off at once to the airport.

There is a horror story titled "The Way Up to Heaven" that I am always reminded of in such circumstances. Written by the British author Roald Dahl, it is about a husband who enjoys torturing his wife by being deliberately late, whether to an appointment, dinner party, train ride, etc. The anxious but docile wife takes this psychological abuse quietly, until one day something happens. She makes plans to fly to France to visit their daughter and grandchildren for a couple of weeks. When the cab arrives to take them to the airport, the wife climbs inside and waits for her husband, who pretends that he has forgotten something in the house and must go back to fetch it. This little prank costs him dearly. He gets stuck in the elevator of his house halfway between the first and second floors. No one hears his calls for help in the empty house. The wife waits anxiously in the cab, worried sick that they would miss their flight. When she sees that they have barely enough time left to make it to the airport, she rushes to the house to get him. She inserts her key into the keyhole and is about to open the door when she hears a sound that makes her change her mind. Calmly, she returns to the cab and tells the driver to proceed to the airport without her husband. By the time she returns from her holiday, her husband has died in the elevator. Did she know that he was trapped? Did she hear his calls for help? Was this sweet revenge for the abuse that she had suffered at his hands? The faint smile on her lips as the cab carries her away to the airport seems to suggest this. I always laugh when I recall this story—partly at myself too.

Amman International Airport, named after the late Queen Alia, had an old, small terminal back in 2011. It wasn't hard to find your way around. I went quickly through security at the entrance to the Royal Jordanian desk. The clerk was polite and professional. I handed him my passport and my e-ticket and he didn't seem to mind at all that I was flying to Tel Aviv or that my passport said that I was born in Israel. I got my boarding pass and hurried to the departure gate on the second floor. The time was 10:30 a.m., and my flight was scheduled to leave at 11:00 a.m. I expected that I would start boarding as soon as I reached the gate, when it was announced over the loud speakers that the flight was delayed to 12:00 noon. Smiling wryly, I said to myself, "Man proposes and God disposes."

The departure lounge was crowded with Muslim pilgrims, most of them elderly, on their way to Mecca. They were dressed in white robes and carried bulging duffel bags. They departed from the same gate, boarding a flight to Saudi Arabia. After they had left, the lounge started to fill with Indian men and women who worked at menial jobs as domestic help, caretakers, cleaners, and unskilled factory laborers in Israel. They looked nervous and had a worried expression on their faces as they sat huddled together. I was astonished to see such a large group of foreign workers on their way to Israel. Israeli society today is so different from the days of my childhood. Among the passengers waiting in the lounge were also a few Israelis who were catching a connecting flight from Mumbai and Colombo to Tel Aviv after an extended trip to India. Israelis love to go to India, as backpackers or in organized tours. They talked excitedly about their experiences and gesticulated wildly, hardly able to contain their enthusiasm.

We boarded at 11:45 a.m. I expected to see exotic flight attendants in traditional Jordanian dress. Instead, the female flight attendants wore bright red skirt suits, similar to those worn by Swiss Air flight attendants. They were all fair-skinned and had blonde hair. "What has happened to the famous Arab houris with big black eyes and silky black hair?" I wondered. These flight attendants looked more Parisian than Middle Eastern women.

The flight took thirty-eight minutes altogether. I looked out the window at the scenery below, watching it change from a yellow, desolate desert with small scattered villages to green fields and dark brown farmland surrounded by heavily populated towns and cities. It was a breathtaking view.

Entering Tel Aviv Ben Gurion International Airport after passing through Amman Queen Alia International Airport was like traveling through a time machine from the past to the future. The difference between these two airports reflected the difference in the level of economic and technological development between the two countries. Ben Gurion International Airport has a modern and sophisticated terminal designed with a great aesthetic appeal. It is also one of the safest and most secure airports in the world.

I walked briskly through the spacious hallways, availing myself of the moving walkways, until I arrived at Passport Control, where an Israeli officer treated my passport to the famous "offensive stamp." I had heard a lot of stories about the Israeli border stamp stigma. It is a serious problem when entering certain Arab countries like Syria, Lebanon, Saudi Arabia, Yemen, and the Persian Gulf states, which refuse people entry if they see the offending stamp in their passports. Officially, it shouldn't be a problem when entering Jordan, Egypt, Tunisia, and Morocco. However, I had personally experienced rough treatment from Passport Control officers in Egypt and Morocco. How would I fare when I returned to Jordan with an Israeli stamp in my passport? It remained to be seen.

On the way out, I changed a hundred dollars into Israeli currency—NIS (New Israeli Shekel)—to pay for cab rides and other expenses. I then went into a phone booth to call my sister Susan and tell her that I had arrived for a few days to visit our brother. She wasn't thrilled to hear my voice on the phone. She wanted to know why I hadn't informed her *in advance* of my arrival. I explained that this was an impromptu trip that I had arranged at the last minute. She said that she was sorry, but she couldn't accommodate me on such short notice. Go figure! Sisterhood can be a great disappointment. Next I called Rachel, my sister-in-law, who was at my brother's bedside in the hospital, and inquired if I could come directly to the hospital. Was my brother awake? Was he allowed to receive visitors? She said that I could come, but sounded tired and despondent on the phone.

Hesitantly, I asked if I could stay a few days in her apartment. She replied that she wasn't sure and would let me know later. I got the feeling that she thought I would be a burden. "Never mind," I said. "You will see me shortly."

I found a cab quickly and asked the driver to take me to Beilinson Hospital in Petakh Tikva. The fare was NIS100, which was quite high. The money I had changed wouldn't last me long. A talkative driver, when he learned that I was visiting my brother at the hospital, expressed his sympathy and best wishes for him. He kindly lent me his cell phone so I could call my friend, Dalia, who lived in Ramat Hasharon. The last time I had seen her was the year before when I had come to Israel to visit my family. I was lucky—she answered the phone. "Shalom Dalia," I said. "Guess who's speaking?" She immediately recognized my voice. "Dalya! How are you? Where are you?" I told her everything in a nutshell. She was very warm and sympathetic, and immediately invited me to stay with her. "We are at home all day today. Come after you visit your brother." And for the first time since I had arrived in Israel, I felt *welcome*.

We reached Beilinson Hospital. Wheeling out my carry-on bag, I entered the Davidoff Center for Hemato-Oncology building, only to discover that the information desk was deserted as Saturday is a day off for these employees. I found a visitor who directed me to my brother's wing on the third floor, and the nurses there directed me to isolation room #4. I had to wash my hands with antibacterial soap and wear a face mask to protect him from contamination. When I knocked on the door, a voice said, "Come in." I stepped inside, and froze.

The man I saw supporting himself on a walker was totally unfamiliar. I thought that I had made a mistake and entered the wrong room. I was about to turn and leave when I saw my sister-in-law in the corner, and I understood.

I am still trying to block this image out of my memory. I want to remember my brother as I had seen him the year before, when we had dinner together at his favorite restaurant in Caesarea, overlooking the sea. It was a rainy day with gusty winds and the sea was dark and restless. He looked youthful, my handsome brother, with a head full of shiny black hair, long thick eyelashes, and dark eyebrows. He talked animatedly about his two granddaughters, aged fourteen and twelve, whom he was looking after because his daughter Inbal was bedridden, her body ravaged by cancer. He cooked meals for his granddaughters, helped them with their homework, and drove them around in his car. He was warm and affectionate toward me and smiled when he talked, but his eyes were sad and clouded with worry. When we hugged and said our goodbyes, we had no idea when we would meet again. The days ahead seemed dark and foreboding, like the sea that raged and roared outside, its waves pounding mercilessly against the shore.

Now my brother smiled feebly and said hello. My eyes welled up and I couldn't hold back my tears. If it weren't for the face mask I would have made a pitiful spectacle of myself. I wasn't allowed to touch him or anything else in the room. Rachel helped him lie down, lifting his legs, which were swollen from his retention of fluids, one by one and placing them on the bed. He was too tired to talk. He lay on the bed, his eyes staring at the television screen that was installed on the opposite wall. From time to time he played with his iPhone. I sat on the bench by the window, next to my sister-in-law. I asked her about my brother's medical treatment, the doctors, and the nurses. She said that they were doing everything they could, trying all kinds of approaches and medications but so far with little results. The transplanted stem cells were ravaging his internal organs. She stayed with my brother all the time, sleeping in his room at night and going home only to shower and change her clothes. She hired a private nurse to replace her when she needed to run urgent errands. I sat quietly, overwhelmed by what I saw and heard. At one point, my brother needed to go to the bathroom. It was a complicated procedure. Some of the needles and tubes that were attached to him had to be disconnected, while others had to go with him wherever he went.

He had difficulty standing on his feet and had to support himself on a walker. The gravity of his condition seemed beyond hope.

I stayed with them until I felt that they were tired and wanted to be alone. I asked for permission to come again the next day and they said that it would be okay. It was after 4:00 p.m. when I left the hospital and took a cab to Ramat Hasharon, where Dalia lived. She had moved there after her first husband, an air force pilot, was killed in a training flight, and had been residing there for the past three decades. During the same period of time, I had relocated several times between Israel, the Netherlands, and the United States. I felt like a "gypsy" compared to her. I had never known the sense of stability, rootedness, and belonging that comes from staying in one single place all the years of your life.

Dalia and her second husband, Yossi, received me with open arms. They had aged and gained a few extra pounds, but their warmth and hospitality remained unchanged. They greeted me with hugs and kisses, and expressed their deepest sympathies for my brother. We chatted at length, updating each other on developments in our lives. After a light supper, they showed me to my room and also gave me their house key so I could come and go freely. That night I retired to bed exhausted, but heartened by my friends' kindness.

The next day I got up early and took the bus to Rishon Lezion to see my mother before heading for Beilinson Hospital, since I was told that my brother would be occupied with doctors' visits in the morning. I had called my mother's Filipino maid the night before to make sure that they would be at home and to ask her to prepare my mother, who suffered from Alzheimer's, for my visit so that she would know who I was. The bus ride was very long; there were numerous stops along the way and an endless stream of passengers got on and off. As usual, the radio was turned on at full blast. Try to get on a bus in Israel where the radio would not be on all the time, broadcasting the news! There are always political and security issues to report about. In between, you can listen to great pop music, both local and Western. *"Kan Galei Tzahal. Ha-sha'a tesha ba-boker"* (This is the I.D.F. radio station. The time is 9:00 in the morning), the broadcaster announced. I smiled to myself, recalling how three days ago I was stealthily listening to it in Sharon's house in Taybeh.

I arrived at my mother's apartment and rang the doorbell. The maid opened the door. My mother was sitting in her rocking chair, looking apathetic. Her face lit up when she saw me, and we hugged and kissed. Her health was failing and her memory fading. She had lost weight and suffered from heart problems. At eighty-six, she was frail and helpless, like a little child. She knew nothing about the critical condition of her only son and the death of his only daughter. We had kept the sad news away from her even when she was still lucid. I talked with her a little, asking how she felt and how she slept at night and what she ate for breakfast. She could answer short, simple questions. Then we played cards. She liked to play rummy and used to be good at it, but this time she didn't play as well as she had the year before. It was another sign of her cognitive decline. She stared at me with hollow eyes and a robotic smile. Her left eye was half-closed, the sight in it dimmed, and her right eye was wide open. She looked scared and confused. I was filled with compassion for my mother—there was no grace or peace for her in old age.

I left my mother around 11:00 a.m. and took the bus to Beilinson Hospital. I stayed there with my brother for twice as long as the day before. He was a little more talkative this time and asked me about my experiences in Jordan. I told him about the Bedouin family I lived with, the village, and my trips to Amman and Taybeh. He listened with interest and remarked that I was courageous to do what I was doing. I felt undeserving of his compliment and wanted to say that there was nothing courageous about my actions. Instead, I said softly that I derived my courage from him. But he replied that he wasn't so courageous and turned his head away. His response sent a stab of pain through my heart. He had always been a fighter who never flinched in the face of adversities. Was what I said insensitive?

Did I hurt his feelings? I felt hopelessly inept and inhibited. How can you express your feelings toward a person you love dearly when you are wearing a face mask and are forbidden to hug him or hold his hand? My tearful eyes and choked voice betrayed the emotions that raged inside me. I paused for a few moments to compose myself, then told him about the harvest of olives in my host family's olive grove and how it reminded me of our childhood, when we used to pick olives together from the trees in our neighborhood and sell them to people on our street to earn a few *grushim* (old Israel pennies). When I asked him if he remembered this, he nodded wordlessly and smiled faintly, but his eyes were sad. I thought with nostalgia of those carefree days but feared that further reminiscing about them would be agonizing for my brother. I gazed at him tenderly, wishing that I had some magic powers to take his pain away, to change the course of his prognosis, and make this grim reality vanish.

My sister-in-law had to run a few errands and I stayed alone with my brother. I was wearing a face mask the whole time and was sweating under it. My brother told me that it was okay to take it off, but I refused. I had come into contact with a lot of people on my way to the hospital and didn't want to expose him to additional risks. I was also careful to wash my hands before entering his room and refrained from touching anything. After my sister-in-law left, my brother looked tired and sank into a silence. He read a little on his iPhone and watched television. There were so many things I wanted to tell him. I wanted to thank him for his emotional support during the ordeal of my messy divorce, to say that I always loved him and looked up to him as my role model, and to ask him to forgive me for any wrong I had ever done him. But I hesitated to speak out. I was afraid to burden him now with my feelings. It would be unfair. It might be construed as an admission on my part that he wasn't going to make it or it might seem as if the sole purpose of my visit was to obtain his forgiveness. Actions speak louder than words. The fact that I was with him now was proof of my love and devotion.

Dr. Corrine, the hematologist, came into the room to check on my brother. She read his chart and looked concerned. His heartbeats were too fast. She told him that she would give him a shot to slow down his heartbeats, and left. When my sister-in-law returned, she helped my brother go to the bathroom: first she sat him up in the bed, then she put his feet down on the floor one by one, and finally she unhooked some of the needles and tubes that were attached to his arms. I was watching the complicated procedure in silence when, suddenly, my brother said, "I'm sorry, Dalya, that I'm giving you my back." His words blew me away and I burst into hot tears, pouring out my anguish behind the protection of my mask. My brother was such a noble soul. In his dire condition, he still thought it necessary to apologize to me. At that moment, I felt terribly ashamed of myself for hesitating to open my heart to him when we were alone in the room.

It was after 4:00 p.m. when I said goodbye and left for the day. I had not eaten anything since the early hours of the morning and bought a bagel with tuna salad and a bottle of water from the hospital cafeteria. The tuna salad tasted stale and sour, but I ate it anyway and washed it down with water. As I left the hospital, I remembered that I had wanted to buy a small radio that would connect me with the outside world during my stay in the remote village of Hamadiyya. I visited a nearby shopping mall but, to my surprise, the shops only sold large radios with attached speakers that were too bulky and heavy to put in my carry-on bag. In Jordan electronic goods are expensive and I didn't know if I would be able to find a small radio with short waves. On the spur of the moment, I bought a medium-sized Sony radio and CD player. To save space, the shop clerk suggested that I take the radio out of the box and put it in a sturdy plastic bag, which I did right away. In addition to being bulky, the box had Hebrew words printed on it and I couldn't take the risk that Umm Ali or one of her children, especially Usama, would see these forbidden letters. I later removed the instruction booklet, which was in Hebrew too, and put them in a zipped pocket in my carry-on bag. I realized that it would be a challenge to travel with this purchase back to Jordan.

The following morning, I traveled once again to Rishon Lezion to see my mother. My sister Susan was there too. We talked about impersonal, mundane things, then took our mother to the park, where a small group of elderly people cared for by Filipino maids had gathered. They sat in wheelchairs, their eyes staring blankly into the distance, their mouths half-open, flies roaming around their heads and landing on their faces. It was a depressing sight. When it was time for me to leave to Beilinson Hospital, my sister insisted on walking me to the bus station, but didn't offer to give me a ride to Petakh Tikva in her own new car.

It was already past noon. I sat in the bus to Petakh Tikva, feeling dizzy and nauseous. The jerky motion of the bus made me feel much worse and I was sweating profusely. I wondered whether these symptoms were caused by some sickness or were merely psychological. Admittedly, I had been deeply distraught by what I had seen and heard over the last couple of days. At the same time, it was the flu season and I was constantly moving around crowds of people. What if I was really coming down with something? My sister-in-law had warned me not to come near my brother if I didn't feel well, lest I should expose him to a viral or bacterial infection. Terrified by the thought that I might put my brother at risk, I called my sister-in-law and consulted with her. She echoed my fears, preferring that I err on the side of caution. I apologized profusely for my indisposition and asked to speak with my brother but he was already asleep. There was nothing else to do but ask her to give him my love and tell him that he was constantly in my thoughts and prayers.

I changed buses to return to Dalia's house in Ramat Hasharon, racked by feelings of guilt and remorse. I was emotionally on the verge of collapse. Was it from the shock of seeing my brother's and mother's grave condition? From fear that the shadows of death were inching ever so closely toward them? The hardest thing, I thought to myself, is when you know what is happening to you. My mother was in a state of blissful ignorance; my brother, on the other hand, was fully aware of his deteriorating condition.

Just then, a woman on the bus got up to speak with the driver. She was in her fifties, with long, light brown hair that hung loose around her shoulders. She stood out in her elegant outfit, stylish shoes, and expensive jewelry. Her appearance and demeanor attracted my attention. She looked like a foreigner rather than a native-born Israeli. I strained my ears to hear whether she spoke in Hebrew or English with the driver. I had a feeling that I knew this woman but I wasn't quite sure. When she returned to her seat across the aisle from me, we made eye contact and I smiled and said in Hebrew, "Are you Keren's mother?" Astonished, she replied with a shrug, "I'm the mother of *a* Keren. It depends on which Keren you mean." She had a distinct American accent in her Hebrew. "Keren Golan," I said. She was stunned. "Who are you?" she asked. "I'm Ziv's mother," I replied. She stared at me in disbelief. In 2005, when my son was a resident at New York–Presbyterian Hospital, he had met her daughter, Keren, who worked there as a secretary. After a whirlwind romance he moved in with her and within a year they got engaged. He gave her an expensive 2-carat princess cut diamond ring that cost $15,000, which we—his parents—had paid for. Keren's mother had organized an engagement party for them in a restaurant in Manhattan, and a small group of family members and close friends were invited. That was when I had first met Keren's parents, a divorced couple of Israeli background. The wedding date was set and preparations were in full swing when my son suddenly broke off the engagement. It was abrupt and harsh, and Keren was crushed. A fight ensued over the engagement ring. She refused to return it and enlisted the support of their mutual friends. Fearing that his image and reputation might be tarnished, my son gave in and let her keep the ring, even though (or perhaps because) he hadn't paid for it with his own money. The breakup was a bitter affair. My son revealed that he had a dark side that I was unaware of. A couple of years later we heard that Keren, who was a tall, pretty, blue-eyed, blonde girl, had married an Indian surgeon and moved to California. Now, after all these years, and of all places, I encountered her mother on a bus ride in Israel. What an incredible coincidence.

"I didn't recognize you," Keren's mother said. I looked in embarrassment at my jeans and sneakers. I had been living out of a suitcase for almost two months now. I bore no resemblance to the elegantly bedecked and bejeweled woman whom she had met at that ill-fated engagement party. "What are you doing here?" she asked. "I'm visiting," I said vaguely. "And you?" "I'm visiting too." "How's Keren?" "She's fine. She has a little girl now," the woman said proudly. The bus was approaching my stop and I had only a few seconds to get to the door. "All the best to you and Keren," I said, standing up. The bus pulled up with a loud screech, and I got off.

As I walked toward Dalia's house, I pondered the vicissitudes of fate. My son had dumped this woman's daughter. But right now, roughly five years after the event, her daughter was already married and the mother of a child, while my son was still single and searching for the perfect relationship. Keren's mother was divorced when we had first met and I was married. Now I was divorced too. "That's life," someone had once said to me. "Everyone gets a turn." But I strongly disagreed. "No, not everyone."

No one was at home when I arrived. I went upstairs to my room and crashed out on the bed. The house, located in a small street away from the route of noisy buses and traffic, was quiet and peaceful. The silence was soothing to my ears and had a calming effect on me. In the evening, I took a walk around the neighborhood, which was situated within walking distance from shops, restaurants, and all the amenities of city life. I came across a falafel stand on the main street—falafel was my favorite childhood food. I looked at it fondly, relishing the smell of falafels and the colorful display of a variety of pickles and salads, but I walked on. Falafels sold on the street are often contaminated and a source of food poisoning. I observed the signs of affluence all around me, in the elegant shops and boutiques, the crowded cafés and restaurants, the fashionable clothes worn by pedestrians, and the expensive cars cruising through the streets. In a phenomenally short time span, Israel had become a prosperous and thriving society.

The following morning, I said goodbye to Dalia and Yossi—and the comforts of their home—and set off on my trip back to Jordan. When I stood before the Passport Control officer at Amman International Airport, I braced myself for a rough treatment. To my surprise, the officer looked at the "offending" Israeli stamp with indifference and said nothing at all. Mechanically, he photographed my face, stamped my passport, and handed it back to me. I heaved a deep sigh of relief and rushed toward the exit hall. When I walked through the sliding doors into the street, I found Anwar, the Peace Corps driver, waiting for me by his car. It would be a long ride back to the village of Hamadiyya.

8 . THE LAST GOODBYE

WITH MORE THAN HALF THE PERIOD OF PRE-SERVICE TRAINING behind me, I felt optimistic and self-assured. Every day I followed the same routine: I was at the girls' elementary school in the morning, and in the Peace Corps classroom or with my host family in the afternoon.

Umm Ali received me warmly when I returned from my trip to "Amman," saying that she had missed me and that the house seemed empty without me. So did her daughters Nawal and Rana. But her son Usama, the jittery army officer, eyed me sullenly. "Where were you?" he asked curtly. I assumed that since he came home only once every fortnight he was uninformed about my trip. I smiled and replied, "I was in Amman." "Where in Amman?" he asked. "At the Peace Corps office," I responded. "Where *is* the Peace Corps office?" he yelled. I finally got it—he was asking for the address of the Peace Corps office! I should have memorized it. What a blunder! His mother and sisters watched us with a puzzled expression on their faces. I could only recall the vague location of the office—I had not concerned myself with the address because I was driven there. I strained my memory. "It's on Jebel Amman, near the Fourth Circle," I said, my heart pounding with anxiety. Usama looked at me with a disapproving frown, then turned around and left. I smiled reassuringly at Umm Ali and her daughters to defuse the tension and went straight to my room.

I wondered if Usama was testing me. Was he going to check on the address that I had given him and on my whereabouts in the past few days? Suppose he entered my room in my absence to go through my things. He would find the certificate of my site assignment to Mu'ta University bearing the name Dalya Cohen, he would find the telephone list of all the volunteers with the name Dalya Cohen among them, and he would find the Hebrew operating instructions for the Sony radio! All of this was enough to expose my Jewish identity! I immediately took these three items, placed them in a separate compartment in my suitcase, and locked it, putting the key in my handbag. We were scheduled to have a center day right after the weekend. I would take these papers with me and store them in the other suitcase that I kept at the training site at Al al-Bayt University.

On Saturday, I visited Fatin, the sister of my first host father Abu Omar. Her parents had grown fond of me and enjoyed my visits. In a small and closed society like the village of Hamadiyya, social visits are an important recreational outlet. Fatin's mother, who had refused to shake my hand during our very first meeting because I was an *ajnabiyya* (foreigner) and a *masihiyya* (Christian), now hugged and kissed me warmly whenever I came and insisted that I have supper with them. We usually sat in the family room and chatted over coffee or tea with Fatin's father, a retired teacher who liked to recite Arabic poetry. On this occasion, he asked me to quote a popular Arabic proverb. I looked at Fatin's mother and said, *al-dunya umm!* (The mother is the world). Fatin's mother beamed with delight. The father said, "I see that you always carry a pen and a notebook with you and write down the new words that you learn. Let me teach you an Arabic verse on this topic: *al-'ilm sayd wa-al-kitaba qayduhu; qayyid suyudak bil-hibal al-wathiqa*. (Literally, "Learning is hunting for wild animals, and writing is the ropes that fasten them; fasten what you've hunted with sturdy ropes.") I loved this couplet and instantly committed it to memory. While Fatin's father was an educated man, his wife was illiterate, a common situation among women of her generation.

As we were talking, the door suddenly opened and Abu Omar came into the room. I remembered that he had told me that he visited his parents every evening. This was a commendable act of filial devotion, but at the same time it meant that Umm Omar and the kids were alone at home. I had observed a marked difference between the family life of my first and second host families. Abu Ali stayed at home every evening after work and every weekend, while Abu Omar seemed to spend most of his evenings away from home. He was surprised, but pleased, to see me. I greeted him cordially and we exchanged the usual pleasantries. Before long, both he and his father started lighting up and puffing away, and the air in the sitting room became stifling from cigarette smoke. I motioned to Fatin that we should begin our TOEFL session. She rose to her feet, muttering excuses for both of us, and we went to her room.

As soon as Fatin and I seated ourselves comfortably on the farshas and pillows in her room, she told me excitedly that she had given up the idea of pursuing a master's degree in English at Al al-Bayt University. Instead, she was going to enroll in a translation program at Zarqaa University. It was a shorter and more practical program in a different location, all of which appealed to her. She was tired of Al al-Bayt University and was looking forward to meeting new people at Zarqaa University. I expressed my support and wished her success. She was making a career choice that would allow her to earn a living, and at the same time would not interfere with the prospect of her getting married and raising a family. Finding a job as an English teacher in a government school in Jordan was nearly impossible— all the positions were already filled. I had heard the same complaint from the LCFs who worked with us. They were university graduates who were hired by the Peace Corps for merely three months, after which they would have to look for another job. Two male LCFs told me that they had worked as waiters and hotel clerks before landing this temporary job with the Peace Corps. The rate of unemployment in Jordan is high, especially among university graduates. Fatin was wisely looking for a profession that would make her more competitive in the labor market. Her parents indulged her: she already had a car, a cell phone, and her own television set. She showed me a new pair of jeans that she had recently bought, though she could wear them only at home but not on the street, where she had to be covered up from head to toe. Arab women's liberation was a complicated phenomenon fraught with contradictions. A car, a cell phone, and a university education were okay—as long as the hijab and abaya remained in place.

My days at the girls' elementary school were mundane. I found the ritual of shaking hands with *every* teacher *every* morning tiresome. The students kept pulling on my arms to get my attention, accidentally wiping their hands on my sleeves, a practice that was tiresome as well. I longed for the day when I would move to Mu'ta University, where things, no doubt, would be entirely different.

The monotony of village life was interrupted by weekly trips to the training site at Al al-Bayt University. As soon as we got off the bus, everyone rushed excitedly to take their laptops out of storage and log onto their email accounts. I was the only person who checked her email account with trepidation in her heart. Would there be bad news about my brother, about my mother, or from Peace Corps Headquarters? I was experiencing tremendous stress from several sources all at once. Worse yet, I could not discuss my worries with anyone.

Shortly after my return from the trip to Israel, Ahmad, the language and cross-cultural coordinator, asked me to take the language proficiency assessment interview that I had missed when I had been away. I was quite eager to do it and find out how much progress I had made so far. To my astonishment, my tester was Rifaat, the homestay coordinator. I wondered if he was qualified to administer this interview. I knew that Ahmad and Eman, the Jordanian TEFL coordinator, had conducted these interviews with all the other J15 volunteers. My interview with Rifaat lasted thirty minutes, during which time I spoke fluently about various topics that he chose for conversation. I was dumbfounded when he graded me as "advanced low." Many volunteers with *minimal* communication skills in Arabic and poor pronunciation had been graded as "advanced," and they openly admitted that their grades were much higher than they deserved so as to encourage them to persist in their efforts. I was deeply disappointed with my grade and couldn't help wondering whether Rifaat's evaluation had something to do with my identity. He had been handling my visa and passport and knew about my recent trip to Tel Aviv. It wasn't so much the grade that bothered me but rather the issue of objectivity. In the summer of 1999, when I was a CASA III fellow at the American University in Cairo, I had an Egyptian language instructor who subjected me to subtle forms of discrimination and made my life miserable. I had learned then that the classroom was far from being a neutral zone, free from bias, prejudice, or bigotry.

I approached Bryan to thank him for allowing me to visit my brother. He expressed his sympathy and best wishes for him, then asked how I was getting along with my new host family. I replied that I liked them a lot and that they were all friendly, except for their elder son, Usama, who worked for the army and regarded me with suspicion, as if I was a spy. I said this jokingly, thinking that Bryan, of all my Peace Corps supervisors, could relate to my experience with Usama. After all, *he himself* had told us that when he had served as a Peace Corps volunteer in Guatemala, he had dated a local girl whose brother regarded him as a spy, even after he had married her and had been her husband of many years. But the minute I said this about Usama, I saw a strange look of heightened alertness come over Bryan's eyes and his expression became tense. I wanted to kick myself for making this remark. How foolish and naive on my part! Perhaps Bryan was in a position to joke about being perceived as a spy while serving as a Peace Corps volunteer, but I certainly was not. I walked away from this encounter with a heavy heart.

On the ride back to my village, the bus driver stopped in the center of Mafraq and we got off to buy sweets and pastries. I bought a bag of pumpkin seeds, which turned out to be very small. As I put a seed between my teeth and tried to crack it, the term *bizr al-mutallaqat* came back to my mind—divorced Arab women cracked these small seeds to allay their worries. I was now doing the exact same thing.

I kept my promise to Latifa and brought her the mechanical pencil she had requested. Elated, she rushed to show it to her classmates. The next day, Abu Omar called me on my cell phone and invited me to come over for lunch on Friday. I accepted, thinking that it was a gesture of gratitude for the pencil. But when I arrived that Friday, Abu Omar wasn't at home and Umm Omar seemed surprised, as if she hadn't been expecting me. I felt embarrassed. After the usual chitchat about school and the kids, she invited me to prepare lunch with her. We cooked chicken topped with layers of dough and potatoes, a dish high on carbs and low on proteins. While we were in the kitchen, Abu Omar showed up and hastened to apologize that he had been tied up elsewhere. He took a USB flash drive out of his pocket and asked me if I could show him how to use it to connect the old computer in the family room to the Internet. I quickly discovered that I didn't possess the know-how for this task, and he was deeply disappointed. It suddenly dawned on me that the reason he had invited me for lunch was so I could fix his computer. During the two weeks that I had stayed with them, I had helped Latifa download a program on the computer, and she was ecstatic about it. This must have given Abu Omar the impression that I was some sort of computer whiz. I was really sorry to disappoint him.

When lunch was ready, we sat on the floor to eat in the traditional way. It was much cozier than eating seated at the kitchen table. As always, Umm Omar served me a portion on a small plate, but the rest of the family ate from the communal tray. Slowly, I dug up the piece of chicken from under the layers of dough and potatoes on my plate, only to discover that I had gotten the chicken neck. I hadn't eaten a chicken neck in the past fifty years. Back home in the United States, I would buy chicken that was already cut up and sorted out in trays of breasts, thighs, drumsticks, or wings. Rarely, if ever, had I seen chicken necks in the meat section of a Giant or Safeway supermarket. Now the sight of the chicken neck, which reminded me of a fish head, gave me the creeps. Abu Omar noticed that I didn't touch it. With a swift movement of his hand, he removed the chicken neck from my plate and put a piece of white meat in its place. It was a kind act and I thanked him. He smiled graciously and encouraged me to eat more. "Umm Omar's cooking is delicious," he declared, and I hastened to praise her cooking as well. Soon after lunch, Abu Omar left and I helped Umm Omar clean up and played with Latifa one of her favorite computer games.

In the late afternoon, I walked back to Umm Ali's house. On my way, I saw a group of village women sitting outdoors. They were shaping cakes out of a mixture of crushed olive pits and olive flesh that had been left over after pressing the olives, and were placing the cakes on the ground to dry in the sun. These cakes, called *jift*, are used as fuel to heat up their homes in the cold winter days. It was a lovely sight of women chatting joyously and bantering as they worked together. Umm Khaled, Mona's host mother, was among them and she called out to me to join the group. I sat on a rock beside her and plunged my hands into the wet mixture, scooping up big chunks that I then rolled into a ball and flattened like a cake. It was fun and I carried on enthusiastically. Umm Khaled looked at me with approval when I told her that I had just visited my first host family. I could see that she appreciated the fact that

I continued to pay my respects to Umm Omar even after I had moved out of her house.

The first week of December was uneventful, except for my "solo teaching" at the girls' elementary school. On a certain day, Eman, the Jordanian TEFL coordinator, and Lupe, a J13 volunteer who assisted her, came to observe me. I didn't put a lot of effort into preparing the class. After all, this was not applicable to my site assignment: teaching at a university is entirely different from teaching at an elementary school. I taught an English lesson titled "Going on a Trip" from the *Action Pack* book to a sixth-grade class. After the class, Eman and Lupe provided me with positive feedback and evaluation.

Around noon, I went home and sat on the balcony to warm myself up in the sun. In the desert, the nights and early mornings are very cold, especially indoors, but the midday sun dispels the chill and then it becomes warm and pleasant. The elevated balcony offered a panoramic view of the village: flat-roofed houses with unfinished foundation columns sticking out from their tops, walled courtyards with olive trees and animal pens, and in the distance the clear blue sky merging with the bleak and dreary desert. I had in my lap a copy of Queen Noor's *Leap of Faith: Memoirs of an Unexpected Life,* which I had been reading in my leisure. After a while, I remembered that I had left my cell phone in my room and rushed to retrieve it. I discovered a new text message from my sister-in-law: "The doctors have connected Shimon to a ventilator and given him anesthetics to keep him asleep." Startled, I ran outside and hid among the trees in the back of the olive grove so that I could call her and speak in Hebrew. By a stroke of luck the call went through and she picked up. She said that my brother couldn't breathe because his lungs were full of fluids. The doctors had told her that there was little hope. She started to cry. I was in shock. I kept saying, "Oh God . . . why? It's so unfair!" My brother had such hard luck. His rare heart condition, then the leukemia, and then the loss of his only daughter. How could his pain and suffering be rationalized?

I couldn't grasp the full meaning of this procedure—the doctors hooking my brother to a ventilator and keeping him asleep—or perhaps I was in denial and refused to acknowledge what this meant. I still believed that some miracle might happen in the last minute to reverse this outcome.

The next day, December 8, was etched forever on my memory. I got up early and was at school by 7:30 a.m., as usual. I had previously arranged another class of "solo teaching" and was anxious to complete this task and go home. At 8:59 a.m., my phone chimed with an incoming message from my sister-in-law: "Shimon is still connected to the ventilator. Today he has high fever, 41°C. The doctors are fighting for his life. I'm pessimistic. So are the nurses." My heart stood still and a deafening ringing echoed in my ears. The teachers asked why I looked so pale and distraught. I managed to say that I had a terrible migraine. Another message came at 11:18 a.m.: "Dalya, if you can come do so, these are Shimon's last moments." I shuddered when I read these words—I could no longer be in denial. I immediately excused myself and left the school.

As I ran home, I wanted to let out a resounding scream, to cry my eyes out, to beat my chest in sorrow, and kick hard against the rocks scattered on the ground. But I couldn't. I didn't have the freedom to show my feelings or give vent to them. I was in an environment where my identity, my history, and the whereabouts of those who were nearest and dearest to me had to be kept secret at all times. There wasn't a single soul that I could turn to in my distress, not even the Peace Corps nurse, who had shown a cold and aloof attitude toward me all along. The pressure of hiding my feelings and keeping them bottled up was unbearable. I had to smile and carry on as usual when inside I was a wreck, overwhelmed with grief, anger, and guilt all at once.

Back in the privacy of my room, I began pacing back and forth like a caged animal, trying to compose my thoughts. I realized that there was no time to lose—I had to quickly arrange another trip to Israel. First, I called Alex Boston to ask for permission to leave immediately to see my brother, and he granted it. Then I called Ahmad, my language and cross-cultural coordinator, to inform him that I was going to Israel again for a few days. Finally I called Lupe, who lived in Amman and had access to the Internet in her apartment, to ask her to book me on the next flight from Amman to Tel Aviv. I requested that she keep the circumstances of my trip and its destination strictly confidential and she was very responsive. She booked me on the only flight to Tel Aviv still available that day, departing at 9:00 p.m. with Royal Jordanian. The itinerary was sent to my email address and I could print it out at the Peace Corps office in Amman, where I would stop on the way to the airport to retrieve my passport, just as I had done on my previous trip. Anwar, the Peace Corps driver, was already on his way to pick me up. I hastily packed a few clothes and essential items in my carry-on bag, then informed Umm Ali that I was going to "Amman" again for a few days. It had been only nine days since my return from my previous trip. I used the same cover story as before: I was getting additional training in connection with my assignment to teach at Mu'ta University. It sounded plausible to Umm Ali, who didn't suspect anything.

Anwar arrived a little past noon and we set off on the long drive to Amman. We were about twenty minutes on the road when my phone chimed with an incoming message from my sister-in-law. It read, "Shimon has passed away." I gave a startled gasp and then buried my face in my hands and wept bitter tears of pain and sorrow. Anwar took the box of Kleenex that sat on the dashboard and placed it in my lap. I wiped my face with a bunch of tissues and said to him in a choked voice, "My brother has passed away." He responded with the traditional Arabic phrase, "*Allah yirhamu.*"[9]

My brother's battle with leukemia had finally ended. He had lost—and we had lost him. If he had not had the stem cell transplant he would have come to the same bitter end sooner or later. The stem cell transplant had held some hope for him. The cruelty of the matter was that the transplant succeeded in treating his blood cancer, but then the grafted stem cells had turned against his body and attacked his vital organs. The rates of this complication, known as GVHD (graft-versus-host-disease) vary between 30–40 percent among closely related patients and donors. The prognosis of beating GVHD depends on how severe it is. In my brother's case, the odds were stacked against him because of his heart condition.

I had wanted to be with my brother in his final moments, but at the same time I had been afraid to. My brother was a beacon of light in my life. I couldn't bear to see him breathe his last. I wanted to remember him as he was in his prime—vibrant, joyful, and handsome—and *not* as he was hooked up to a ventilator, looking like a shadow of his former self. He wouldn't have known if I had been there or not anyway. Most likely, he would have preferred not to have me present. Such private and intimate moments were reserved for, and could only be shared with, the person closest to him—his wife, Rachel. She had been there with him, all the way to the very end.

When their only child, Inbal, was diagnosed with Stage 4 breast cancer, she had been in her mid-thirties. She underwent aggressive rounds of chemotherapy that ravaged her body and robbed her of her looks. She decided early on that she didn't want anyone except her parents, her husband, and her daughters to see her in this condition. She wanted everyone else, both friends and relatives, to remember her as she had been in her prime. This was her expressed wish and it had to be respected. She passed away on January 23, 2011. I remember the sad message that my brother had sent me. It simply said, "Shalom Dalya. Sorry to tell you. Inbal is not with us anymore. Love, Shimon." My brother barely survived one year after his daughter's passing. May father and daughter rest in peace and may their memory be for a blessing. Amen.

The ride to Amman was imprinted on my mind as a nightmare. I had eaten a cup of yogurt mixed with oatmeal shortly before we left and it didn't sit well with me. Perhaps it was the bumpy road and heavy traffic that made me feel queasy. Anwar kept pressing on the brakes abruptly, throwing me up and down, backward and forward, and in doing so shaking my stomach and sense of balance. Or perhaps it was the shock of my brother's death that was causing this reaction in me. My stomach started turning and churning and I felt the food rising to my throat. I asked Anwar to pull over, but he couldn't stop in the middle of the road. Meanwhile, I was getting dizzier and queasier from the jerky motion of the car. I closed my eyes and held tightly onto the grab handle on the ceiling of the car. The thought that I would vomit in the car filled me with panic. Just as I was about to lose control, Anwar announced, "We've arrived!" and pulled up in the parking lot of the Peace Corps office building. I flung the door open, ran toward the farthest corner of the parking lot, and threw up uncontrollably, emptying the entire contents of my stomach. Afterward, I felt feeble and shaky and could hardly stand on my feet. Anwar helped me get to the Peace Corps office and seated me on a chair. Mat came over and suggested that I lie down on the sofa in Bryan's office, which happened to be unoccupied that day. I dragged myself through the hallway and up the stairs into his office, and collapsed on the sofa. When I closed my eyes, I felt the room spinning rapidly around like a twister and pulling me into its empty center. I tried to open my eyes, but it was to no avail. The spinning was relentless. All that shaking in the car had disrupted my sense of balance. A similar episode had happened to me once on a visit to New York City. It was a very hot day and I was looking for an apartment with a real estate agent. We went in and out of buildings and rode up and down in elevators, when suddenly I became dizzy and couldn't hold my head straight or stand on my feet. I had the feeling of being in the middle of a vortex that was spiraling faster and faster and drawing me into its hollow center. I ended up canceling all my plans for that day and returning home. This was *not* an option now. I *had to* make it to the airport.

I pulled myself together and called my sister-in-law, asking her when the funeral would take place. Traditionally, a Jewish burial is held within twenty-four hours after the death occurs. She told me that she had delayed the funeral until Sunday, December 11, to give my younger sister, who lives in Australia, enough time to arrive. When I inquired whether she wanted me to come to her apartment, she replied that she had many arrangements to make in connection with the funeral and the *shiva* (Jewish custom of seven days of mourning for a deceased person) and wasn't sure whether she would be staying in her house in Caesarea or in her apartment in Kiryat Uno. I commiserated with her over the loss of our beloved Shimon and wished her strength in the days ahead.

Next, I had to arrange for a place to stay in Israel. Finding a hotel room in Tel Aviv wouldn't be easy now, when we were so close to the Christmas holiday and the rates per night would be exorbitant. Who should I call on? My Alzheimer's-stricken mother and my sister Susan were not an option—I needed to be in a stress-free and supportive environment to make it through the difficult days ahead. Once again I called my friend Dalia and was relieved when she answered the phone. I told her that I was on my way to Tel Aviv and explained the circumstances. She said simply, "Dalya, your room is waiting for you. Come here straight from the airport." This was Dalia, always welcoming me with open arms and a compassionate smile.

I rested in Bryan's office for as long as time permitted, then went to Mat's office to print out my itinerary and retrieve my passport. I informed him that I would be traveling on my own dime once again, because I didn't want to bother my sister-in-law in her dark hour with filling up reimbursement paperwork on my behalf. But I only had traveler's checks on me, with almost no cash left. I needed to call American Express in the United States to inquire how I could cash them. Because this was a long-distance call, Mat directed me to Alex's office to use his phone. Alex seemed puzzled by my request, but politely relocated himself to the sofa so I could place the call. As I stood by his desk with my back toward him and the phone in my hand, waiting to be connected with American Express customer service, my eyes roamed over the desk. I noticed a large group picture with the head shots of the J15 volunteers. "This is probably in prepara-tion for our swearing-in ceremony at the end of the month," I thought to myself. I saw the faces of Theresa and Claire and Lora . . . and Rob and Will . . . and Megan and Ben and Ruby—everyone, *except me*. My photo was missing. How strange. Surely I must have overlooked it among the many faces. I turned my head to glance at Alex. He was sitting on the sofa with the same puzzled expression on his face, as if he was unable to fathom something. "What's troubling him?" I won-dered. Just then, the voice of a customer service representative came through, interrupting my thoughts. He said that it was very difficult to cash an American Express check in Jordan or Israel because they had closed most of their offices in these countries, but anyway gave me two phone numbers that I could try in Tel Aviv. I hung up, thanked Alex, and left his office. In my rush to get everything in order for my flight, the absence of my head shot from the J15 group picture escaped my mind.

By the time I was ready to leave, Anwar had gone home and another driver named Usama was assigned to take me to the airport. The ride with him was much smoother, perhaps because he drove an SUV and not a small passenger car. We arrived at the airport at 6:15 p.m., and I repeated the check-in procedure, already familiar from my trip nine days earlier. Unlike the previous time, the lounge by the departure gate was not full. There were a few shabby-looking Filipino passengers, no doubt foreign workers employed as domestic help, cleaners, and caretakers in Tel Aviv. I had two hours to wait for my flight. I sank into an armchair and tried to rest and regain my strength. I had a splitting headache, perhaps from hypoglycemia. Except for a cup of coffee in the morning and the yogurt that I had thrown up, I had not eaten anything all day. I went to the kiosk in the corner of the lounge and bought a cheese sandwich and a bottle of water, but neither the food nor drink could alleviate my headache or grim mood. We took off on time, served once again by female flight attendants who looked more Parisian than Middle Eastern women. We landed safely in Tel Aviv Ben Gurion International Airport at 9:45 p.m.

I was astonished to see that the terminal was quiet and not busy at all. Normally, it is teeming with an endless stream of passengers. The Christmas rush, during which thousands of holidaymakers pass through this building daily, had apparently not begun yet—perhaps it was not due for another week. I walked briskly through the empty hallways and arrived at Passport Control, where an Israeli officer stamped my passport for the second time in less than two weeks. Exiting onto the streets, I found a cab quickly and asked the driver to take me to Ramat Hasharon. It was close to 11:00 p.m. when I arrived at Dalia's house. Both she and her husband, Yossi, had stayed up to wait for me. They hugged me warmly, commiserated with me on my brother's passing, then ushered me to my room to get some sleep. "We can talk more in the morning," they said gently.

I crashed out on the bed. I was completely drained, physically and emotionally.

In the morning, Dalia offered me a ride to Tel Aviv, where she worked at a pharmacy. I readily accepted, as I needed to locate a bank or hotel to change my American Express traveler's checks to Israeli currency. When Dalia heard that I was low on cash, she immediately took out her wallet and gave me NIS250, saying, "Let me know if you need more money." She then consulted with her co-workers on where I could cash my checks. The rate of exchange differed from one institution to another, sometimes significantly. "The best place is the post office," they said unanimously. There was a post office within walking distance from her pharmacy. I set off at once, found the place, and obtained the cash.

It was mid-morning on a Friday, a short workday in Israel. I walked to Dizengoff Center and browsed in a couple of bookstores, but I wasn't in the mood to read or buy anything. I had the key to Dalia's house, so I got on a bus and returned to Ramat Hasharon. I was glad to find Yossi at home—I felt an urgent need for human company—and we ate lunch together and chatted pleasantly. Every now and then I tried to call my sister-in-law on her cell phone, but got no reply. Yossi looked astonished and I felt embarrassed. "She must be very busy," I said to him apologetically. "She probably has a million things to attend to for the funeral." He nodded in sympathy. At long last, she answered the phone, saying that she was on her way from Caesarea to Kiryat Uno. If I could come to the intersection of Herzelia and Ramat Hasharon within the next half hour, she could pick me up from there. Yossi kindly offered to give me a ride there, and we set off immediately.

We hugged each other tearfully when we met. My heart was overflowing with compassion for my sister-in-law, Rachel. Within a year, she had lost both her daughter and her husband. Now all she had left was her two granddaughters. As we drove toward Kiryat Uno, she told me that my sister Tami was expected to arrive from Australia later in the afternoon. The last time I had seen Tami was when I had come to Israel from the Netherlands to sit shiva for our father, who had suddenly died of a heart attack. Now we were going to meet again on another somber occasion—the funeral and the shiva of our brother. I wondered what Tami, who was twelve years younger than me, was like now. Throughout her childhood, I had been like a second mother to her, enveloping her with my affection and attention. After she had gotten married and had relocated to the other end of the world, we lost touch. The huge distance—the Pacific Ocean—which she had put between us, became physically and psychologically a formidable barrier to cross.

We arrived at my brother's apartment in Kiryat Uno. It felt strange to enter it without seeing him there. The year before, when I had come with Susan for a visit, he stood waiting for us on the balcony and waved enthusiastically as we got out of the car. He rushed to open the door and hugged and greeted us warmly; he floated in and out of the kitchen to bring us refreshments; and he proudly showed us around his new apartment. He had bought it so that he would be close to Beilinson Hospital, where he was being treated. Everything he owned he had worked hard for and earned with the sweat of his brow.

I helped Rachel carry the bags of groceries that were in her car up to their apartment on the sixth floor, and then we borrowed a few chairs from the building's community room in preparation for the many visitors that would come during the shiva.

Tami arrived around 4:00 p.m. and we went down to the street greet her. When she saw Rachel, she rushed toward her and the two of them broke into tears and hugged each other for a long time. I scrutinized my younger sister with interest. She had changed a lot over the years that I hadn't seen her. I saw a mature woman in her early fifties, with sunken cheeks, wrinkles around her mouth and eyes, and an expression of deep sorrow on her face. She had not been told that Shimon had already passed away when she boarded the plane from Melbourne to Tel Aviv. She had flown with the vain hope that she might still see him. Susan broke the news to her when she picked her up at the airport, and she was still in shock. Tami approached me and we hugged each other with some awkwardness that characterizes a long separation, then we went up to the apartment.

Over the next two days, Saturday and Sunday, Rachel and Tami were practically inseparable. They would sit together, eat together, and retreat to the master bedroom to speak with each other in subdued voices, shutting me out. On the one hand, I felt left out; on the other hand, I was glad that Rachel had someone to lean on in her hour of need. Tami, a math teacher in a high school in Melbourne, had a two-month term break, so she could stay for an extended period of time and provide Rachel with emotional support. I was amazed to see how much she had changed over the years. Gone was the impetuous and judgmental girl that I remembered. She was courteous and considerate, her demeanor quiet and reserved. This was a different Tami, a Tami I had not known and had missed all these years. She was very careful not to say anything that might be construed as criticism against any family member, even when Rachel had lost her self-control and said, in my presence, that she would never forgive Susan for being so egotistical and uncaring during the many weeks that Shimon lay in the hospital; not once had Susan offered to help her, even though she owned a car and lived close by. Tami tried to calm Rachel down without disparaging Susan. I observed all of this in astonishment.

On Saturday morning, Tami, Susan, and I visited our mother. It was a rare occasion in which all of us, the three daughters, were together with our mother. Mother was in a good mood, lucid and funny, but our own mood was gloomy and the occasion somber. We stayed until Mother got tired and needed to rest. We then entrusted her to the care of her Filipino maid and took our leave.

In the evening, when the Sabbath had ended and the stores reopened, Rachel, Tami, and I went to a supermarket to buy more refreshments for the shiva.[10] I used this opportunity to buy a couple of notebooks for myself, as I was keeping a journal and had run out of writing paper. We spoke little on the way. After returning to the apartment, Tami stayed in her room to work on the eulogy that she had prepared for Shimon's funeral. I sat at the computer and tried to write something too, but the words failed to flow out of me and form on the screen. I was depressed, stressed out, and disoriented all at once. Worse yet, I felt like an outsider. I feared that my words, like my presence, might not be welcome. After many failed attempts, I gave up. Instead, I wrote Miri a short letter, telling her that my brother had passed away and that I had flown to Israel to attend his funeral.

I had hoped to reconnect with Tami after all these years, but her attention was now focused solely on Rachel. I felt like a fifth wheel on a wagon, completely useless and redundant.

The funeral took place on Sunday at 1:00 p.m. in the cemetery of Caesarea, where Inbal was buried. We left the apartment early in the morning because Tami wanted to stop on the way at Khevrat Kadisha in Or Akiva,[11] where Shimon's body was being prepared for the burial, to say her last goodbye to him. Susan and her husband were supposed to follow us in their own car, but at the last minute Susan claimed that there was something wrong with their car engine and insisted on riding with us in Rachel's car. Her husband protested that she was imagining things, but, as always, she made him bend to her will. I got the distinct impression that she had fabricated this story so that she could ride with us in the same car—it was a reflection of her controlling personality. The situation became awkward and highly charged. Rachel looked annoyed, but said nothing. The five of us were squeezed into her small car: Rachel in the driver's seat, Susan's husband next to her, and the three sisters in the back seat. I sat by the window; Susan, who is corpulent, sat in the middle; and Tami sat on her other side by the window. There was a tense silence. Before long, the bickering began. Susan's husband felt hot and opened the window beside him. Susan complained that she was cold and that the wind was blowing in her face. She yelled at him to close the window, but he left a crack open. She yelled at him again. Rachel nervously turned on the air conditioning. "It's set too high. Can you please lower the thermostat?" Rachel lowered it. There was a brief silence. "Now it's set too low. Can you please raise the thermostat?" And finally, "Do you mind turning it off?"

We arrived at Khevrat Kadisha in Or Akiva, where Shimon's body lay in shrouds, waiting to be transported to the cemetery in

Caesarea. Tami went inside to say her goodbyes while we waited outside. When she emerged, her eyes and nose were red from crying. Again, she and Rachel hugged for a few moments, while we looked on in silence. Afterward, we climbed into the car and continued the drive to Caesarea.

Caesarea is one of the prettiest towns in Israel. The blue sea, Roman antiquities, and towering palm trees are a splendid sight. My brother had loved this place, which is far away from the hustle and bustle of the big city, Tel Aviv. We stopped in the town center and each of us bought a bunch of flowers to put on his grave. Since it was too early to proceed to the cemetery, Rachel took us to their house so we could wait there. The house looked neglected: the front yard was overrun with weeds, all the potted plants had withered, and the patio was littered with dry leaves and rotted dates that had fallen from the palm trees. It was eerie to come to the house and not see my brother there. He had always been the first to welcome his guests with a warm hug or a firm handshake. He had loved his house and taken great care of it, making all kinds of improvements with his own two gifted hands. We stayed on the patio, where it was cool and breezy. I went inside to freshen up before the funeral. When I passed through the living room, my glance fell on a shelf stacked with DVDs that was attached to the wall. I approached with interest and browsed through the movies—Israeli films are one of my passions. I came across a DVD titled "Shiva" (referring to the Jewish ritual of seven days of mourning). I had seen this film when it was released in 2008. It is a disturbing story about an Israeli family that sits shiva for the eldest brother who has unexpectedly passed away. Instead of uniting the family members, the shiva ritual only accentuates the divisions among them—all kinds of tensions, conflicts, and grudges between the siblings, as well as between their spouses, suddenly emerge and come to a head. The story is set in the middle of the first Gulf War and Saddam Hussein's Scud missile attacks on Israel, a background that heightens the sense of crisis of this family, which faces enemies from both within and without. The film's subject matter and uncanny resemblance to my own family dynamics shook me. A feeling of despair washed over me.

We finally left for the cemetery, a secluded area surrounded by leafy trees and green shrubs. A large crowd consisting of relatives, friends, colleagues, and acquaintances had gathered. The black Khevrat Kadisha van was parked at the entrance to the graveyard. At the appointed time, the funeral procession began. Shimon's body was removed from the van and carried on a bier by four men. The rest of us followed slowly behind. The procession entered the cemetery and headed toward a small clearing with a stone table in the center. The bier was placed on it and we gathered around for the eulogies. Shimon's body, wrapped in a white shroud, appeared small and slender. The rabbi asked the closest relatives of the deceased to step forward. Rachel, supported by Tami, moved forward. Susan grabbed my arm and moved forward with me. The rabbi proceeded to make the traditional cut in the shirt collar of each of us as a sign of mourning. Then the eulogies began.

The first eulogy, a warm and heartfelt tribute, was by Shimon's longtime boss at the medical equipment company where he had been the general manager for twenty years. The second eulogy was by Rachel; it was tearful and emotional and she could hardly finish reading it. The third was by Tami, a sensitive and moving speech that revealed how much she cared for Shimon. Then Shimon's best friend, Avi, spoke. I knew him back in the days when they were roommates studying together at the Technion (Israel Institute of Technology) in Haifa and I was serving in the I.D.F. at Kibbutz Hasolelim in the Upper Galilee, a location that enabled me to visit them now and then. His eulogy, like those that preceded it, emphasized what an exceptional man Shimon was: a loving husband and father, a devoted son and brother, a loyal friend, a talented engineer, and, above all, an exceedingly *modest* person. He never boasted about his accomplishments and never showed off his knowledge.

He was wise, generous, and compassionate, with a big heart and a unique sense of humor. Many mourners, men as well as women, wept openly, tears rolling freely down their faces.

Throughout the eulogies, I was in a daze. The finality of my brother's death suddenly sank in. I didn't know that he had touched so many lives and was loved and appreciated by so many people. Even the I.D.F. had sent two representatives, officers in uniform, to pay their respects. Weighed down with grief, my throat constricted and I had difficulty breathing. I wanted to shift my weight from one foot to another, but I couldn't. All this time, Susan was clutching my arm forcefully and leaning heavily on me. Her tight grip antagonized me. I felt chained to her like a prisoner, unable to move at will. Choked with emotion, I struggled to maintain a dignified posture and breathe normally.

After the eulogies, the procession moved toward the freshly dug grave. Shimon's body was slowly lowered into it and encased by slabs of stone. One by one, people threw a spade full of earth on top of the stones—it is considered a mitzvah to do so. After the grave was filled with earth, the rabbi recited the Kaddish (a prayer said in honor of the deceased) with a minyan.[12] Three wreathes of flowers were laid around the mound of earth that marked the fresh grave, and we fetched our own bunches of flowers to put on top of it. As I was bending over Shimon's grave with my flowers, Susan suddenly yelled at me, "Don't put flowers there! Bring them over here." Her words stung me like poison ivy. I was aghast that even here, at the cemetery, she sought to boss people around. Before I could respond, Tami snapped back, "*She* wants to put *her* flowers *there!*" Her voice was sharp and impatient. It was the only time I had seen Tami lose her reserve. In my heart, I thanked her for coming to my rescue, even though she referred to me as "she" in my presence.

I asked Rachel to take me to her daughter's grave so I could put flowers on it too, and we walked a few rows of graves away to where

Inbal was buried. Father and daughter were now united. May their souls be bound up in the bond of life, and may they rest eternally in dignity and peace. Amen.

It was an intensely emotional afternoon. Many mourners gathered around Rachel to express their condolences, before dispersing, little by little. As we prepared to leave, I took one last look at the fresh grave and whispered, "Goodbye, dearest brother. We miss you terribly."

The car ride back to Kiryat Uno passed in silence, except for a few snappy exchanges between Susan and her husband. I looked at Rachel with concern, wondering why she was in the driver's seat instead of Susan's husband. Each of us was wrapped up in our own thoughts. I was thinking that when my father had passed away, I didn't feel like I had been orphaned. But now, with both my father and brother gone, I felt like a total orphan, even though my mother was still alive. My kind and caring brother had been a protective and guiding force in my life. He had a strong sense of loyalty and morality and refused to meet with my ex-husband or speak with him after the scandal of his betrayal and double life broke out. On more than one occasion, he had asked me if I needed financial help, and I knew that I could always count on him. We grew up as Irish twins, always together, he being just one year my senior. I have a picture from our days in kindergarten, where I'm anxiously holding his hand in a class full of little children. I always looked up to him as a role model. In my dysfunctional family, he was my *only* role model. Perhaps if I had followed more closely in his footsteps, I would not have married the wrong guy. He had had strong reservations about the husband I had chosen and had never trusted him. He saw through his endless lies, his empty promises, and his narcissistic personality. My brother was honest, reliable, and honorable—everything my husband was not. After my divorce, I realized that I had lived with an impostor for so long that I no longer knew what a *real* man was.

We arrived in Kiryat Uno in the late afternoon, and Susan decided to stay with us. We didn't expect many visitors at the apartment, as visitors usually start arriving the day after the funeral. Indeed, only one person showed up, a friend of Rachel's from her workplace, and the two of them retreated to a corner of the living room to talk. Tami went to her room to rest, and so did I. I wasn't so much tired as I wanted some time alone to process the day's shattering event. Two hours later, when Tami and I returned to the living room, Rachel's friend was still there, and so was Susan, indefatigable, reading a book. Her husband looked cooped up and desperate to leave. To pass the time, Tami and I sat at the kitchen table to drink a cup of tea. I thought this would allow us to exchange a few words, but Susan got up immediately to join us. After a few casual remarks, Tami asked us to tell her some stories about Shimon's childhood. She had missed those years of his life because when she was born, Shimon was already thirteen. I was eager to reminisce about Shimon; after all, we had grown up together as Irish twins. But Susan monopolized the conversation. I waited patiently for her to finish talking so that I could say something too, but she went on and on, without allowing me to get a word in edgewise, as if she had known our brother intimately as a little boy and was the highest authority on the subject. In reality, Susan was three years older than Shimon. She had left home when she was thirteen to live on a kibbutz, and had married at seventeen. When Shimon was ten and I was nine, Susan no longer lived with us. I, on the other hand, had lived with him in our parents' house until he turned eighteen and left to study in Haifa. Susan's continuous monologue was getting on my nerves. I didn't hear one story that I had not known or heard from our mother before. I gave up and went back to my room.

As I sat in my room, it occurred to me that I should write down my childhood recollections of Shimon and send them to his wife and Tami. I knew a chapter in his life that neither of them shared. My brother was my playmate and closest companion throughout the years of my childhood and youth. We attended the same kindergarten and the same elementary school. Even our Bat-Mitzvah and Bar-Mitzvah were celebrated together on the same day in one big party, because when I turned twelve, he turned thirteen—the respective ages at which this ceremony is held for girls and boys in Israel. When I was in high school, he went to an all-boys' vocational school and occasionally asked me to set him up with girls from my class. I introduced him to my best friend, Varda, and they dated for a while. He was my math tutor and I was his English tutor. At eighteen, he went to Haifa to study mechanical engineering at the Technion, and the following year I was drafted into the army and volunteered to serve in Kibbutz Hasolelim in the Upper Galilee, a three-hour bus ride from where he lived. I loved to surprise him with a big bag of oranges and grapefruit, freshly picked from the kibbutz orchards. He lived with his friend, Avi, in a rented room in an apartment belonging to a difficult landlady. He told me that he used to give her half the amount of oranges that I brought him so as to please her . . . Tears welled up in my eyes. There was so much to recollect and so much to say, but no opportunity to say it.

Rachel's friend, as well as Susan and her husband, had finally left, and the three of us remained in the living room together for the first time after the funeral. I was eager to connect, to reach out and touch, but I quickly discovered that Rachel and Tami wanted to be alone. Two is company; three is a crowd. They had things they wanted to share with each other, but not with me. I decided to give them space and made myself scarce, retreating to my room for a while. When I came back, they had vanished into the master bedroom. I could hear them talking in subdued voices. I lingered in the living room, not knowing what to do. When they emerged, they ignored me and headed directly for the kitchen, still talking in subdued voices. I wished them goodnight and retired for the night.

As I lay in bed, I considered the possibility of leaving the next day. I had received permission from the Peace Corps to stay for the entire shiva, but I had also made a flight reservation for the day after the funeral. I could stay on or leave. I pondered the situation. I had attended the funeral and paid my respects to my brother. Rachel had no use for me as Tami was there to support her. The two of them got on well together. I was unneeded, if not downright unwanted, so why impose myself on them? As for Susan, the fact that I had stayed with a friend rather than with her on two successive visits to Israel said it all. I had to acknowledge the plain truth: there was little warmth or contact between us, the remaining siblings. Bereavement can unite family members—or accentuate the divisions and lack of cohesion among them. My presence served no purpose. I decided to leave.

I deeply regretted that Tami and I had no opportunity to talk and wondered how she felt about me. Her demeanor was reserved and guarded. She didn't ask me any personal questions. Perhaps she didn't want to open old wounds—or perhaps she didn't want to reconnect. She was very polite, to be sure, but other than exchanging casual remarks such as "How did you sleep?" "Are you jet-lagged?" "Would you like a cup of tea?" we didn't have any real conversation. Perhaps blood ties don't matter as much as the amount of time spent together. Since her relocation to Australia, Tami and I had not spent any time together.

The next morning I got up early and prepared to leave. I called a cab to pick me up at 8:30 a.m. and take me to the airport. Both Rachel and Tami didn't seem surprised and didn't express any disappointment at the news of my departure. I assumed that if Rachel hadn't already told Tami about my whereabouts, which I had asked her to keep confidential, she would probably do so after I left. I called Susan to say goodbye, dreading her prying questions, but was relieved when she didn't answer the phone and left a voicemail instead. When my cab arrived, I hugged Rachel and my sister and wished them strength in the days ahead. Tami walked me to the elevator lobby. As we stood there waiting for the elevator, I uttered the traditional Jewish phrase, "May we meet on a joyous occasion the next time." She looked at me with a somber expression on her face and said,

"I don't think so." Startled, I asked, "Why?" She replied, "Mother's health is failing. She's getting weaker all the time. She may not be around much longer." The prospect of coming to Israel for another shiva dismayed me. "We've got to stop meeting like this," I said with a deep sigh. Just then the elevator arrived. We hugged again and said our goodbyes.

As the cab sped through the highway toward the airport, I stared blankly ahead, my mind preoccupied with the events of the last three days. The loss of my brother was an enormous blow to my family. He was its backbone, its *matzpen* and *matzpun*.[13] His absence had left a huge void that could never be filled. With his passing, the weak ties that bound my family had become even looser. I thought of my Jordanian host family, of their strong sense of cohesion and solidarity, and felt a great admiration for this deeply rooted Arab value orientation. For Arabs, it is an inviolable axiom: the family is sacred and above all else. Without a family, a person is a tree without roots, a trunk without braches, a leaf in the wind ...

The flight back to Jordan was uneventful, except for the rough treatment that I received this time from the Passport Control officer at Amman International Airport. He took one look at the "offending stamp" in my passport and declared that I needed a new visa to enter Jordan. He was rude and hostile. When I showed him that I already had a valid visa, he started yelling at me and waved his arms threateningly. I showed him the sticker of the Peace Corps on the cover of my passport, thinking that perhaps this might calm him down, but he only got madder. Who was I to argue with him? As a last resort, I told him that I was going to call the Peace Corps safety and security coordinator, Samir. I took out my cell phone and started dialing his number when the Jordanian officer relented, reexamined my visa, and reluctantly stamped my passport. So the stories about the "offending stamp" were true after all. I realized that two trips to "Disneyland" in less than two weeks were enough to arouse the wrath—and suspicions—of the Jordanian Passport Control officers.

When I walked out of the exit hall into the street, I found Waleed, another Peace Corps driver, waiting for me. I climbed into his car and we began the long drive back to the village of Hamadiyya.

Umm Ali couldn't understand why I hugged and kissed her so warmly when I arrived. "I missed you," I said to her. She smiled graciously. I noticed the marked progress in the construction of Usama's house over the few days that I had been away. I knew that Umm Ali was supervising the construction workers (all Egyptians) and cooking for them at the same time. I complimented her on her good work and mentioned in passing, "It's a pity that daughters don't stay in their parents' house after marriage and only sons do." I had no idea that I had touched a raw nerve. Suddenly, Umm Ali burst into tears, saying that she missed her mother, who had passed away a year and a half earlier. She told me that her mother had lived in the village near the boys' elementary school and that she used to visit her every day. She said that when a woman grows old, she is ashamed to ask her son to help her wash herself or get dressed, but she is not ashamed to ask her daughter to perform such intimate services for her. She was very sad about the loss of her mother. I commiserated with her, and all of a sudden my floodgates opened and my face was covered in tears. Umm Ali thought that I was crying because of her. How I wished that I could open my heart to her and tell her about my own sorrows! *My private life was a secret and a taboo.* I cried for my brother, for my father, for my divided family, and for my lonely and orphaned self. I cried silently, hot anguished tears, releasing my bottled up grief for a few fleeting moments, before I abruptly pulled myself together. *It would be foolish to expose myself now.*

Umm Ali took me by the hand and offered to give me a tour of Usama's house. She proudly showed me around the structure, pointing to the location of the kitchen, the living room, the master bedroom, and the children's room. Usama was there, pouring water on the concrete ceiling with a garden hose. He glanced at me briefly but didn't greet me. I assumed that he still regarded me as a spy. Perhaps he had entered my room in my absence and had found something. I had removed all the papers that bore my last name from my suitcase and placed them in my other suitcase at the training site. But who knows? Perhaps I had overlooked a tiny detail . . . But no, if he had found anything, he certainly wouldn't be standing there pouring water on the concrete ceiling with a garden hose . . . He would be raising hell. I quickly dismissed this paranoid thought from my head.

I was impressed with the size and design of Usama's house, which included a master suite complete with its own bathroom. I wondered where he got the money to build all this—it surely didn't come from his meager army salary. Oh yes, Peace Corps money, of course. It was why he put up with me in the first place. I smiled to myself. The tour came to an end, and Umm Ali and I walked hand in hand back to the old parental home.

My paternal grandparents, Rahamim and Lulu Abudi, after arriving
from Baghdad in Israel, circa 1951.

A greeting card featuring my father, on the left, and my maternal
great-uncle Haim. The Hebrew words on the card say: Happy New
Year. Haifa, Israel, 1942, which is the year that my father came to Israel.

My mother Ahuva Shami, aged approximately sixteen,
in Baghdad, circa 1941.

My father Shawqi Abudi, in his early twenties,
in Baghdad, circa 1940.

My parents, in Tel Aviv, in 1967. They had met and married
in Israel, circa 1943.

My brother Shimon and myself in kindergarten, circa 1952.
My brother, in a sailor's shirt, is seated in the front row, and I am
seated next to him on the left.

My brother and myself, wearing Purim costumes, circa 1957.

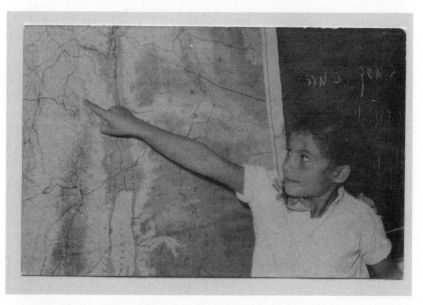

Myself, in a geography lesson in the third-grade of elementary
school, in the town of Lod.

On Israel's tenth Independence Day, the municipality of Lod issued
a special certificate to every child in town who was born in the year
that the Jewish State was established.

My brother, Shimon, in the summer of 1994.

My brother's daughter, Inbal, in the summer of 1994.

Myself, in basic training in the I.D.F., in the summer of 1966.

Myself, in Kibbutz Hasolelim in the Upper Galilei, in 1967.

Myself, in Utrecht, the Netherlands, circa 1972.

Myself, in Potomac, Maryland, circa 1997.

Myself, today, in a traditional Arab dress.

9 . MY PERMANENT
SITE

I WELCOMED THE MONOTONY OF MY DAYS IN THE VILLAGE AFTER the tumultuous time that I had been through. We had two weeks left until the end of our pre-service training: one week of practicum, and the final week—the highlight of the entire program—a trip to Amman to attend the "supervisors conference," followed by a visit to our permanent sites. We looked forward to this conference, set for December 19 and 20, when we would meet the principals of the schools at which we were assigned to teach. We would then travel to our designated towns and villages to see our apartments and sign the leases. In the meantime, we continued to follow the same routine in the village. However, with the language proficiency test and solo teaching already behind us, the enthusiasm with which we applied ourselves to the practicum had diminished.

On December 15, we had a center day. As usual, when we arrived at the training site I rushed to take my laptop out of storage and checked my email account, only to find *no* urgent messages awaiting me this time. None at all! There were some newsletters from websites that I was subscribed to, but that was all. I couldn't believe my eyes! For the first time since my arrival in Jordan, I felt *normal,* just like the rest of the volunteers—no crisis and no pressing issues to attend to. I quickly dropped Miri a note: "Guess what? I logged onto my email account today and, for the first time in weeks, there was no bad news! No 'fire' to extinguish and nothing to stress about! I can easily get used to this!" I went to class feeling a huge surge of relief.

As I passed through the hallway, I ran into Natalie. She stopped me and offered her condolences on my brother's passing. Stunned, I remained speechless for a moment. "How do you know?" I asked when I finally found my tongue. "I overheard it," she replied. I became alarmed. If there was a rumor or gossip circulating about me, then my identity and safety might be compromised. "From whom?" I inquired. She refused to divulge, saying, "I wanted to be nice to you. But now you want to know something that I can't tell you." She wanted to be nice? This came across more like an act of bullying on her part than an act of courtesy. We hardly ever spoke to each other. In fact, there had been an undercurrent of tension between us since the flight from Frankfurt to Amman, when she had sat next to me. Now, she was telling me that she possessed sensitive information about me. How did she come by this information? Natalie was in the same village with Angela, who had become close with Mona. Angela and Mona might have talked about me, perhaps over the phone, and Natalie could have overheard them. But how did Mona know? Perhaps from Walaa, our LCF, who might have heard it from Rifaat or Ahmad, or perhaps Anwar the driver? I was deeply worried. All these people were supposed to *protect my identity* and keep my personal information *confidential.* You never know what a leak of confidential information might lead to. Wasn't this how Kate Puzey's tragedy had come to pass? In March 2009, she was found with her throat slit on the front porch of her house in a village in the West African nation of Benin, after an email with a sensitive report that she had sent to her Peace Corps supervisors was *not* handled confidentially, even though she had specifically asked them to keep it anonymous. My friend Miri constantly feared for my safety in Jordan. "If your Jewish identity is discovered, you might end up with a knife in your back or your chest. Don't forget that Palestinians carry out stabbing attacks on Jews in Israel all the time, in the street, in the marketplace, in the bus station, even while riding in a cab," she said. I pondered whether I should bring this matter to Bryan's attention, and after careful consideration decided that I should not rock the boat. But my sense of being on shaky ground had intensified.

That morning, I received my ATM card from Sultan. It confirmed to me that I was regarded as a regular member of the group, and I cheered up. Later, I also received the written report about my solo teaching, which was full of positive comments, and it further lifted my spirits. After lunch, the entire J15 group gathered together to vote for two representatives who would give a speech at the swearing-in ceremony. Will was chosen from among the guys and Veronica from among the girls. I noticed that Mona's face was crestfallen. She had expected to win the vote but failed.

Everything seemed to be on track. Still, when I returned to my village, I couldn't help thinking that something was terribly amiss in this great undertaking. I had joined the Peace Corps out of a sense of idealism. I wanted to be of service to humanity. I wanted to transcend issues of race, religion, and nationality, to become part of a larger, global family. Instead, I found myself living like a fugitive on the run, having to hide my true identity and lie about it, lest I get caught and suffer the consequences. This didn't make sense. Could I live like this for two whole years? For the first time since my arrival in Jordan, I began to have serious doubts.

In preparation for the swearing-in ceremony, we had to take pictures of our host families and submit them to the Peace Corps office. They were meant for the certificates that the host families would receive from the Peace Corps in recognition of their gracious hospitality. Umm Ali looked forward to this event. She told me that she couldn't wait for the day when she and her family would put on their best clothes and travel to the training site at Al al-Bayt University to attend the ceremony. Her eyes sparkled and her face beamed with pride as she imagined her family's name being announced and the certificate being handed to them. I was touched by her enthusiasm and realized how much the swearing-in ceremony meant to her too. We agreed to get together on a Saturday afternoon, when Abu Ali and all the children would be at home, to take pictures.

At the appointed time, we gathered on the balcony to pose. Dressed in traditional Arab garb, Abu Ali and Umm Ali sat on chairs, surrounded by Nawal, Rana, Ziyad, Adil, and Huda. Olive trees and flat-roofed houses appeared in the background, and beyond them in the distance loomed the desert. Umm Ali and Abu Ali stared solemnly at the camera, their heads held high, their posture straight, and their hands resting in their laps. Nawal and Rana, wearing hijabs, stood behind them, smiling bashfully. They were flanked by Ziyad and Adil, who were grinning broadly, while little Huda stood in the front with a baffled expression on her face. I snapped several pictures of the family in slightly different positions and then gave the camera to Nawal so she could include me in some of the photos. We were in a festive mood. The much-anticipated conclusion of our journey together was near at hand.

December 18 was our last center day. At the end of the last technical session, we rushed out of the classroom screaming with joy. Two groups, the YD (youth development) and SE (special education), who had already attended the supervisors conference the week before, got on minibuses that took them back to their villages, and my TEFL group remained at the training site.

The next morning we boarded the bus to Amman, filled with nervous anticipation. At this two-day conference, we would meet the Jordanian principals at whose schools we were assigned to teach for the next two years. I would meet Dr. Zaydan, the vice dean of the College of Arts at Mu'ta University, who was also a professor of English. We were instructed to wear business attire and be well groomed. Naturally, we were anxious. Would my supervisor be a nice person? Would he or she like me? Would I make a good impression? It was much like going on a blind date.

When we arrived in Amman we were taken to Orchid Hotel, where we stayed one night. Located in the heart of a commercial and shopping center, the Orchid is one of the luxury hotels in the city. It was certainly a far cry from the Palmyra, where we had stayed on arrival in Jordan. We assumed that this expensive accommodation was chosen in honor of our Jordanian guests. After checking in, we had a lavish lunch, and at 2:00 p.m. the conference began. Dressed in a black pants suit with a name tag saying "Dalya Seymore" pinned to my lapel, I looked for Dr. Zaydan. All the other female volunteers had female supervisors, and all the male volunteers had male supervisors. I was the *only* female volunteer paired with a male supervisor. It was an awkward situation, mitigated only by the fact that I was an older woman and thus deemed beyond sexual temptation.

I found Dr. Zaydan sitting by himself in a secluded corner of the conference room. I smiled and greeted him. He extended his hand to shake mine, and I took my cue from him and shook his hand. Dr. Zaydan was in his late forties, short, dark-skinned, and mustached. He began to chat in English, asking me about my background. I told him that I had earned a doctorate in Arabic with a minor in applied linguistics from Georgetown University, and a master's degree in English from the State University of Utrecht. I had taught at the University of Amsterdam, where many of my students were Arabs from North Africa, and at the University of Maryland. In fact, I had also taught at the Hebrew University of Jerusalem, where many of my students were Palestinian Arabs, but could I mention this to him? Of course not. "You look Middle Eastern," Dr. Zaydan remarked. "Where are you originally from?" "The Netherlands," I replied, nervously awaiting his reaction. He didn't seem suspicious. "The Dutch have assimilated a lot of ethnic groups from Indonesia, Curacao, and more recently from Turkey and North Africa," he said knowingly. I nodded repeatedly in agreement.

Dr. Zaydan mentioned that he was from a small village by the Dead Sea, not far from the border with Palestine. *Palestine or Israel?* I wondered, as I tried to picture the map of Jordan in my mind to figure this out. I remembered how this map was drawn on the outer wall of the girls' elementary school in Taybeh: all the territories west of the Jordan River up to the Mediterranean Sea, then north of the Sea of Galilee up to the border with Syria, and then south of the Dead Sea up to the border with Egypt, were marked as Palestine, thus completely erasing any trace of Israel. Was he referring to this kind of map? Dr. Zaydan asked me if I had ever been to the Dead Sea. I shook my head, feigning ignorance. In fact, I had been several times to the Dead Sea—on the Israeli side, of course. But could I tell him that? I had to pretend that I had never seen the Dead Sea, period. He remarked that it is a must-see place, and I nodded enthusiastically. At least I didn't have to lie on this point. Inwardly, I felt hopelessly conflicted. I had always prided myself on my honesty and integrity, and here I was, compromising these qualities in compliance with Peace Corps instructions. Was this justified? And how long could I keep up this charade?

Dr. Zaydan had received his elementary and secondary education in Jordanian schools, earned his PhD in applied linguistics from the University of Malaysia in Kuala Lumpur, traveled widely in the Arab world, and spoke several Arabic dialects. We discovered that we had several interests in common, among them a passion for travel and a love for Arabic and world literature. I was impressed by his friendly and respectful demeanor. He was thoroughly professional and never asked me any prying questions such as, "Are you married?" "How old are you?" "Are you a Christian?" "How much money do you make as a teacher?" It seemed to me that he was pleased with my academic background and my experience as a teacher who is at ease with Arabic language and Arab culture.

The welcome speeches began. Alex and Bryan delivered their speeches in English and Lana translated their words into Arabic. Next, Sultan and Lana delivered their speeches in Arabic and translated their own words into English. Only a few participants in the conference were fluent in both languages. I noticed that whenever I laughed at jokes made in Arabic, some fellow volunteers eyed me enviously—they could not follow what was said. We then engaged in a round of introductions designed to break the ice between the volunteers and their supervisors. Each volunteer had to introduce his or her supervisor in Arabic to all the participants and each supervisor had to introduce his or her volunteer in English. The volunteers struggled with Arabic pronunciation, syntax, and vocabulary, while the supervisors struggled with the English, a situation that generated a lot of laughter. When my turn came to introduce Dr. Zaydan in Arabic, I spoke fluently, pronouncing the tough guttural consonants *'ayn*, *ha*, and *kha* with ease and finesse. I heard exclamations of *mashallah* (indicating amazement) from the Jordanian supervisors. I smiled and turned my face toward my Peace Corps supervisors, Alex and Bryan, confident that I had done them proud. To my consternation, Bryan gave me a cold, penetrating look and Alex stared at me with an aloof, puzzled expression, just like the one I had seen on his face when I was in his office, trying to call American Express from his desk phone. My smile vanished and my heart sank. A sudden sense of foreboding washed through me.

We proceeded to engage in a team-building activity. Each group of participants seated around the same table had to construct a tower from a hundred pieces of plastic straws and two meters of tape within twenty minutes; the group that would manage to build the highest and sturdiest tower would be declared the winner. Dr. Zaydan and I sat alone at a table in a secluded corner of the conference room, almost hidden from view by big white columns. I had the impression that Dr. Zaydan had deliberately chosen this particular spot so as not to be seen seated with a female stranger. In our own little team of two, I let Dr. Zaydan be the architect of the tower construction and contented myself with being his assistant, handing him straws, placing them where he pointed, or fastening them with a piece of tape. After all, this was a *patriarchal* society and I had to be careful not to infringe on his sense of masculinity. We didn't win, but we managed to build a fairly high tower.

The first conference day ended at 6:00 p.m., and we were free to spend the evening as we pleased. By now—the final days of our pre-service training—most of the volunteers belonged to small subgroups that planned their leisure activities separately, and they vanished from sight the minute we were dismissed. I went to the lobby and ran into Lupe, who was taking a few girls to City Mall to do some shopping. I had nothing else to do so I joined them. We took a cab together and split the fare among us. I wasn't prepared for what awaited us at City Mall. It was another side of Amman that I hadn't seen before: the affluence, luxury goods, and consumerism. Judging by the names of the shops and the colorful displays in their brightly lit windows, you couldn't tell whether you were in Jordan, the United States, or Western Europe. The ground floor was dominated by the famed French department store Carrefour. The other three floors housed numerous boutiques and shops of local and global brands, from clothing, shoes, and jewelry to optics, toys, and electronics, as well as elegant restaurants and cafés, cinemas, and even banks. The mall was packed with shoppers, young and old, veiled and unveiled women, girls dressed in traditional Arab attire and in modern Western clothes, men with their wives and children, and teenagers with their friends. These were well-to-do Jordanians with money to spend, not the poor Bedouins of my village. We checked out the prices of items in various stores and found out that they were much higher than in the United States. After a while, this replica of Euro/American malls started to bore me, but my companions, who happened to be Natalie and Angela, wanted to continue shopping until our curfew time of 10:00 p.m. I realized that I was stuck. Peace Corps safety rules warned female volunteers against traveling alone at night by cab. I had to wait for them until they were ready to leave so that we would return together to the hotel. I had a throbbing headache from the jumble of noise, music, and voices around me, and the repeated rides up and down the escalators made me queasy. Natalie and Angela had endless energy and moved from store to store, trying on shoes, boots, blouses, and sweaters. I realized that tagging along with others had been a poor idea and that from now on I should plan my own leisure activities, in line with my own interests and abilities.

The next morning, I ran into Nabila, the elementary school principal whom I had met in Taybeh during my site visit with Sharon. We ate breakfast together, along with Claire, who was assigned to teach at her school. Despite her initial preference for an older volunteer, Nabila was pleased to have Claire teach at her school. "Her eyes reflect such innocence," she said to me in Arabic, glancing at Claire, who had no idea what we were talking about. Nabila congratulated me on my assignment to Mu'ta University, praising the institution for its high academic standards and beautiful campus. I was delighted to hear this and eager to embark on the site visit and see everything with my own eyes.

We began the second conference day with a session that was devoted to defining mutual expectations: the supervisors were asked to define their expectations of the volunteers, and the volunteers were asked to define their expectations of the supervisors. These expectations were then compared. The idea was to establish realistic expectations of each other and to set the boundaries of what we could and should do for each other. Next, the supervisors remained in the conference room for a meeting with Sultan, and the volunteers convened in a separate room for a briefing on financial and housing matters by Mat, the Peace Corps management and operations officer. We learned that we would be getting a settling-in allowance of JD340 ($480) and a monthly allowance of JD189 ($266). The Peace Corps would pay the monthly rent on our apartments and we would receive an additional JD15 ($21) for utilities, JD10 ($14) for our cell phones, and JD17 ($24) for leave. Altogether, these were modest amounts that required careful budgeting on our parts to make both ends meet. Most of us had been using our American credit cards and ATM cards to supplement our expenses even during our pre-service training. If we planned to travel around Jordan on vacation, we would surely need to draw on our own funds. The more stuff a new volunteer could "inherit" from a departing volunteer, the better off he or she was. We had a lot of questions, to which Mat didn't always have a ready answer because he was new at this post, having recently arrived in Jordan. I raised my hand to ask a question. Mat ignored me. I tried again, but he kept ignoring me. I found an opportunity to speak up and quickly asked my question. He answered me curtly and with reluctance. What's wrong with this guy? I asked myself, feeling snubbed and slighted.

We returned to the conference room for additional sessions, focusing on the first three months at our permanent sites. We were asked to develop a three-month action plan with our supervisors, taking into consideration that, during this period, we would only be required to observe classes but not teach. Our goals would be to get to know the school system, adjust to our new communities, settle in our new apartments, and complete all the necessary safety and security arrangements. It was nice to know that we had a three-month grace period before assuming teaching responsibilities. We also received the leases that we had to sign with our landlords and were told to inspect our apartments carefully. The day before, I had approached Bryan and asked him to ensure that the name they put on my lease would be Seymore and not Cohen. I was relieved to see that this was done properly and reassured by the fact that I had received a lease like everyone else, as this confirmed to me once again that all was well. Finally, Bryan and Alex delivered the closing remarks and handed each of us a certificate of participation in the conference. On this certificate, as on my lease, my name appeared as Dalya Seymore.

After a quick lunch, Dr. Zaydan and I set off on our journey to Mu'ta University. As a stranger of the opposite sex riding alone in a car with a Jordanian man, I was an exception. A popular Arabic proverb states, "When a man is alone with a woman, the devil is the third party," implying that it is inevitable that sexual temptation should arise. Dr. Zaydan drove a comfortable Hyundai car, property of the university. I didn't know whether to sit in the front or the back. To sit next to him in the front would imply familiarity, which was culturally inappropriate, but to sit in the back would be to relegate him to the status of my driver, which might offend him. Dr. Zaydan saw my hesitation and signaled to me to sit in the front. We had a long drive ahead of us, going south. Mu'ta University is located in the town of Mu'ta, which is 120 km south of Amman and 15 km south of Karak. Depending on traffic, it would take us two and a half to three hours to get there. We spoke little in the car. I passed the time looking out the window at the scenery. We were driving in the desert along King's Highway. Parched, stony terrain, with small scattered villages surrounded us and stretched into the horizon. The monotony of the scenery and the motion of the car made my eyelids heavy. I was embarrassed to nap in Dr. Zaydan's company and forced myself to stay awake. We arrived at our destination around 5:00 p.m., and Dr. Zaydan proceeded to give me a quick tour of the campus.

I was delighted to see how beautiful my permanent site was. The center of the campus was dominated by an octagon-shaped pond with a fountain in the middle. Stone benches surrounded the pond, inviting students to sit and relax in the open air. The ground between the various buildings was covered with paving stones and interspersed with palm trees and small areas of grass that imparted freshness and coolness to the place. Clean, elegant, and peaceful, the campus looked like a haven in the midst of the foreboding desert. Male and female students walked around, looking well dressed and groomed. I was taken with the modern and aesthetic architecture of the buildings; it was so different from the grave and stern look of the buildings at Al al-Bayt University. Founded in 1981, Mu'ta University comprises two separate sections: one civilian, and the other military. The military section was surrounded by a high wall and military police guarded its gated entrance.

At the end of the tour, Dr. Zaydan took me to see the faculty residential area and check out my apartment. Located within a few minutes' walk from the center of the campus was a group of low buildings, each one comprising three apartments arranged in a row. Olive trees and oleander trees surrounded the buildings, giving them privacy and shelter from the sun. The layout of the place and the greenery reminded me of a small kibbutz—I had lived in one and visited many others. Dr. Zaydan opened the door to a middle unit in one of the buildings and declared, "This is your apartment. You will sleep here tonight and tomorrow. The housing staff left you some food in the refrigerator and there are blankets in the bedroom." I looked closely around. We were instructed to inspect our apartments carefully before signing the lease, so that we could note down anything that was missing or broken and in need of repair. It was a one-bedroom apartment cluttered with shabby furniture. There were three twin size beds in the bedroom, without sheets or pillows. The yellow foam mattresses had blood stains on them and seemed to be infested with fleas and bedbugs. Patches of plaster had fallen off from the walls, exposing the gray mortar and concrete building blocks. Several old chairs and side tables stood in the living room, covered with a thick layer of dust. The kitchen was equipped with a cooking stove and a small refrigerator, and there were some cups and dishes in the cupboard. I opened the bathroom door and took a quick peek. Holy moly! There was a commode! And there was central heating throughout the apartment! In the brutal winters of this region, this was a real luxury. I felt quite lucky. True, the place was terribly neglected: the walls were dirty, the carpets torn and soiled, and the curtains faded and frayed. But with hard work and some investment it could be made into a cozy home.

Dr. Zaydan was in a rush. There was a graduation ceremony of English major students that he had to attend. He locked the apartment and gave me the key. We hurried back to the campus and entered a building called al-Sala al-Abbasiyya, where the celebration was already in progress. Loud oriental music and a festive crowd of students greeted us. Faculty members and professors of English—all mustached men in dark suits—were seated in the front row. Dr. Zaydan introduced me to Dr. al-Qasim, dean of the College of Arts, and to Dr. al-Mazini, head of the English department. I was prepared to place my right arm across my chest and utter the traditional greeting, as is customary between strangers of the opposite sex, but they extended their hands to shake mine and so I shook their hands. They eyed me inquisitively. I assumed that they had expected a blonde, blue-eyed American woman, not a distinctly Middle Eastern–looking woman. We exchanged a few pleasantries but could hardly make ourselves heard over the din of the crowd and loud music. Each graduate whose name was announced approached Dr. al-Qasim, shook his hand, and received his or her diploma. Then all the guests clapped their hands and let out shrill trills of joy. The female students were a diverse group that included veiled girls, girls dressed in traditional Arab garb, and girls wearing modern Western clothes. High-heeled boots, tight pants, and fitted jackets were conspicuous enough to turn male heads around and attract their attention. Trays with sweets and pastries were passed around. Cell phones were raised in the air to snap pictures. Several male graduates were lifted onto the shoulders of their friends, who sang and danced with them. The music got even louder. The air was thick with cigarette smoke, and I could feel the muscle around my airways tighten up. With an apologetic cough, I rose to my feet and went outside for a breath of fresh air.

The sun was setting. I realized that soon it would be dark, everyone would go home, and the campus would be deserted. A J13 volunteer who had taught at a Jordanian college told me that the disadvantage of living on campus is that at the end of the day, when the students go home, the place becomes empty and dreary—there is nowhere to go and nothing to do. It's not like when you live in a village and can visit neighbors or friends in the evening. A Peace Corps volunteer who lives on a university campus experiences a greater sense of loneliness and isolation than a Peace Corps volunteer who lives in a village. I thought about the two nights that awaited me in the neglected apartment that was assigned to me. The idea didn't appeal to me. There were no sheets or towels and the bloodstained mattresses looked gross. I was in a bit of a fix. All the other J15 volunteers were invited to sleep in the homes of their principals, but in my case, because Dr. Zaydan and I were of the opposite sex and he lived by himself in the faculty residence on weekdays, this was impossible. What was I to do? Suddenly I recalled the names of the J14 couple, Dave and Anne, who had recently relocated to this campus from the town of Tafila. Why not call them and ask if I could stay with them for two nights?

I had met Dave and Anne at our site announcement ceremony at Al al-Bayt University. They had introduced themselves to me upon hearing that I was assigned to Mu'ta University and we had exchanged telephone numbers. I managed to reach Dave on his cell phone and asked if I could sleep two nights in their apartment. He replied that he would have to check with Anne and would let me know. I hung up and waited nervously. A few minutes later he called back to say that it was okay, and I breathed a sigh of relief. We agreed to meet in front of al-Sala al-Abbasiyya building. I went inside to inform Dr. Zaydan where he could find me, and left quickly.

Dave spotted me first and waved. He said that although I looked Middle Eastern, there was still something different about me, perhaps it was my demeanor. I was dying to ask what was striking about my demeanor. Deep down, I knew the answer, so I just smiled and nodded in acknowledgment. We walked toward his apartment, located in the campus staff residential area, which comprised a group of two-story buildings with two apartments on each floor. We entered a nice building surrounded by a green lawn and leafy trees and climbed the concrete stairs to the second floor. Dave and Anne had a lovely two-bedroom apartment that they had "inherited," along with most of its furnishings, from the J13 Peace Corps couple who had last served at this site. I had heard of them and regretted their departure because they were exactly my age.

I thanked Anne and Dave for their hospitality and explained my peculiar predicament to them. My supervisor couldn't host me because he was of the opposite sex, and the apartment assigned to me was unfit for use. They were sympathetic and eager to exchange personal observations and experiences with me. Dave prepared a pot of tea and Anne poured it into cups. We sat in their cozy living room and chatted animatedly. Within minutes, I learned the reason for their relocation from their original site to this place.

Anne was a special education volunteer in Tafila. She had witnessed an incident of child abuse at work and reported it to her supervisors. The report had caused a stir in the town, and the Peace Corps, fearing for her safety, decided to remove her from that site. After what had happened to Kate Puzey in Benin in 2009, they felt compelled to take this course of action. Kate Puzey had been found slain in her house after she had reported to her supervisors that a local male teacher at the village school was molesting female students. The tragedy—and scandal—caused a public outcry and the conduct of the Peace Corps came under sharp scrutiny. An official investigation was launched into the case amid allegations of many other incidents of rape, murder, and cover-up, and the failure of the Peace Corps to protect its volunteers. In November 2011, a month after my J15 group had arrived in Jordan, President Obama signed the Kate Puzey Peace Corps Volunteer Protection Act, aimed at protecting Peace Corps whistleblowers and improving the treatment of victims of violence and sexual assault. In view of all these developments, it was no wonder that the Peace Corps office in Amman was anxious to evacuate Anne and Dave from Tafila.

Anne said that at first the Peace Corps wanted to terminate her service altogether and send her and Dave back to the United States. Neither she nor Dave had expected such an extreme reaction and were unprepared for it. They had to plead with the Peace Corps to let them stay in Jordan and complete their service. Finally, the Peace Corps agreed to relocate them to another site in Jordan, where no one knew them. I wondered why they had chosen this location, which is about an hour drive from Tafila. Perhaps the campus environment was considered more secure and tolerant than that of a town.

Anne and Dave were in their early thirties. Dave was a lawyer by profession and Anne planned to go to graduate school when they returned to the United States. She said that the year they had spent in Tafila had been very stressful for her. Tafila is a conservative town and she was the only woman walking around without a hijab, a situation that, in her view, had antagonized the townspeople and made them hostile to her. She remarked that when her group, the J14, went through their pre-service training, the mood among the volunteers was somber and depressed. She was amazed to see how upbeat the mood was among the members of my group, the J15, when she had attended our site announcement ceremony. She also mentioned that four volunteers from her group had quit the Peace Corps after being a few weeks in pre-service training. I was astonished to hear all this. The Peace Corps staff didn't share this information with us.

I asked Anne and Dave if they wanted to see my apartment and help me inspect it, and they agreed at once. We left their apartment and walked toward the faculty residential area, located just a little way from their neighborhood. *How lucky that I would be living in close proximity to them,* I thought to myself. *If any one of us needs help, we are within a stone's throw of each other.* It was pitch-dark inside the apartment and I had to grope for the light switch on the wall. When I flipped it on, Anne and Dave gasped in surprise. They didn't expect to see a furnished apartment, even though everything was dirty and shabby. "Dalya, this is unusual," they said. "Normally you have to start from scratch." We found a piece of paper with operating instructions in English attached to the cooking stove. Anne concluded that the former resident must have been the pervious Peace Corps volunteer who had left abruptly after one year of service because of health issues. We inspected the apartment and made a list of things in need of repair. They suggested removing the old wall-to-wall carpeting and placing area rugs on the tiled floor. The apartment would have to be painted and the shabby furniture discarded. We opened the refrigerator to see what food was left there for me. There was pita bread, a bowl of yogurt cheese, and a plate with sliced baloney. I asked Anne if she wanted to take this food to her apartment. She said, "Yes, why not?" We took the food, locked the front door, and left.

Back in their own apartment, Dave prepared pasta with tomato sauce for supper and invited me to share it with them. After supper, they went to work on their individual assignments and I took a hot shower and retired for the night in the spare room. It was almost 10:00 p.m. and I had to be ready at 8:00 a.m. the next day. I lay down on the farsha that they had placed for me on the floor and snuggled under the covers. The blanket was thin, but the central heating was on and the room was quite hot. I slept peacefully and soundly.

The following morning I got up at sunrise and prepared myself for a long day crammed with meetings. I put on a fresh shirt and the same black pants suit—it was the only one in my possession. Jordanians attach a lot of importance to clothes and personal style of dress, not only for reasons of modesty but also as a reflection of one's class and social status. "Dressing down" deliberately in faded, distressed jeans or scruffy clothes, as people tend to do in the United States, is inconceivable. Unfortunately, with the small number of outfits available to me while living out of a suitcase, I couldn't impress them. In the kitchen on the countertop, I found several canisters with tea, Turkish coffee, instant coffee, white sugar, and brown sugar for my choosing. Before I had gone to bed, Anne had asked me what I ate for breakfast, and I replied that a cup of coffee would be enough. This was a very kind gesture on her part. I made myself my usual morning cup of Turkish coffee and drank it with delight. It was the one thing that I was glad had remained a constant throughout my time in Jordan.

The air was chilly in the morning—it always is in the desert—and I was shivering with cold. Dr. Zaydan was supposed to pick me up at 8:00 a.m. and I hoped that he would come on time. He lived off-campus in a small and isolated residential area built for university employees with large families. He arrived late and immediately apologized, explaining that he had stayed up into the night to work on a linguistic paper that he was preparing for publication. He drove the short distance to the center of the campus and parked in a cramped space reserved for faculty and staff. We entered the Humanities building, which contained auditoriums, classrooms, and lecture halls, and also housed the dean's office and other administrative and departmental offices. Dr. Zaydan showed me his two offices, one in his capacity as the vice dean and the other in his capacity as a professor of English. They were both small and simple, but equipped with a telephone and a computer. He also took me to the office of technical support and introduced me to Abdullah, who would be indispensable to me in all matters pertaining to my computer and Internet connection.

A series of meetings awaited us, the first of which was with the dean, Dr. al-Qasim. His office was a sunny, spacious, and elegantly furnished room, accessible only through his secretary's room. Several professors of English, all mustached men in dark suits, aged fifty and over, had already gathered there. The dean was tall, fair-skinned, clean-shaven, and distinctly younger than his colleagues, perhaps in his mid-forties. He greeted me courteously and extended his hand to shake mine. The other men took their cue from him and shook my hand too, eyeing me inquisitively. We exchanged pleasantries and refreshed ourselves with hot drinks, served by a tea man who had brought in a tray loaded with cups of coffee and tea. The dean addressed me in English, inquiring about my education, area of specialty, and teaching experience. He was impressed with my PhD from Georgetown University. Jordanians have a high regard for this institution not only because it is one of the eight Ivy League schools in the United States, but also because King Abdullah had attended the School of Foreign Service there in 1987. The dean mentioned that he had earned his PhD in comparative literature from Ohio University. Suddenly, out of the blue, he asked, "Where are you originally from? Is …?" I knew that *he knew* where I was from because Lana, the education program manager, had emailed him my resume. Before he could finish enunciating the word "Israel," I interrupted him and said, "The Netherlands, but my family arrived there from Spain." I heard the other men in the room remark in Arabic *wadih alyayha* (meaning, "It's obvious," a comment directed at my Middle Eastern appearance). The dean turned toward them quickly and said emphatically, "Dalya speaks Arabic fluently." It was a gentle way of warning them that I could understand what they might say in Arabic. They looked a bit embarrassed.

The dean was eager to know who else the Peace Corps was sending to Mu'ta University. He was under the impression that another volunteer was on the way. I wasn't aware of this. "Perhaps Danny," I speculated. The Technical University in Tafila, to which Danny was assigned, was in the throes of angry student demonstrations and his supervisor couldn't make it to the conference in Amman. The Peace Corps office had canceled Danny's site visit until the social unrest on the campus subsided. Perhaps in the meantime they had assigned him to Mu'ta University. "Who's Danny?" Dr. Zaydan asked. "He's the tall slim guy whose supervisor didn't make it to the conference in Amman," I said. "You mean the Chinese guy?" Dr. Zaydan asked again. "Yes," I confirmed. "Oh, he's Chinese?" the dean said, his voice betraying his disappointment. "He's Chinese American," Dr. Zaydan hastened to correct himself. But the damage was already done. Asian people are looked down upon in Jordan, where they are associated with foreign workers who do menial jobs as domestic help or cleaners in hotels and restaurants. This is a source of constant aggravation and frustration for Asian American Peace Corps volunteers, who have to cope with demeaning and disparaging attitudes on the part of the local people. Danny was not only a very nice guy but also one of the few J15 volunteers with formal training in teaching English as a foreign language, having recently obtained his master's degree in this field.

The dean asked if I had a chance to see my apartment. He wasn't sure whether it was accessible because the painters had been working there for the past week and the place was a mess. Astonished, I said that I had seen the place but there was no sign of painters. It turned out that the apartment Dr. Zaydan had shown me was the university's guest apartment, and it was meant just for the two nights of my site visit. I was assigned a four-bedroom apartment in the same building where Dr. Zaydan lived, in that isolated residential area off-campus. I was extremely disappointed to hear that. A suitable apartment was crucial for my smooth adjustment to my new environment and success at work. It would be unpleasant to live in an empty four-bedroom apartment far away from the campus. The Peace Corps settling-in allowance covered only the basic necessities. Most volunteers who were stuck with big apartments ended up furnishing only one room and leaving the rest of their apartments empty. Besides, how would I walk this long distance to my classes in the winter when it snowed? And in the summer when it was sweltering hot? I asked the dean if I could get a one-bedroom apartment on campus. He said that he would have to check with the housing office about it. Reluctantly, I requested to see the apartment before the end of my site visit. Dr. Zaydan said that he would get the key and take me there later.

From the dean's office we went directly to the office of Dr. al-Mazini, head of the English department. By now the hallways were already crowded with students who were attending morning classes. They smiled at Dr. Zaydan and greeted him cordially, stealing inquisitive glances at me. I could tell that he was well liked by his students. We walked a short distance and arrived at the office of Dr. al-Mazini, a grave-looking man in his early fifties. Dr. al-Mazini had a long and distinguished career: he was formerly the head of the military section of Mu'ta University, and in his younger days he had served with Prince Abdullah, now the king, in the Special Forces of the Jordanian army. A picture of them standing side by side wearing military fatigues and holding assault rifles was proudly displayed on his desk, visible to all visitors.

Dr. al-Mazini inquired about my education and teaching experience and, like the dean, regarded me appreciatively when he heard that I had graduated from Georgetown University. Having ascertained that I had the necessary academic qualifications, he proceeded to discuss the subjects that I would teach the next semester. He was particularly interested in courses on English literature, both prose and poetry. He talked about teaching nine to twelve credit hours per week, which meant three to four courses per semester. His own area of specialty was applied linguistics and discourse analysis. He showed me the syllabus of a course that he had taught the previous semester and it was an impressive piece of work. I wondered whether I would be able to prepare three to four syllabi in the short time span available to me—just four weeks—and at the same time settle into a new apartment that needed to be furnished. The move from my village to my permanent site was set for January 4, 2012, and the new semester was scheduled to begin on February 6. In contrast to my fellow volunteers, who were given a three-month period to observe classes in their schools before starting to teach, I was expected to start teaching right away. I noticed that Dr. Zaydan looked concerned. He was probably thinking what I was thinking: that Dr. al-Mazini had not attended the supervisors conference in Amman and was unaware of the Peace Corps guidelines. I decided to check with Bryan about the workload that I had just been assigned.

After this meeting, Dr. Zaydan took me to observe an English comprehension drill in one of his classes. It was a large group of about forty students in their early to late twenties, all of them girls, except for one guy. The girls were not the faceless and shapeless females that you see and read about in the newspapers. Most of them were dressed in Western-style clothing and wore hijabs; only a few were veiled and covered in black flowing abayas. Dr. Zaydan introduced me to his students as a Peace Corps volunteer and gave them the opportunity to ask me questions. One girl raised her hand and asked in a puzzled tone of voice, "Why did you come to Jordan?" She had never heard of the Peace Corps before—its history, mission, or service. I explained to her what the Peace Corps was about. I saw skeptical expressions on many faces. They seemed to say: *Since when does the United States do anything for the sake of Arabs? The United States always sides with Israel and wages wars on the Arabs.* Another girl raised her hand and asked why I had chosen to come to Jordan of all countries. I replied that Peace Corps volunteers don't get to choose where to serve; they are assigned according to their specific skills, which are matched with the needs of specific countries, and they have to show flexibility and willingness to serve wherever they are placed. I was glad to come to Jordan because I had a keen interest in Arab culture and society and hoped to learn a lot about them during my stay. But the girls continued to eye me critically. A woman traveling alone without a male companion or a male guardian is regarded as an anomaly in this conservative society. I realized that I would have to work hard to win their trust and acceptance. Suddenly, I felt scared and unsure of myself. *What if I fail? What if they discover that I am Jewish and a Sabra?* The military section of the university was just around the corner. *What if a Palestinian student recognizes my Israeli accent? Will I be found stabbed to death or with my throat slit?*

When the class ended, I went to the university library to browse in the English books section. I searched for classics of American and English literatures, anthologies of poems and short stories by male and female authors, and translations into English from world literature. I was pleased to discover that the library was well stocked. I sat at a computer terminal, typing authors' names into the search box and checking which of their works were available throughout the many university libraries in Jordan. On a sudden whim, I typed my own name and clicked search. I almost fell off my chair when the results came up on the screen—my books were available in almost every university library in Jordan! Cohen or no Cohen, when a book carries the name of an acclaimed publisher like Oxford University Press, it is purchased without discrimination. Mu'ta University library had my book, *Matter of Fate*, as did Yarmouk University in Irbid and the University of Jordan in Amman. I felt a huge sense of accomplishment. At a time when I was bogged down by feelings of self-doubt, this was a great boost to my morale. "You can do it, Dalya," I said to myself as I left the library.

I entered the Humanities building and made my way through the crowded hallway on the ground floor, where students were roaming between classes. Suddenly I heard a voice call out my name. It was Janine, the Asian American J14 volunteer who had lived with Mona's host family the year before. She was serving as an English teacher in an elementary school in a village nearby and as part of her free-time projects she came to Mu'ta University once a week to tutor students in English conversation. We hugged and chatted for a few minutes. She looked unhappy and frustrated. The attitude of the local people to her ethnicity was a source of constant aggravation for her. She congratulated me on my site assignment and asked how I liked the campus, eying me enviously. Lately, I had been getting this kind of reaction a lot. After all, I was going to be a lecturer at an acclaimed Jordanian university, I was going to teach credit courses to adult students, and I was going to get an office equipped with a telephone and a computer. All of this meant a lot of prestige. To me, this meant a lot of *hard work and responsibility,* but this side of the matter hardly crossed the minds of those who wished that they were in my shoes. The grass always looks greener on the other side of the fence!

It was well after midday when I arrived at Dr. Zaydan's office. He had a couple of hours to spare and offered to take me on a car ride to Karak. I reminded him that I needed to see my apartment. We went to the housing office to retrieve the key but it wasn't there; the painters had taken it so they could get into the apartment early in the morning. Dr. Zaydan suggested that we stop by the apartment later in the day and invited Abdullah, the computer technician, to join us on the car ride. Abdullah sat in the front next to him and I sat in the back. I felt awkward but I understood why Dr. Zaydan had asked Abdullah to tag along: it was culturally inappropriate for him to be seen alone with a female stranger in his car. If he could avoid it, he would.

We drove through the main street of the town of Mu'ta. The sights were similar to those of any other Jordanian town: small retail shops, cafés and restaurants, bakeries, grocery stores, and a souk. This particular town is famous for the location of a battle in 632 CE, in which the armies of Islam fought for the first time with Christianity and lost. We left Mu'ta and continued toward Karak to see its famous Crusaders' castle. The fortified castle, which dominates the town, was a battleground between the Crusaders and the armies of Saladin, whose statue stands in the town center. The old section of Karak has a tricky system of very narrow one-way streets and we arrived there at the busiest time of the day when everyone was out shopping and having lunch. We couldn't find a parking place, so we drove around the ancient castle and looked at it from the car windows. I wished that I had my camera with me to take a few pictures—I hadn't brought it along because I didn't want to look like a tourist and I assumed that I would have many more opportunities to take pictures in the future. Dr. Zaydan pulled up near a food stand and Abdullah jumped out to buy us sandwiches. He returned with a bag of *laffas:* wraps of flatbread spread with hummus. Although it was very greasy and doughy, I ate one, as I was hungry. We then headed back to the university, where I was expected to meet with the dean for the second time.

When I arrived, the dean was unavailable, so I sat in his secretary's office to wait. The secretary was a short, plump, and pompous woman with a big gap between her upper front teeth. She had company—her little daughter, aged eight, and another woman with her seven-year-old daughter. Having nothing to do, I eavesdropped on their conversation—I had become a shameless eavesdropper in my voracious curiosity to learn what the local people felt and thought. Regrettably, I didn't pick up any interesting nuggets of information. The two women talked about their daughters' end-of-term exams at elementary school. I understood from their remarks that they were related. I was quietly watching the two girls at play, when suddenly the secretary's daughter took a printed sheet of paper, shoved it rudely in my face, and ordered me in Arabic, "Read this to me!" Her tone of voice was bossy, as if I was her maid. I glanced at the paper and saw that it contained instructions in English on how to operate a water heater. I pushed it away from me and replied in Arabic, "This is technical English." Instead of reprimanding her daughter for being impolite, the secretary lauded her: "Praise be to God! My daughter can tell that the page is printed in English!" I continued to watch the two little girls: the secretary's daughter was dark, loud-mouthed, and a spoiled brat, while the relative's daughter was fair, soft-spoken, and well-mannered. I was marveling at the differences between them when the dean finally popped his head in the doorway and invited me in.

During the first thirty minutes that I sat in the dean's office, there were constant interruptions. First, the telephone rang and he engaged in a long conversation; then a middle-aged man came in for a job interview, which was conducted in front of me; next a student showed up with an urgent request; and finally the plump secretary strutted in with her spoiled daughter. She asked the dean to give her three days off from work so she could help her daughter prepare for her end-of-term exams at school. I listened to her request in amazement. Her daughter was in the second grade of elementary school, not high school! While the mother was talking with the dean, the daughter looked around the office and saw a half-full glass of water sitting on the dean's coffee table. Without asking for permission, she grabbed the glass and drank all the water. Neither the mother nor the dean said anything. To my astonishment, the dean approved the secretary's request! As I sat there observing all these social interactions, I couldn't help but feel, once again, as if I had fallen "down the rabbit hole."

The dean impressed me as an astute, progressive, and easygoing person. I could see how well he handled his staff and various visitors. After the secretary had left he turned to me and apologized for keeping me waiting, saying that his administrative duties as a dean consumed most of his time. He mentioned that his wife had been an English teacher but was now a stay-at-home mother raising their five children. He asked me how I liked Mu'ta University, and I replied that I loved it. How had my meeting with Dr. al-Mazini gone? I told him that we had discussed the courses that I would teach the next semester and had agreed on fiction by women writers, the art of the short story, and literary theory and analysis. He was pleased to hear that I could add new courses to the program of the English department. Suddenly, the smile on his face vanished and he remarked in a critical tone that the previous Peace Corps volunteer had left after just one year. How long was I planning to stay? "Two years, inshallah," I said. "And if you are satisfied with my work, perhaps another year." He remained silent and his expression was grave. A sudden feeling of uneasiness washed over me.

I brushed my uneasiness aside and broached the subject of my housing again, requesting a one-bedroom apartment on campus. The dean said that he would look into this matter and see what he could do about it. As we signed the lease, I mentioned that I hadn't seen the four-bedroom apartment yet, and he wanted to know why. Just then Dr. Zaydan entered the office and joined the conversation. He apologized that the key to the apartment was still unavailable and offered to show me his own apartment instead, as all the units in that building were identical. I shook hands with the dean for the last time and we exchanged parting salutations, using the traditional phrases *ma'a salaama* (so long) and *ila l-liqaa,* (until we meet again).

Once again, Abdullah dutifully tagged along with us as we left the campus and drove to an isolated residential area comprising several high-rise apartment buildings surrounded by the desolate desert. Devoid of grass, trees, or shrubs, the place looked bleak and dreary. There was no elevator in the building that we entered and we climbed the narrow and dimly lit stairs up to the fourth floor. Dr. Zaydan's apartment consisted of four big bedrooms plus a living room, a kitchen, and two bathrooms—one with a squat toilet and one with a commode. The place looked empty, shabby, and depressing. Dr. Zaydan's wife and children lived in a village by the Dead Sea, about 45 km from Mu'ta University. Dr. Zaydan stayed here during the weekdays and went home on the weekends. I struggled to hide my disappointment. Perhaps I would manage to persuade the housing office to give me a smaller, one-bedroom apartment on campus.

Earlier, the dean had instructed Dr. Zaydan to take me to dinner, at the university's expense. Out of courtesy, Dr. Zaydan asked me whether I preferred Jordanian, Middle Eastern, or Western food. I replied that Jordanian food would be fine—I didn't want to trouble him since he had been running around with me all day. In fact, I could have done without dinner altogether but I knew that if I said this, he would be offended.

We dropped off Abdullah, who was eager to go home, and drove to a restaurant in the town of Mu'ta. It was a small and cramped place, but popular among students. The waiter seated us at a table near a group of Malaysian girls wearing hijabs. Dr. Zaydan greeted them in Malay, proud to display his knowledge of their language. The menu was brought to us and I ordered chicken with rice and a salad but Dr. Zaydan ordered only a cup of tea. He claimed that he had been invited for dinner at the home of one of his students later in the evening but I immediately suspected that he didn't have enough money to order dinner for two. When the food arrived, I invited him to share my plate with me and he ate with relish. This confirmed my suspicion that the real reason he hadn't ordered dinner for himself was that he didn't have enough money. Teaching at Mu'ta University was a prestigious job, but not a lucrative one. He would be reimbursed for his expenses at a later date, after submitting valid receipts. Regrettably, the food was poorly prepared—the chicken was burned, the rice bland, and the salad stale. I ate very little, even though I was hungry. To calm my growling stomach, I drank a cup of hot tea.

We chatted about various topics. The more I got to know Dr. Zaydan, the more I liked him. He was a serious, modest, and good-natured man, with an enormous sense of responsibility. As my supervisor, he would be of great help to me in planning my classes, dealing with students, and adjusting to campus life. And yet, that same, single thought tormented me time and again: what would happen if he found out that I was Jewish and a Sabra? Dr. Zaydan seemed to be the kind of person who would be torn between a sense of loyalty to his people and a sense of responsibility for my safety. It would be unfair to put him in such a predicament. But was it fair to put me in this predicament, where I felt constantly conflicted and guilty about the lies I had to tell the people I respected?

After dinner, Dr. Zaydan dropped me off at the apartment of Anne and Dave. He would pick me up at 6:00 a.m. the next day and take me to the bus station in Mu'ta, where I would begin my journey back to the training site at Al al-Bayt University. Anne and Dave were busy that evening, working on projects for their respective supervisors at the special education and youth development centers. I had some work to do too: I had to fill out my "action plan" for the first three months at my permanent site. I was supposed to do this with Dr. Zaydan but we had been so busy all day that we never got round to it. Fortunately, I had a pretty good idea of the multiple tasks that awaited me in the next three months. As soon as I finished this work, I retired for the night, exhausted from the long and eventful day. I lay down on the farsha, buried my head in the pillow, and went to sleep.

But I didn't sleep well that night. My abdomen itched terribly and I kept scratching myself. In the morning I checked my abdominal skin and discovered several red spots that were sore, swollen, and itchy. I realized that I had been bitten by fleas that were in the farsha. This is a common problem in the hot countries of the Middle East and I had experienced it before in my travels to Egypt, but this was the first time that I had encountered it in Jordan. The homes of my two host families in the village of Hamadiyya, Sharon's apartment in Taybeh, and the hotels in which we stayed in Amman had no fleas. I washed up and dressed, packed my carry-on bag, and tidied up the spare room before I walked out of the apartment, closing the door gently behind me. I would call Anne and Dave in the evening to thank them for their hospitality and warn them about the fleas in the farsha.

It was chilly and windy outside and I shivered with cold as I stood alone in the empty street waiting for Dr. Zaydan to arrive.

I felt sorry that he had to get up so early in the morning, but he was extremely duty-bound and had insisted on taking me in person to the bus station in Mu'ta. A long trip awaited me back to the training site at Al al-Bayt University. With luck, it would not exceed five hours—it all depended on how long it would take for each bus to fill all its seats. Dr. Zaydan arrived on time and took me to the mosque area in Mu'ta, where the bus to Amman was parked, waiting for passengers. He wrote down my cell phone number and my next arrival date, January 4, 2012. I thanked him warmly for all his help and for being such a gracious host, and we shook hands and exchanged goodbyes. As he drove off, I felt lucky to have him for a supervisor: our personalities meshed well together and we would surely make a good team.

I chose a window seat, leaned back with my eyes closed, and dozed off as soon as the bus started moving. When I woke we were already on King's Highway and the town of Mu'ta was far behind us. A young woman in her early thirties, wearing a hijab and Western-style clothing, was sitting beside me. We smiled at each other and began to chat. I learned that she was single, that she worked as a laboratory technician at Mu'ta University, and that her name was Jihan. I said to her, "You have the same name as the former Egyptian First Lady, Jihan Sadat." She laughed and said, "You seem to know a lot about the Middle East." She stayed on campus from Sunday to Wednesday and at her parents' house in Amman from Thursday to Saturday. She came across as being affable and I exchanged phone numbers with her, pleased that I would have a friend when I moved into my apartment on campus.

The first leg of the trip went smoothly, and we made it to Amman Janubi bus station in just two hours. From there I took a cab to Amman downtown Raghadan bus station, which provides public transportation to the north of the country. I boarded the bus to Mafraq, arriving there around noon, and rushed to get on the next bus to Al al-Bayt University. It filled up with students quickly and set off without delay. I got off at the south gate of the campus and walked briskly toward the Peace Corps training site, located opposite the Faculty of Islamic Law. I was famished and the timing was perfect—I arrived exactly on time for lunch.

Lunch at the training site had become an important source of nutrition for me over the past couple of months. The food was always the same but it was balanced, tasty, and plentiful. I sat with my fellow volunteers in the courtyard of the classrooms building, chatting and warming ourselves up in the sun as we ate. The dominant topic of conversation was of course the visit to our permanent sites. Many girls expressed fear about being lonely and isolated in remote villages, but I didn't share this fear. I had always been able to be by myself and fill my time with meaningful activities—but then again, I was in a different age group.

After lunch, we had a site visit debrief and an opportunity to share our experiences in sector-based groups. The leases that we had signed with our landlords and the "action plans" that we had prepared for the first three months of service were collected. I ran into Bryan in the hallway and told him that I hadn't been able to inspect my apartment at Mu'ta University and had no idea about its condition. To my astonishment, he was indifferent, as if this didn't matter. I was even more astonished when I mentioned that I had stayed with Anne and Dave during my site visit and he said that he already knew about it. I had made the decision to stay with them on the spur of the moment. How had he learned about it? A sudden feeling of uneasiness washed over me. I got the impression that if I merely sneezed, everyone near and far would instantly know about it.

Our last technical session that day was with Samir, the safety and security coordinator, on the topic of allegations. He discussed at length the risks involved in making allegations about wrongdoing, both to the accused and the accusing person. We were advised to be cautious when we reported theft, physical abuse, sexual harassment, and so on to our supervisors because of the danger that this might pose to our safety and security on the one hand and to the reputation of the accused on the other hand. Kate Puzey's tragedy was the elephant in the room but her name was never mentioned. We were given specific scenarios to analyze in small workgroups. Throughout the session, Samir emphasized the "no gossip" policy as the prerequisite for a safe and secure environment for volunteers of all backgrounds. I thought of Natalie and what she had "overheard" about me. It bothered me, but I kept my mouth shut. I didn't want to stir up trouble for anyone in my group.

Finally the session ended, and with it our pre-service training.

It was Thursday, December 22, 2011. The American Embassy in Amman had invited us to celebrate Christmas with their staff on December 24. Over the past few days, we had been secretly buying Christmas gifts for each other. I had bought a warm scarf for John, who complained that he was always cold, at Carrefour department store in Amman's City Mall. On December 26, we were going to have an orientation session at the Peace Corps office in Amman. I had already been there a couple times in connection with my trips to Tel Aviv and was superficially acquainted with it. On December 29, we were expected to take our final Arabic proficiency interview, but it was an informal assessment and we had nothing to worry about. We all looked forward to January 3, 2012, the day of our swearing-in ceremony—a festive occasion marking the conclusion of three months of grueling pre-service training. Finally, on January 4, we would move from our host families' homes to our own apartments at our permanent sites.

Everyone was jubilant at the end of this last technical session. The period of pre-service training is regarded as the hardest part of the Peace Corps mission and has the highest rate of drop-out. Our group, the J15, was unusually resilient—we had no drop outs at all.

While waiting for the buses to arrive and take us back to our villages, many volunteers took their laptops out of storage and logged onto their email accounts to check their messages. This time, I didn't bother. All my trials and tribulations were now behind me. The issue of the email that had come a couple of months earlier from Peace Corps Headquarters about my background check didn't even cross my mind. It was such a long time ago and I hadn't heard anything since then. No news is good news, as the saying goes, is it not? I was certain that everything had been sorted out and straightened out or else they wouldn't have allowed me to come so far. Would they?

Congratulations!

Dalya Cohen

The beginning is the most important part of the work
Plato

Your New Community:

Region/Governorate: Karak

Town: Mu'ta

Population: 18,000 approximately

Distance from Amman: 120 km

Did you know... the significance of Mu'ta comes from the battle that took place there at the time of Prophet Mohammad.

Your University :
Name: Mu'ta University

Telephone: 03-2375540

No. of Professors: 21

No. of students: 700

Some Background:

Mu'ta University is located in the south part of Jordan in a small town called Mu'ta in Al Karak Governorate , it was founded on 22 March 1981 by Royal Decree, to be a national institution for military and civilian higher education. The University campus is located in the town of Mu'ta which is 15KM away from Karak city and 120 Km far from Amman.

You will be expected to be helping university students in their English through conversational classes as well as organizing activities and courses for students to improve their English. You will be handling your own classes as well as assisting professors in some of their courses and do some extracurricular activities.
You will be living on campus in the faculty residence in a great furnished apartment and you will have an office in the English department/Arts Faculty equipped with a desk, telephone, computer and internet for your use!
You will be the second TEFL Volunteer in Mu'ta University! The first volunteer left after a year for medical reasons. You will have a J14 couple working and living on campus with you but they are in a different departments since they are Youth Development and Special Education Volunteers. There are tons of opportunities for you to cooperate together and work on secondary projects!

All the best!
Lana

My site assignment.

Mu'ta University

Peace Corps Jordan

Certificate of Participation

For

Dalya Seymore

Jordan 15 Supervisors Conference
Amman, December 19 - 20, 2011

Alex Boston
Country Director

Lana Al Momani
Education Program Manager

Certificate of participation in the supervisors conference in Amman, issued to me under the name Dalya Seymore.

The Peace Corps training site on the campus of Al al-Bayt
University in Mafraq, with the square and "barracks-looking"
buildings around it.

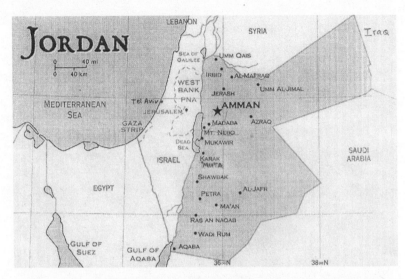

My travels around the Kingdom.

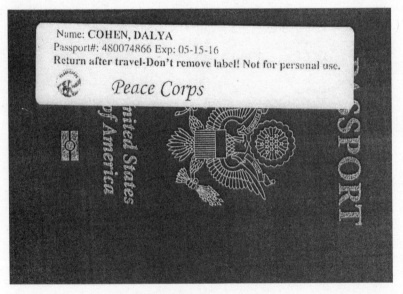

My Peace Corps passport.

Page 27 in my Peace Corps passport.

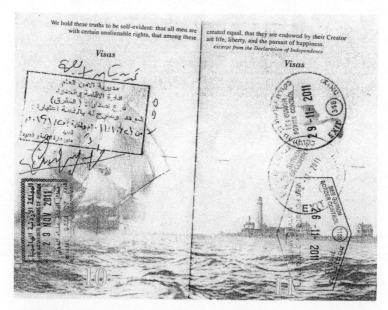

"Offending" Israeli stamps next to Jordanian stamps. In Israeli
dates, the day comes first, then the month, then the year.

More "offending" Israeli stamps next to Jordanian stamps.

10. THIS CAN'T BE TRUE

IT WAS ALREADY DARK OUTSIDE WHEN THE BUS DROPPED ME OFF in the village of Hamadiyya. I made my way cautiously along the dirt road leading to my host family's house, trying not to step on sheep dung and chicken droppings. Umm Ali and her daughters welcomed me back with hugs and kisses, eager to hear all about my trip. When they asked about my visit to Mu'ta University, I replied simply that I was *mabsoota* (pleased). They wanted to know when they would receive the formal invitation to the *takhrij*, the swearing-in ceremony, and which one of their photos would appear on the certificate that they would receive from the Peace Corps for serving as my host family. I told them that I had selected the photo in which Huda was sitting on my lap. Of all her family members, Umm Ali in particular was looking forward to this event. Her face lit up and she danced with joy when I said that the ceremony was set for January 3.

Her childlike enthusiasm touched me. We chatted for a while, then I went to my room to rest.

I lay down on the farsha, reflecting on the events and experiences of the past few days. I felt an oppressive sense of anxiety mingled with gnawing loneliness. I had not made any close friends during the pre-service training. I wondered if this was because of the age gap between me and the other volunteers. Lora, my roommate at the training site, who was fifty years old, hung out with the young girls. Mark, who was in his seventies, stuck with the guys. I was a loner. No doubt, it was an innate tendency of mine, but the need to hide my identity intensified this tendency and had led to my isolation. I wished that there were people close to my age in the group. The J13 group had about ten volunteers who were in their sixties; they traveled together around Jordan and organized social activities for themselves. Sharon had told me this when I had visited her in Taybeh. I needed to develop more social contacts. Perhaps I would find friends among the female faculty and staff at Mu'ta University. Jihan seemed nice and interested in getting to know me. This would be a good start.

The pre-service training was over. I felt like patting myself on the shoulder—I had survived this grueling period. I had persisted in the face of stresses and challenges that no other volunteer had experienced, having to adjust to two different host families in a short time, to conceal my Jewish identity, and to cope with the tragic loss of my brother. I had endured rough living conditions in a poor village in the desert and proved that I was made of a tough mettle and that I was not a quitter. Now I was just a few days away from the much-anticipated swearing-in ceremony, the culmination of my hard efforts, when I would proudly take the oath of service. With this pleasant thought floating in my head, I drifted into sleep.

I woke up to the sound of forceful banging on my door. I was startled. Throughout my long stay in this house, no one had ever banged on my door, let alone in the middle of the night. I heard the voice of Umm Ali saying, "Dalya, wake up! There's a phone call for you!" I scrambled to my feet and turned on the light. It was well after 10:00 p.m. I hurriedly opened the door. "Who wants to talk to me?" I asked. "Sultan," she replied. I became alarmed. This was highly unusual. "Why didn't he call me on my cell phone?" I asked in astonishment. "He told me that he tried but couldn't get through to you," she said. I immediately checked my cell phone. It was fully charged but there were no missed calls registered on it. Sultan was clearly lying, which made me even more alarmed. Struggling to maintain my composure, I thanked Umm Ali, closed the door, and hastened to call Sultan. He answered at once. "Hello Sultan," I said, my heart pounding so hard that I thought he could hear it on the other end of the line. "What's up? I'm told that you tried to call me and couldn't reach me. My phone is on and has been by my side all this time." "Well," he said, fumbling for words, "when I dialed your number I got a recorded message that you're out of reach." Out of reach? Sultan was lying again. My level of anxiety rose one notch higher. "What's the matter?" I asked. "Bryan wants to talk to you," he said. The situation was getting more bizarre with every passing minute. If Bryan wanted to talk to me, then why didn't he call me directly? Why did he use Sultan as his messenger? I hung up and called Bryan, who answered immediately. "Alex wants to talk to you," he said tersely. "Wait for him to call you." This was absolutely insane. It was now after eleven o'clock at night. Couldn't they wait until the morning? The lies and phone calls back and forth between unnecessary messengers had been bad enough and now I was expected to sit by the phone and wait for Alex to call me at this late hour?

After what seemed like an eternity, Alex called. "I'm afraid I have bad news for you," he said. "I received a message from Peace Corps Headquarters informing me that you didn't pass the background check." "What does this mean?" I asked, dumbfounded. "You're going home," he said bluntly. "Going home? When?" I uttered in disbelief. "Tomorrow," he declared.

I was in utter shock. My ears started ringing and my hand nearly dropped the phone. "What's the rush?" I managed to say with difficulty. "The swearing-in ceremony is just a few days away. I've completed the entire pre-service training. Let me stay for the ceremony. Then I'll go back to straighten things out." "No," he said. "I can't let you stay. You have to leave immediately." This was absurd. Was he telling me the truth? Perhaps he was lying just like Sultan. "Can you please forward this message that you received from Peace Corps Headquarters to me?" I asked. "No, I can't do this," he replied. "This is all a terrible mistake," I insisted. "What has come up in my background check that requires my immediate departure?" "I don't know," he said. "They don't share this information with me." "But this is so cruel and unfair," I pleaded. "I was in the application process for almost a year and I waited another six months for my departure date. They had plenty of time to conduct my background check within that period. They should have completed it *before* sending me overseas. Don't I have the right to defend myself and appeal this decision?" "No," he said. "As a volunteer in training, you don't have any rights. As a sworn-in volunteer you do." I was shattered. "First they put me through three months of grueling pre-service training and then they tell me to leave?!" I protested in a choked voice. "That's why I kept pressing Peace Corps Headquarters to hurry up with the conclusion of your background check," he said self-righteously. "What?" I gasped in dismay. "You *pressed* them to hurry up? If your objective was to send me home *before* the swearing-in ceremony, then why did you let me go through the entire pre-service training program? You could have spared me all this hardship and heartache!" Alex's remark hit me hard. I felt betrayed by the very authority figure that I had trusted to help and support me. Now that he had inadvertently revealed his role in this dramatic development, he was unwilling to talk to me anymore. "I don't make the rules, Dalya. Based on the results of your background check I have no choice but to send you home. Mat will call you in the morning with the logistics."

I was reeling from the news. Alex didn't seem to care about the physical, psychological, and emotional impact that his shocking announcement would have on me. The manner in which he broke the news to me, calling me in the middle of the night after a bizarre telephone set up, lacked tact, civility, or consideration. Couldn't this have waited until the morning? Couldn't he have told me all this in a face-to-face meeting? I had been available to them at the training site all afternoon—in fact, I had only returned from there a few hours ago. All of them—Sultan, Bryan, and Alex—had seen me there. And before that they had seen me at the supervisors conference in Amman. They had smiled at me and shaken my hand and let me travel to Mu'ta University to meet with the dean and sign the lease for my apartment, knowing full well that my fate had been sealed! What a charade! I now understood why they had stared at me so disturbingly when I had presented Dr. Zaydan to the participants in the supervisors conference, and why Mat had ignored me when I had raised my hand to ask a question in his technical session, and why Bryan had shown no interest in my report about not having inspected my apartment . . .

I was devastated. I collapsed on the farsha, muttering over and over again, *This can't be true . . . This can't be true . . .* I had put my utmost trust in the Peace Corps, regarding it as one of America's finest and most respected organizations. But the ABC News 20/20 investigation into the murder of Kate Puzey, which had aired on January 14, 2011, uncovered many disturbing stories about the culture and policies of the Peace Corps. Former volunteers went public with their ordeals. There were charges of rape, murder, and cover up; sexual assaults on female volunteers that had been swept under the rug by the agency and dealt with a "blame-the-victim" attitude; and volunteers who attempted to report problems or abuse met with bureaucratic hurdles and a lack of compassion on the part of Peace Corps officers. My story would be just one more sad testimony among many others. I had made so many sacrifices to serve in this agency: I passed up a good job opportunity; I spent a lot of money on medical exams and a packing list; I worked so hard to make it through the pre-service training, putting up with malnutrition, sleep deprivation, and unsanitary conditions; and I endured risks to my safety on account of my Jewish identity. I had weathered all of this and hadn't quit because I was *wholly committed* to Peace Corps service. Now, when I was just about to reap the fruits of my labor, I was told unceremoniously to go home!

I didn't shed a single tear. I was numb with shock. I lay on the farsha in the darkness of the night, contemplating the lack of humanity of an agency whose claim to fame rests on rendering service to humanity. For week after week they had kept me in the dark, choosing not to communicate or share any information with me. Now, after they had dealt me such a harsh blow, they wouldn't even tell me what issues were found in my background check or on what basis I was suspected of being involved in "intelligence activities," thus denying me a chance to defend myself. It was so surreal, so Kafkaesque. It was as if I was watching a horror movie about a helpless woman caught in the grip of brutal forces—except that the woman was *me*, not a stranger, and it was my stark reality, not a fantasy.

I didn't sleep a wink that night. When the first rays of light began to filter through the window of my room, I got up and started packing my things. Drained of energy, I went to the kitchen to make myself a cup of coffee. Umm Ali came after me as soon as she heard my footsteps in the hallway. She looked worried and bewildered. She must have suspected that something serious had happened from all those phone calls in the middle of the night. She greeted me with *sabah al-kheir* in a hesitant voice, scrutinizing my face for any clues, then asked me directly why Sultan had called so late the previous night. I pretended that it was a small matter. "There is a change in the program," I said. "I need to go to Amman again for a few days of training." I paused for a moment, and then added, "I don't follow the same program as the others in my group because I've been assigned to teach at a university." She looked at me silently, her expression still worried. I smiled reassuringly at her. "When are you leaving?" she finally asked. "Today," I replied. "I don't know exactly at what time yet." My demeanor was nonchalant. She accepted my explanation without asking any further questions and went back to her room.

Mat called around eleven o'clock in the morning. It was late and my nerves were frayed from the long wait. In an authoritarian tone of voice, as if he was the sheriff in charge of enforcing court orders, he informed me that I had to be ready with my bags by 2:00 p.m. He would come in person with Usama the driver to escort me out of my host family's house and take me to the Peace Corps training site at Al al-Bayt University, where I would collect my second suitcase from storage. Then I would ride with him to the Peace Corps office in Amman to sign various papers and retrieve my passport. Afterward, Usama would take me to a hotel in Amman, where I would wait for my flight, scheduled to leave after midnight to Washington Dulles International Airport via Paris, where I would have a five-hour lay-over. This meant a grueling trip of more than seventeen hours, start-ing after midnight. I had not slept a wink since this nightmare had begun, and I was near exhaustion. I said to Mat, "Couldn't you at least book me on a direct flight or a daytime flight?" He responded that this was all he could get, considering the limitations he had: to put me on an American carrier, to buy me a one-way ticket, and to get me on the next flight out on one of the busiest days of the year—Christmas Eve. In my state of shock and confusion, I hadn't realized that I would be flying on Christmas Eve.

I had a hard time processing all this information. Mat didn't bother to ask if I had a place to go to when I arrived in Washington, DC. He didn't offer to book me a hotel room there or to send my itinerary to a friend or relative so that I could meet a familiar face at the airport. Nobody seemed to care if I got off the plane and slept in the street, as long as I was *out* of *Jordan today*. But, at that very moment, what infuriated me the most was Mat's intention to come with Usama the driver to "escort me out" of my host family's house. It was crass, tactless, and uncalled for, and I strongly objected to it. "My host family doesn't know you. They have never seen you before. This would arouse suspicions. I told them that I was going to Amman for a few days. I don't want this to become a scandal for them and a topic of gossip in the village. They know Usama the driver, and he is enough. I'm not going to be escorted like a criminal out of my host family's house, in plain view of all their neighbors." My plea fell on deaf ears. The "sheriff" refused to budge. As soon as I got off the phone with him, I called Alex. "I don't want Mat to show up on my host family's doorstep," I said firmly. "Why add insult to injury? What purpose would this serve? It would only invite gossip and speculation and ruin my host family's reputation." He backed down in the face of this argument and said that he would instruct Mat not to come with the driver. I then broached the topic of confidentiality. I asked Alex to keep this affair confidential so as to protect my host family's reputation. He replied that only he, Bryan, Sultan, and Mat were involved in this affair and that it would be kept confidential. I took his words with a pinch of salt. All that had happened had undermined his credibility.

I started to tidy up my room. I wanted to leave it clean and neat for Umm Ali. I sorted out my books and papers and put them in plastic bags because they didn't fit into my suitcase. I would try to squeeze them into my other, larger suitcase that was kept at the training site. I worked like a robot, my mind refusing to accept this bitter turn of events. Dozens of questions swirled in my head. Why did the Peace Corps send me to Jordan? Had no one in that office read my resume? Why had they sent me overseas *before* completing my background check? They had had plenty of time—a year and a half—to look into every nook and cranny of my life in order to decide whether I qualified for Peace Corps service. Why did Alex allow me to go through the entire pre-service training program, only to remove me when I had made it to the finish line? Why did he let me go through the hellish period of pre-service training only to kick me out when I arrived at the fininshing line? Why did he press Peace Corps Headquarters to conclude my background check *before* the swearing-in ceremony? The unfairness and callousness of the whole situation filled me with anger.

I reached for my cell phone and dialed Alex's number. I wasn't going to give up what I had worked so hard to attain without a fight. He answered at once; apparently he was expecting some resistance on my part. I went straight to the point. "I don't think this is fair," I said. "I was sent here by the Peace Corps after a lengthy application process and a lengthy waiting period. I completed the pre-service training successfully and fulfilled all my tasks. It's unfair to send me home now. What's the rush anyway? Tomorrow is Christmas Eve. Let me stay for the swearing-in ceremony and then suspend me until I clear the issues in my background check." He refused. "I can't do that," he said tersely. "Why?" I demanded to know. "Because once I make a decision, it's irreversible," he declared. *Irreversible?!* Even God Almighty reverses his decisions from time to time, as the Bible tells us, but not Alex the country director? "But I deserve a chance to defend myself," I insisted. "Just yesterday, in the concluding technical session of our program, Samir and Bryan drilled into us the pitfalls of making allegations without due diligence and the necessity to proceed with caution to avoid damage to innocent people. I've *never* been a spy and I've *never* been involved in intelligence activities— unless I've been doing something in my sleep all these years that I'm not aware of. Please give me the benefit of the doubt and let me stay a few more days. I will leave immediately after the swearing-in ceremony." My plea fell on deaf ears. "No," he said, unmoved and unfeeling. "You must leave tonight."

Even inmates on death row have the right of appeal. I didn't. Employees are usually not laid off before Christmas so as not to ruin their holiday. I was. True, I was Jewish and I didn't celebrate Christmas; I celebrated Hanukkah, the Festival of Lights, which falls at the same time as Christmas. None of this mattered. Alex wanted me out. *Tonight.* I recalled that two weeks earlier, when I had placed a call to American Express from his office in Amman, I had seen a large group picture with the head shots of the J15 volunteers lying on his desk. But my head shot was not among them. This meant that I was *not* going to be at the swearing-in ceremony. But why? Perhaps he was afraid that I would become a "blemish" on his record, a sordid scandal of "espionage" on his watch. This was his last year at this post—he would be leaving Jordan in the summer. Or perhaps he had not taken a shine to me. I had little contact with him throughout the pre-service training. In our few interactions, he appeared aloof and cold and rarely spoke to me. By contrast, I had pleasant interactions with other supervisors: Lana, the education program manager, was appreciative of me, Eman, the TEFL coordinator, was pleased with my solo teaching, Ahmad, the language and cross-cultural coordinator, was friendly and often chatted with me, even though he knew I was a Sabra, and I had a good rapport with Dr. Zaydan and Dr. al-Qasim... What would all these people say when they heard about my sudden departure?

I had three conversations with Alex on that day, Friday, December 23. They were all unproductive. He refused to forward to me the email that he claimed he had received from Peace Corps Headquarters with the message that I didn't pass the background check; he refused to tell me what issues had been found in the check; and he refused to delay my departure from Jordan. I felt as if I was banging my head against a brick wall.

I finished cleaning my room and returned my key to Umm Ali. I told her that I would be moving from "Amman" directly to my apartment on the campus of Mu'ta University. I would be leaving her house a few days earlier than what had been stipulated in her hosting contract, which expired at the end of the month. My host family benefited from all my absences because they didn't have to feed me on those days. In this large household, with so many mouths to feed, it was no small matter. Still, I had no doubt that Umm Ali genuinely liked me and enjoyed my presence. We had many pleasant conversations and interactions, and hosting an American "daktora" gave her a sense of pride and added to her prestige among her relatives and friends. She and her family were kind to me and treated me well. Her face was crestfallen as she gazed at my room, now emptied of all my belongings. I tried to act normal, smilingly assuring her that I would stay in touch and visit often—but on the inside I was a complete wreck.

Usama arrived around 2:30 p.m. I hugged and kissed Umm Ali and her daughters for the very last time, shook the hands of her sons, and we said our goodbyes. Abu Ali was not at home. Usama helped me load my bags into his car, and I climbed into the front seat and sat beside him. As he started to back up slowly toward the road, Umm Ali came out of the front door and watched us, with little Huda holding her by the hand. She stood there as a last farewell—her figure, dressed in her favorite burgundy robe, was erect, her head, covered in *isharb*, was held high, and her expression was solemn. As I looked at her, my eyes became misty. She waved at me and I waved back at her until she disappeared from view. The image of her standing there with her little daughter and waving goodbye was etched onto my memory. I knew that we would never see each other again. I believe that, deep down, she knew this too.

We drove to Al al-Bayt University, a short thirty-minute car ride away. When we arrived at the Peace Corps training site, we found Mat and Sultan waiting for us in the parking lot. We walked in silence toward the storage room in the men's dorm building, where I tried to squeeze all the stuff in my plastic bags into the two suitcases and a carry-on bag that were at my disposal. It wasn't an easy task. Back home in the United States, I had used space bags to pack my things, which saved a lot of room in my suitcases. But to reuse them I needed a vacuum hose to suck the air out of the space bags, a tool that wasn't available to me here. I took several bulky items, among them my pillow and a blanket, and left them behind for the other volunteers. Sultan came by and politely asked if I needed any help. I said, "No. I just need to go to the bathroom." He said, "Why don't you use the men's bathroom. There's no one here today." The men's bathroom was at the end of the hallway, whereas the women's bathroom was across the courtyard in the other building. I thanked him and went to the men's bathroom. I was astonished to see that it was much cleaner than the women's bathroom. I remembered reading somewhere that studies on the myths and realities of public bathrooms revealed that men's bathrooms were generally cleaner and contained a significantly lower amount of bacteria than women's bathrooms.

I finally managed to fit all my stuff into my two suitcases, the carry-on bag, and a small shabby bag that had been discarded by a member of the J13 group. I was worried that my luggage would exceed the weight limit imposed by the airline and that I would encounter problems at the check-in desk. Sultan helped me carry my bags back to the car. On the way to the parking lot, he asked me gently how I wanted him to explain my disappearance to my host family and the other J15 volunteers. I stood still, fumbling for an appropriate response, when suddenly the enormity of the misfortune that had befallen me overwhelmed me and I broke into tears. I had carried myself with reserve and dignity throughout this harrowing ordeal—this was the only time that I had lost my composure in front of others. I turned my back to him, buried my face in my hands, and wept silently. For a few fleeting moments, my anguish washed out in hot, bitter tears. Then I regained my self-control. In a weak voice, I told him that it would be best if he said that I had to leave because my mother had become ill. Taking care of a sick old parent is considered an inviolable obligation in Arab culture and would be accepted as a valid reason for my disappearance. It would save Umm Ali's reputation—and perhaps mine as well. Sultan seemed genuinely sorry for me. Could he be trusted to keep this affair confidential? I wasn't sure. The day before, he had lied to me repeatedly over the phone. When we reached the parking lot, he said a hurried goodbye and left.

Mat, Usama, and I set off on our way to Amman, riding in silence. I watched the scenery from the car window, trying to take it all in for the last time. I regretted not having taken more pictures during my stay, pictures that would remind me of all the places I had been to. Deep down, I knew that I would never return here.

We arrived at the Peace Corps office in Amman in the late afternoon. When we entered, I found Laurene the nurse waiting for me. She looked piqued and impatient. Having to come to the office on a Friday, which is a day off from work, was a great inconvenience and *I* was the cause of it. She gave me a bunch of medical forms and circled some tests that I should do on my return to the United States. She claimed to know nothing about the circumstances of my sudden departure but I didn't believe her. As usual, she was cold and aloof toward me. In the middle of her explanation, I had to take a call in the other room. When I got off the phone and returned to her office, she was already gone. The forms lay on her desk with a note. She wasn't going to waste her precious time waiting for me.

My telephone conversation was with Lien Galloway, senior advisor to the General Counsel at Peace Corps Headquarters in Washington, DC. I asked her what had gone wrong with my background check, but she refused to tell me, stating that the information wasn't her "property" to give; it was the FBI's. When I inquired how I could obtain it, she said that I would have to make a Freedom of Information Act (FOIA) request. I demanded to know why the Peace Corps had *not* conducted my background check *prior to* sending me overseas and why I was *not* allowed to participate in the swearing-in ceremony now that I had completed the pre-service training. She had no answers, no explanation, and no apology for me.

I returned to Mat's office. I had had nothing to eat or drink all day except for my cup of coffee at Umm Ali's. I had not had any sleep since the night before when they had awakened me with their bizarre series of phone calls. I was hungry, thirsty, and distraught. I could barely follow what Mat was saying to me. He was going over my account: I had been given an allowance of JD22 for a period of two weeks but only five days had elapsed from this period; therefore, I owed the Peace Corps nine days of allowance money, which he calculated to be the sum of JD14. I listened to him in disbelief. I was sitting there, famished, dehydrated, and traumatized, on the point of total collapse, and he was talking to me in nickels and dimes! Perhaps he was only doing his duty but I didn't expect such pettiness. I had flown to Tel Aviv twice at my own expense and saved the Peace Corps the sum of $1,300 on flight tickets, for which I was entitled to be reimbursed, and now he insisted that I pay back the Peace Corps JD14, which equaled the trifling sum of $19.60! He had even demanded that I sign a form to this effect! I didn't want to argue. It would be beneath my dignity.

The toughest form was yet to come. I had to choose between "resignation" and "administrative separation," which would define the nature of my departure from the Peace Corps. Two cruel options. I didn't want to resign and I didn't deserve to be removed from service. I couldn't make a choice. Mat called Bryan to ask for his opinion. Bryan thought that "resignation" sounded better for future employment prospects. Reluctantly, I signed the resignation letter and handed it back to Mat. He heaved a deep sigh of relief. What was *he* sighing about? Was he afraid that I would give him a hard time? Now I had a burning question for which I wanted an answer. I looked him straight in the eye and said, "When we were at the supervisors conference in Amman, did you already know that I would be sent home?" He dropped his gaze and replied, "Yes, I knew. It had already been decided." My gut feeling had been right all along! That was why he had snubbed me when I raised my hand to ask a question in his technical session. That was why Alex and Bryan had stared at me so disturbingly when I introduced Dr. Zaydan to the participants in the supervisors conference. And that was why Bryan had shown no interest in my report about the condition of the apartment that I had received from Mu'ta University. The awful manner in which I had been treated cut me to the bone.

It was almost 6:00 p.m. and Mat was still not finished with me. There were more forms to fill out and more releases to sign. "All this paperwork," I sighed in exhaustion. "Can't this wait?" "No," he insisted. "You must complete everything now, or else I can't give you back your passport." I felt like a hostage who had been forced to collaborate with her abductors under duress. He repeated this threat whenever he saw me hesitate about signing a form that he placed before me. He instructed me to return my cell phone to Samir on the way to the airport and my Peace Corps passport and ticket stub to Peace Corps Headquarters in Washington, DC. I signed all the papers that he handed me automatically, barely cognizant. I was desperate to leave his office and go to the hotel, where I could finally get some rest. I had barely three hours to spare before embarking on my grueling flight back to the United States and I urgently needed something to eat and drink. If the last twenty-four hours were a nightmare, the next twenty-four hours would be hell.

At long last we completed all the paperwork. I rushed out of the office into the parking lot, where Usama was waiting for me in his car. On the way to the hotel, I asked him to stop by a convenience store so that I could buy some food and bottled water. As he navigated through the heavy traffic in the streets, I wondered whether he would be discreet about what he had seen and heard, or whether he would divulge the day's events to his colleagues. The matter was completely out of my control.

The Canary Hotel is an old building without elevators in central Amman. Because I had several pieces of luggage and would stay only for a few hours, I was given a room on the ground floor that belonged to one of the hotel's employees. As usual, I had to surrender my passport to the desk clerk for the duration of my stay, a procedure that I had encountered in both Egypt and Jordan. It was around 7:30 in the evening when I entered my room, which was tiny and furnished sparsely with a bed, a chair, and a small refrigerator. There were men's clothes lying on the bed and a large shopping bag that contained two big bottles of Johnnie Walker Scotch Whiskey. When I opened the refrigerator to put my bottled water inside, I found a six-pack case of Heineken cooling on the shelf. The consumption of alcohol is forbidden in Islam but it is readily available in the modern city of Amman, where there are many bars for customers who wish to get a beer or a glass of wine or other alcoholic drinks. I quickly ate an apple to soothe my hunger and collapsed on the bed in utter exhaustion.

I had barely any time to rest when the shrill ring of the telephone woke me up. It was Alex, informing me that he and Samir were waiting for me in the lobby, ready to escort me to the airport. I glanced at my watch—it was only 9:45 p.m. and I had to be on the move again. I scrambled out of bed and dragged my weary body into the bathroom to wash my face. In the mirror, a ghost with no resemblance to my former self stared back at me. My face was gaunt and drawn, my eyes were hollow and with dark circles, my complexion was pallid, and my expression was dazed. I looked like someone who had just emerged from a horrific car crash. I tried to fix my face and spruce up my appearance, but it was to no avail. Forget it—let them see what they had done to me! I put on my jacket and wheeled my suitcases to the lobby, where Alex and Samir were waiting impatiently, looking grim and sullen. I had inconvenienced them and practically ruined their day off. They had left their cozy homes at this late hour in the night to take me to the airport. Were they afraid that I might run away? I stood before them, a frail, tired, shaken woman. They didn't ask, "How do you feel, Dalya? Are you well enough to fly? Did you have something to eat or drink? Is there anything you need for the trip?" Three months of dedicated hard work and not one word of sympathy or kindness.

We climbed into the car. Samir sat in the driver's seat with Alex beside him and I sat in the back like a convicted felon, escorted by two security guards. The road to the airport was pitch-dark. We drove in silence. Samir kept fidgeting in his seat. After a while, he turned the radio on and set the volume at full blast. Was the silence getting on his nerves? There were a lot of speed bumps on the road. Every time he drove over one of them, I was jolted up and down in the back seat. I held onto the grab handle on the ceiling of the car with all my might, trying to avoid the repeated shaking, terrified that it would disrupt my sense of balance and trigger another episode of dizziness and queasiness. After a rough ride that seemed to last forever, we arrived at the airport and entered the terminal together. At the door to the departure hall, we were stopped. Samir pleaded with the security guard to allow him to accompany me to the check-in desk, using various forms of entreaties in Arabic, but the security guard flatly refused. I realized that Samir and Alex were terribly afraid that I *might not* get on the plane and would somehow manage to *sneak out* of the airport. That was why they had taken me to the airport themselves and why they now insisted on waiting behind the glass doors until I completed the check-in process. I felt sorry for them as I left them standing there, looking nervous and frustrated. As far as I was concerned, they had delivered the "package" to the "shipper" and had accomplished their mission.

The departure hall was crowded with travelers. I had never seen it so packed before—I had passed through it twice in the past couple of months. I waited a long time in line by the Air France desk, which served Delta passengers. When my turn came, the check-in clerk declared that my two suitcases were over the weight limit, while my third bag was under the weight limit. He demanded that I step aside and distribute the weight evenly between the three bags. With great difficulty, I pushed the heavy trolley to a place where I could open my bags and move items around. When I had finished, I waited in line all over again. The check-in clerk allowed me to check one bag free of charge and demanded payment for the other two, one of which was actually the responsibility of the Peace Corps to cover.

I was directed to pay the fine at yet another desk, where the clerk moved at an excruciatingly slow pace. When I had finally completed the check-in process and received my boarding pass, it was already past midnight.

As I stood on the escalator ascending to the departure gates on the upper level, I glanced in the direction of the glass doors where I had left Alex and Samir but there was no sign of them. They must have gotten tired of waiting and gone home. The bizarre spectacle of the two of them peering hard through the glass doors with worried looks on their faces was the last glimpse I had of them. I smiled wryly to myself as it suddenly occurred to me that I wouldn't be the only person who would have a sleepless night tonight.

The lounge by my departure gate was teeming with happy passengers on their way to celebrate Christmas in Paris. I was probably the only wretched person among them, deeply traumatized and disoriented. All I prayed for now was to have this grueling trip behind me. I just wanted to get home.

The flight left at 1:40 a.m. It was packed full. I was astonished to see that most of the passengers were Arabs, rather than foreign nationals. I occupied an aisle seat next to an elderly Jordanian couple. The husband, who had a kind face and a small frame, sat in the window seat and his wife, who was corpulent and rather plain-looking, sat in the middle. Her fleshy thigh spilled into my seat, taking up a good portion of it, while her arm and shoulder rested on me. I gently asked her to move a little bit. Her husband smiled at me apologetically. During the flight, he was very attentive to his wife, asking the flight attendant to bring her a pillow and a blanket as well as water and tea. It was evident that he cared for her a great deal. However unattractive, she was his queen, absolutely adored and protected. I thought of Frank Sinatra's song, "You're Nobody till Somebody Loves You." I had once asked my friend, Varda, a clinical psychologist, if she agreed with this statement. She didn't; she thought it far more important that you love yourself.

We landed at Paris Charles De Gaulle Airport at 5:00 a.m. local time. I had a long layover before my connecting flight to Washington Dulles International Airport at 12:40 p.m. Luckily, I didn't have to change terminals or transfer my luggage, which was checked right through to my final destination. The lounge by my departure gate was completely deserted at this early hour of the morning. I lay across a row of three armless chairs, closed my eyes, and tried to grab some sleep. I hadn't slept a wink on the plane—I had never been able to sleep on flights. Scenes from the past three months flashed across my mind like a broken film reel, repeating themselves over and over again. I tried to make sense of what had happened to me, to find a purpose or meaning in it, but failed.

Time crept by at a maddeningly slow pace. I lay on the chairs for a while, stood up and paced around the lounge, lay down again, then repeated the pattern. I was agitated and restless. I ate an apple and some crackers, constantly watching the clock on the wall. Meanwhile, the lounge was getting fuller and noisier. Families with little children, groups of excited teenagers, young men and women, and elderly people, all carrying bulging duffel bags and tote bags, were on their way to the United States to celebrate Christmas. I sighed with despair. It would be a packed flight, long and arduous.

We boarded the plane around noon. Three Japanese children sat next to me, while their parents sat across the aisle from them. I watched the family with interest. The mother was Japanese but the father looked European. When he talked with the flight attendant, I detected a heavy Italian accent in his speech. The kids spoke Italian with each other and with their parents but American English with me. During the entire flight, their father was extremely attentive to them—he chatted with them, played video games with them, and took care of their needs. The mother buried her head in a book and was completely uninvolved. I was intrigued. An Italian father, a Japanese mother, and American-raised children. This unique family seemed totally at ease with its ethnic, cultural, and linguistic diversity.

The flight to Dulles Airport lasted longer than usual, nearly nine hours, due to strong winds. Unable to sleep, I passed the time by listening to music, watching movies, and reading the magazines that were placed in the seat pocket. The air in the cabin was hot and smelled foul, the seats were narrow, and the leg room was a tight squeeze. We were served a high-carb, unsavory, complimentary meal. I ate a roll of bread with a salad. I had already lost weight during the pre-service training and now it seemed like I had lost another couple of pounds just over the past few days. My pants were getting looser on me and I kept tightening my belt to hold them in place. My body must have taken a hard beating from all the stress and deprivations that I had endured in Jordan. I wondered what kind of medical issues I might have developed during this period.

At 3:00 p.m. local time on Christmas Eve, we landed at Dulles Airport. I merged into the large stream of passengers who headed toward Customs and Immigration, where an overcrowded hall awaited us. I felt nervous when I stood before the US Immigration officer and handed him my passport, fearing that he would tell me to step aside and take me for an interrogation. I wondered whether I would be placed on the NSA checklist at airports from now on. Would I also have to worry about being stopped by a police officer when I drove my car? The officer stamped my passport and uttered the usual "welcome home" greeting. My fears vanished and a surge of relief swept through me. Those two heartwarming words lifted my spirits and brought me back to reality. I was now in the "land of the free and the home of the brave." I had no reason to be paranoid—no one was out to get me or had a reason to hate me. I was safe and sound, surrounded by thousands of other immigrants like me, all with peculiar accents and distinct ethnic features. A smile lit up my face as I hurried to the baggage claim area to collect my bags, which had made it safely from Amman through Paris to Washington, DC. A fellow passenger helped me pick them off the carousel and put them on a trolley and, pushing the heavy load with great effort, I proceeded lightheartedly to the street exit.

The clear blue sky of a mild winter day received me. There was little traffic about and the street was quiet—a relaxed mid-afternoon on Christmas Eve. The dispatcher at the taxi stand found me a cab quickly. "We're going to Potomac, Maryland," I said to the driver, who smiled and replied, "Yes, ma'am." I leaned back in my seat, opened the window a crack, and let the cool wind blow over my face. The cab seemed to glide through the highway—there were no speed bumps, no horns honking, and no noisy exhaust pipes spewing black smoke into the air. Whenever I returned to the United States from a trip abroad, I always marveled at how quietly the traffic flowed in the streets. My thoughts shifted to my house. Tomorrow was Christmas Day and I had no food, no phone or Internet connection, and no working car at home. When we got off the Beltway and were headed west on route 190 toward River Road, I asked the cab driver to continue to Potomac Village and stop by Safeway so I could buy some groceries. It was almost 6:00 p.m. and quite dark when the cab driver finally pulled up by my townhouse. My hand trembled as I fumbled in my handbag for the key to the door. With bated breath, I inserted it in the keyhole, unlocked the door, and pushed it open.

The first thing that struck me when I stepped inside was the silence and solitude that reigned over the place. During the past three months, I had been surrounded by people day and night. I had lived in a large household that comprised twelve members. I had followed technical sessions with a group of thirty-eight volunteers. I had observed and taught classes at the village girls' elementary school, which was crowded with students and teachers. I had never been alone. All of a sudden, I was surrounded by silence and solitude—the distinctive characteristics, not necessarily undesirable, of being single and living on my own.

I flew into a flurry of activity. I brought my bags into the foyer and rushed to turn on the central heating, the water valve, the cooking gas valve, and the circuit breaker of the electric water heater. I then went from one kitchen appliance to the next, from the refrigerator and microwave oven to the washer and dryer, and plugged each one into a power outlet. I would contact Verizon after Christmas Day to ask them to renew my phone, Internet, and television services. I went to the garage to check on the condition of my car. After sitting idle for so long, the battery was dead—exactly as the mechanic at my auto repair shop had predicted.

I went upstairs to my bedroom, changed the sheets on my bed, then stepped into the bathroom and took a long hot shower. I washed my hair twice and scrubbed my body thoroughly, savoring the sensation of unlimited hot water running over my skin—a real luxury that I had taken for granted. After my shower, I put on a fresh pair of pajamas and went straight to bed. It felt strange to lie on a bed instead of a farsha on the floor. The mattress felt too soft, the down blanket too light. I didn't need to wear gloves, socks, or a sweater to keep me warm. It felt odd, as if something was missing.

I fell asleep as soon as my head hit the pillow. I woke up in the middle of the night, completely disoriented. *Where was I? Why was I lying in bed and not in my sleeping bag on the floor? Was I in a hotel room in Amman?* I groped in the dark for the light switch of the lamp on the bedside table and flipped it on. Light filled the room, revealing modern teakwood furniture and a white ceiling fan. I looked around in puzzlement, trying to connect the dots. Suddenly, all my memories came flooding back. I sat up in the bed, held my head in my hands, and stared blankly into space.

II. THE QUEST FOR
THE TRUTH

CHRISTMAS DAY WAS A WRETCHED DAY IN MY LIFE. I WAS IN A DAZE, UNABLE to process what had happened. I swung between anger and despair. How could the Peace Corps be so callous and unfair? How could they put me through the wringer and then tell me that I didn't qualify? Why hadn't they conducted my background check *before* sending me to Jordan? During the year and a half that elapsed between the dates of my application submission and my departure, I had allowed them to look into every nook and cranny of my life, from my health records and financial obligations to my personal history and divorce agreement. They had received my resume and every single form and document that they had requested. They had failed to process my application in accordance with the sequence of stages delineated in their booklets. The Peace Corps *Volunteer Handbook* clearly states on page 2: "*After* you have been nominated and *before* you are invited to serve, the Peace Corps initiates an investigation of your background, as required by law for all volunteers and staff." Similarly, it is plainly written in their *Be a Volunteer* brochure that the eligibility review, which includes a background check, is part of stage *four* in the application process and comes *before* extending an invitation to serve to qualified candidates, which is stage *five* in the application process. But in my case, the background check had come *after* they had already invited me to serve, *after* they had already sent me overseas to Jordan, and *after* I had already completed the entire pre-service training program there. This was absurd! Worse yet, after they had *failed* to conduct my background check timely and had decided so belatedly that I didn't qualify for service, they had *denied* me the right of appeal by hastily removing me from the swearing-in ceremony just a few days before it was due to take place. Was this fair? They had unceremoniously sent me home, spiriting me off to the airport in the middle of the night under escort, as if I were a convicted felon! Was this proper treatment?

From a state of anger, I would swing into a state of despair. I had a dream—to serve in the Peace Corps. For the past two years, I had lived in preparation for Peace Corps service. I had passed up a good employment opportunity in my field, I had engaged in volunteer work in my community, I had spent a considerable amount of money on medical tests and a packing list. Suddenly, this dream was crushed, shattered into pieces. When this dream crumbled, I lost the meaning and purpose that it gave to my life. It was as if I was thrown into a black hole. The psychological shock to my psyche was profound; the disruption of my life total. How was I to pick up the thread of my life?

I lay on my bed in the dark in utter misery. I wanted to escape into sleep but sleep eluded me. I tossed from side to side, kicked the blanket away, then pulled it over my head, but it was to no avail. I looked at the time; it was 3:00 a.m. I climbed out of bed and went downstairs to unpack my bags, hoping that this activity would distract my mind and give me some relief. I was sorting out the contents of my bags when I accidentally dropped a heavy key chain on the tiled foyer floor right by one of the impact sensors of my alarm system. In the stillness of the night, the noise sounded like the shattering of a window pane and the alarm went off. I rushed to the phone to report the false alarm to the monitoring center, only to discover that the phone was dead! What to do? At this early hour on Christmas Day, I couldn't knock on my neighbors' door and ask to make a phone call. The monitoring center would alert the police and an officer would be dispatched to check on my house. Sure enough, a car pulled up on my driveway fifteen minutes later, its headlights shining through the glass windows by my front door. Two police officers approached, holding flashlights. I rushed to open the door. "Good morning, officers," I greeted them. "I just came back from a trip abroad and accidentally set off my alarm system. I'm sorry to have troubled you. My telephone service has been disconnected, so I couldn't call the monitoring center to cancel the alarm." The police officers poked their heads in the foyer and saw my bags with the airline tags still attached to them. They smiled and said, "We're glad to see that you're okay and that no one is trying to get away with your stuff on Christmas Day. Happy Christmas!" "Happy Christmas," I replied. "And thank you for coming."

I closed the door and went to the kitchen to make myself a cup of coffee. My thoughts drifted back to Jordan. If two police officers had appeared on my doorstep in Jordan at 5:00 a.m., I would have freaked out. It would have meant only one thing: that they had come to arrest me. Jordan is not a democratic country. I was not an American citizen by birth but by naturalization. I was born and raised in Israel, had served in Israel Defense Forces, and had close relatives who lived in Israel. Given my background, the Jordanian authorities could easily allege that I was involved in intelligence activities. If the Peace Corps believed that I was involved in intelligence activities, who would blame the Jordanian authorities for alleging the same thing? Most likely, I would have been thrown into jail to rot there and die ...

Suddenly the enormity of the risk that I had taken in agreeing to serve in Jordan sank in. How could I have been so naive! Even *Arab* citizens disappear all the time in their own home countries—all of them police states—and are never found or heard from again. Let alone a foreigner like me, Jewish and a Sabra to boot!

The fact of the matter was that, for nearly three months, I had lived under a false identity. I pretended that I was Christian and that my last name was Seymore. I was told to do so by my Peace Corps supervisors so that my safety and efficacy as a Peace Corps volunteer would not be compromised. I was not who I appeared to be—I was an impostor. Who wouldn't assume that I was a spy?

In reality, having to conceal my Jewish identity all this time was not as simple as I thought it would be. I was confronted with many difficult situations. I had to feign indifference when I heard racist remarks about Jews or expressions of hatred toward Israel and a desire to see it wiped off the map. The image of the map of Jordan, as it was drawn on the outer wall of the girls' elementary school in Taybeh, with the names and frontiers of all its neighboring countries but with no trace of Israel, remained seared in my memory. I had to take refuge in the bathroom when I saw the anti-Semitic cartoons, with grotesque and hateful portrayals of Jews, which the children of my first host family watched on their computer. I had to ignore such disturbing incidents and not react to them out of fear that revealing my feelings would blow my cover. Little by little, this had become detrimental to my emotional and psychological well-being.

Never before had I needed to conceal my Jewish identity. In Israel, I grew up as a Jew among Jews. In the United States, I live in a Jewish-friendly suburb, where Hanukkah is publicly celebrated along with Christmas. Suddenly, in Jordan, I found myself in a situation where I had to renounce any connection to Judaism. I thought that this was not a big deal. After all, I was a *modern* Jew:

I drove on Shabbat, I didn't keep kosher, and I didn't fast on the prescribed days. But I was wrong. Judaism is not merely a set of religious laws and rituals; it is a history, a culture, and a nation. It bothered me to dissociate myself from these facets of my personality. I wanted to be *me,* to express my core self. I longed to talk about my background—where I was born, grew up, and went to school. Ben, a fellow volunteer of German parentage, talked freely about his background. But I had to bury my past, my roots, and the rich experiences that made me who I am. Toward the end of my stay in the village, I started to sing Jewish prayers in the privacy of my room, especially *Hashkiveinu adonai eloheinu le-shalom* and *Avinu malkeinu.* I didn't care if my host family heard me. Did they know the difference between Hebrew and Dutch? I could always say that I was singing in Dutch. I had also started inadvertently to blurt out words in Hebrew when I spoke Arabic. The two languages are so closely related that it was easy to mix up their vocabularies, especially when I was tired or absent-minded. Obviously, I was *not* made of "good spy material." This even happened to me once when I was talking with Usama, the suspicious son of my second host family. Instead of using the word *laa* (Arabic) for *no,* I said *lo* (Hebrew). I was horrified when it happened, but he didn't notice. I told myself that the people in my village were not educated enough to catch such slips of the tongue, but university students were and surely could. Teaching three to four courses per semester meant interacting with 120 to 160 students each semester. Inevitably one of them, especially if he belonged to the military section of Mu'ta University, would have discovered my identity. I recalled that when Dr. Zaydan had introduced me to his class, the first question that a female student had asked me was, "Why did you come to Jordan?" Her tone of voice expressed suspicion and distrust. Where was I to begin? With my Iraqi-born and raised parents? With my lifelong passion for Arabic and fervent desire to understand my neighbors, to communicate with them, and coexist with them? Would she have believed any of this if I had told her?

In the late 1970s when I relocated with my family from the Netherlands to the United States, I was once invited for dinner at the house of a Silver Spring rabbi whose child and mine were classmates at the Charles E. Smith Jewish Day School. The rabbi's wife asked me what I did in my free time. When I told her that I was studying Arabic language and literature at Georgetown University, she looked at me disapprovingly and said in a critical tone, "How can you do this? Don't you feel a conflict of loyalties? Don't you feel that you betray your people by devoting your time and energy to the enemy who wants to annihilate you?" I was taken aback by her response. *What a narrow-minded attitude,* I thought to myself. *Didn't she understand the importance of knowing thy neighbor? Of opening a dialogue? Of building a bridge between two warring nations?* And here I was, several decades later, still hoping to make a difference and still facing suspicion and distrust, from all sides.

For the last three months, then, I had lived in a bubble of illusions. Sooner or later this bubble was bound to burst, though I hadn't expected the Peace Corps to be the agent to burst it. I wondered if there was more to this affair than met the eye. Were there perhaps other, hidden motives for my disqualification? I was keenly aware that I was *different* from all the other volunteers in the J15 group. I was the only person who was not a native-born American citizen. I was not merely Jewish but a Sabra, apparently the first Sabra who was sent to serve as a Peace Corps volunteer in Jordan. I was also the only person with a doctoral degree and the only person who spoke Arabic fluently. I was different. I attracted attention, not necessarily positive. Then the issue of my background check came up, further singling me out. I wondered why the country director had never bothered to sit and talk with me so as to assess my personality and motivation. The fact that he had to *press* Peace Corps Headquarters to hurry up with the conclusion of my background check suggested that they were not ready yet; perhaps they had some doubts and needed more time. But time was exactly what they did *not* have on their hands and could *not* afford to lose, because then I would make it to the swearing-in ceremony and would have the right of appeal. They didn't care about the predicament that they had put me in or the terrible shock that I got when they had sent me home unceremoniously. All they cared about was protecting the image of the Peace Corps. But in their zeal to prevent an apparent "espionage" scandal, they had created another scandal—unfair and callous treatment of a volunteer.

Admittedly, I was getting tired of all the secrecy and deception. It was stressful and detrimental to my well-being. I also felt that it was wrong to mislead my host family—it had become a moral issue that tormented me. I longed to say to them: "I'm Dalya Cohen, not Dalya Seymore." They deserved to know the truth, and I deserved to be true to myself.

It is a great tragedy that Arabs and Jews, who trace their lineage to the same ancestor—the patriarch Abraham—have been off and on at war in Palestine for a hundred years. As the descendants of half-brothers Ishmael and Isaac, we are "first cousins." We look alike, we live in proximity to each other, and we speak closely related languages. We are both *ahl al-kitab* (People of the Book).[14] When will this senseless conflict end?

The lyrics of John Lennon's song, "Imagine," sprang to my mind. I had translated this song into colloquial Jordanian with the help of my first host father's sister, Fatin. Lennon's vision of a world with no possessions, religions, or countries, where there is nothing to kill or die for, expresses a universal yearning for peace. Softly, I began to hum it to myself.

Imagine . . . imagine that my true identity had been discovered. What would have happened to me? I might have been butchered like a goat by some fanatic Jihadist or Hamasnik, or the Peace Corps would have had to evacuate me in a hurry. Perhaps it was inevitable that sooner or later I would be sent home. Perhaps I was lucky to be safe and sound in my own home. Perhaps this was all for the better . . .

I stared blankly at the dregs of coffee in my cup, lost in my train of thought. I desperately needed to rationalize what had happened to me so that I could cope with my anger and frustration. I also needed to find some *closure* or else I would never have peace of mind. I resolved to get to the bottom of this. After Christmas, I would contact Peace Corps Headquarters, the OPM (US Office of Personnel Management), and the FBI to request a copy of my background check under the Freedom of Information Act. I would not rest until I discovered the truth.

I passed Christmas Day in isolation, disconnected from the outside world. I roamed around my townhouse, thankful to God that I had a place to come back to. Imagine if I had leased out my townhouse before I had left, thinking that I wasn't coming back for two years! No one at the Peace Corps office had asked me if I had a place to go to after I got off the plane at Dulles Airport; for all they cared, I could sleep in the street and beg for alms. It didn't matter to them if I became ill from this shock, fell into a terrible depression, or developed severe maladjustment problems. Their only concern was to get rid of me as fast as possible.

My home was my only solace. What a relief it was to go to the bathroom and not have to squat, to prepare my own meals, to take long hot showers, and to sleep in a bed—in short, to enjoy the comforts of modernity. But, deep down, I knew that all these comforts could not make up for what I had lost—or rather, what had been taken away from me: my dream, my trust in the Peace Corps, and my belief in American justice and fairness.

I could have remained shut up in my house for days if it were not for urgent maintenance activities that I had to carry out. In a way, having to deal with practical matters was therapeutic for me.

It distracted my mind from dwelling on the same agonizing topics. The day after Christmas, I went to my next-door neighbors
and asked to use their telephone. I called a road service truck to
jump-start my car so that I could drive it to my auto repair shop
to have the battery replaced. I called Verizon and asked them to
renew my telephone, Internet, and television services. I also called
my friend Miri to tell her that I was back from Jordan. She thought
that I was joking—she couldn't believe it. She immediately assumed
that the Peace Corps had sent me back out of concern for my safety
and security. How ironic! I told her that I would give her the details
when we got together. I had to call an exterminator to get rid of grain
moths that were flying all over my kitchen, and I had to mail my
Peace Corps passport and ticket stub to Peace Corps Headquarters in
Washington, DC.

I managed to complete all these tasks within a few days and had
nothing else to occupy myself with. I felt disoriented, aimless, and
restless. I was tormented by persistent questions: What were the
issues they had found in my background check? Why wouldn't they
disclose them to me? How could I clear my name if I didn't know
what I was accused of? I had to find the answers to these burning
questions.

I called Lien Galloway, senior advisor to the General Counsel at
Peace Corps Headquarters, and requested to meet with her, but she
refused to see me. I tried to speak to someone else in that office, but
failed. The staff was uncooperative, unsympathetic, and unwilling
to give me any information. They were there to protect the agency,
not the returned volunteers. I realized that I was facing a wall of
silence. Only a FOIA (Freedom of Information Act) request could
break this silence. I called the Office of Personnel Management
(OPM) and asked for instructions on how to submit a FOIA request.
I was told that it would take several months to get a response because
they received numerous requests every day and were backed up. I
decided not to waste any time and submitted my request at once. On

December 28, four days after my return, I faxed my FOIA request to the Office of Personnel Management, asking to get a copy of the background check that was conducted about me in connection with my Peace Corps application. I had taken the first step. Now I had to wait patiently for their response.

The following days I holed up at home, avoiding contact with people and shutting myself off from the world. I just ate, slept, and watched television. I would wake up in the middle of the night, my body's internal clock still synced up with the Jordanian standard time, and think to myself, "Now my fellow volunteers are having their final language proficiency interview," or "Now they are having their last immunization shots." The hardest night was Tuesday, January 3. I looked at the date and said to myself, "Now they are being sworn in as Peace Corps volunteers." And the next day I said to myself, "Now they are moving to their permanent sites." I was disconsolate and weighed down by a sense of defeat and failure. My self-image and self-esteem were at rock bottom. I kept asking: Why do bad things happen to good people?

One night, as I was vegetating in front of the television, I happened to see the movie *A Serious Man* by the Coen brothers. I was glued to the screen, instantly identifying with the hero, a Jewish professor of physics for whom everything suddenly goes wrong. His wife betrays him with his best friend; anonymous letters of complaint against him are sent to his department head and threaten his application for tenure; his son, who is about to celebrate his bar-mitzvah, is into drugs; his teenage daughter steals money from his wallet for a nose job; and his useless, unemployed brother exploits him. The harder he searches for an explanation for the series of misfortunes that have befallen him, the more futile his attempts seem. He goes to three rabbis, asking them, "Why do bad things happen to good people?" but receives no satisfactory answer. Powerless, perplexed, and beleaguered, he watches his life unravel, unable to make sense of it. In the final scene, his doctor calls him, asking to see him immediately about the results of his chest X-ray; at the same time, a massive tornado rapidly approaches his son's school, where his elderly teacher fumbles for the right key to open the emergency shelter for the students. Then the movie ends. I had anticipated some kind of epiphany at the end, but there was none.

I was deeply moved by this film. I felt that the hero's numerous tribulations and desperate search for clarity resembled mine. But if the struggle to find meaning and purpose in life is futile, then how are we supposed to live our lives? Seize the day? Live only for the moment? Grab what we can while we still can? I watched the movie again on pay-per-view, looking for some clues. I noticed an epigraph at the beginning of the movie. It was a motto by Rashi, the famed Jewish Biblical commentator of the Middle Ages. It said, "Accept with simplicity everything that happens to you." I was mystified. What did Rashi mean by this? Resign to your fate? Make no attempt to resist or struggle, no matter what happens to you? Should I, then, not pursue a FOIA request? Give up the quest for the truth? Rashi's advice didn't sound helpful to me. I felt that it advocated a defeatist approach to life.

Over the next few days, I continued to sprawl out on the couch in front of the television, passing the time in a mindless way, when I came across the movie *Fair Game.* It is based on the story of Valerie Plame, a CIA covert agent whose name was deliberately leaked to the press in 2003 by White House officials in retaliation for public criticisms made by her husband, Joseph Wilson, against the second Bush administration's case for invading Iraq on the grounds that Saddam Hussein possessed weapons of mass destruction. Valerie Plame had worked for the CIA for eighteen years and was well regarded in her job. But when officials in the White House wanted to discredit her husband, they had no qualms about destroying her career. On the same day that her name was leaked to the press, her superiors at the CIA told her that she was suspended and that she had to leave her office immediately. They didn't protect her or offer her any help. They dropped her like a hot potato.

I knew the story and had followed it closely when it unfolded in the newspapers, but seeing it now as a feature film carried a special message for me. I said to myself: "If this is what was done to Valerie Plame, after eighteen years of dedication to her work, then who am I to complain about what was done to me after a couple of months of hard work? Valerie Plame is an all-American woman, born and bred in the USA, while I am an immigrant and a member of a minority group. Perhaps I should relativize, compare my misfortune to other people's misfortunes, and then follow Rashi's advice. *Life is unfair.* Isn't this what we teach our children at school? Even in this free and democratic society, the individual can be victimized, whether intentionally or unintentionally, by government agencies. Valerie Plame sued those who were responsible for her ordeal. Should I follow her example?"

I went online and googled "lawsuits and claims against the Peace Corps." I was stunned by the results that I got: pages full of detailed charges and complaints of former volunteers against the Peace Corps for discrimination, cover up, medical negligence, failure to provide adequate protection, failure to offer adequate counseling to victims of assault, incidents of rape, homicide, and even suicide that were swept under the rug. Philip Weiss's 2005 book, *An American Taboo: A Murder in the Peace Corps,* explores the murder of Deborah Gardner by a fellow volunteer in 1975 in the tiny island nation of Tonga, focusing on the role of the country director in obtaining the release of the perpetrator from prison and Peace Corps efforts to cover up the scandal. Then there was the three-part ABC News 20/20 report on the murder of Kate Puzey in Benin as a result of confidentiality breach on the part of her supervisors. The report brought to light other cases of assault, sexual and otherwise, against female volunteers and Peace Corps attempts to keep word of these cases—and their apparent mistakes in them—quiet. I had no idea that the Peace Corps had come under sharp public criticism. I had regarded it as an iconic institution that represents the best and noblest values of

American society. But those reports painted a picture of a flawed agency with callous bureaucrats who go to extremes to protect its image and reputation.

I sank deeper into depression. I had no support system to help me cope with this crisis. The Peace Corps offers returned volunteers only three therapy sessions to deal with maladjustment problems, which is nowhere near enough to attempt to solve them. My depression was exacerbated by delayed grief over my brother's passing. I hadn't been able to mourn for him properly while I was in Jordan. Now all my bottled-up pains and sorrows burst out and overwhelmed me. My poor emotional and psychological state took a toll on my physical health. I suffered from high blood pressure, irregular heartbeats, palpitations, night sweats, insomnia, skin allergies and infections, muscle spasms, spells of blurred vision, and ringing in my ears—it seemed as if my entire immune system had collapsed. In the space of three months I had seen more doctors and specialists than I had seen in the past ten years. My medical bills began to pile up, adding to my worries. I was trapped in a vicious circle: the more distressed and depressed I was, the more medical problems I developed, and the more depressed I became. I had to break out of this vicious circle.

One Saturday in late February, I took the first step to come out of my isolation: I went to Shabbat morning service in my synagogue. There was snow and sleet on the roads, but I drove anyway. I felt terribly anxious and insecure. How would the rabbi and members of my congregation receive me after such a long absence? I had a high regard for this inclusive and innovative conservative Jewish synagogue. They had embraced me during a dark time in my life, when I was going through a bitter divorce, and had given me a new sense of belonging to a larger, collective family. The congregation had a vibrant cultural life with a strong emphasis on female participation, including a dynamic sisterhood on whose board I had served until shortly before my departure. I had gotten to know many of the regular congregants and befriended them.

There was a low turnout that morning on account of the weather. I was greeted warmly by the small gathering. People came up to me, hugged and kissed me, and asked how I was doing and where I had vanished to. I said briefly that I had been traveling out of the country and had also gone to Israel in connection with my brother's passing. They expressed their condolences and welcomed me back. I participated eagerly in the service, feeling a deep need to nourish the roots of my identity. After the service, we had a Kiddush followed by a light lunch—and an opportunity to mingle and chat.

Attending the Shabbat service had lifted my spirits, but as soon as I returned home, I felt depressed again. My best friend, Miri, a major source of support for me, had gone to Italy with her husband to celebrate her sixtieth birthday. She knew what had happened to me and encouraged me to become active again—to go out of the house, meet people, and look for a job. Reaching out for help, I invited a fellow congregant home and unburdened my heart to her, saying that I had recently suffered a major setback and didn't know how to move on. She advised me to stop torturing myself about the past. *Self-doubt is poison.* Instead, I should find my passion and focus on it. "What do you like doing, Dalya?" she asked. I said that my hobbies were Latin dance, movies, hiking, traveling, and reading and writing, although I hadn't been able to read or write lately because I couldn't concentrate. She suggested that I take up Zumba classes, join a hiking club, and become a member of the Smithsonian Associates, which offers a wide variety of educational and cultural activities. She asked if I was interested in dating, remarking that I was still young and pretty and shouldn't remain alone. I said no—I didn't have the emotional energy to invest in a relationship at this time. A sensitive and sympathetic lady, she shared some of her own difficult life experiences with me. I enjoyed her company and her visit cheered me up, but as soon as she left, I felt depressed again.

February is the shortest month of the year, but to me it seemed unbearably long. My days were filled with medical appointments and

I came to know the health care system in the United States pretty well—it is costly, but not necessarily efficient or effective. Patients are ushered in and out of the doctor's office every ten to fifteen minutes and told to come back again in a few weeks. One doctor even had an assistant buzz her to tell her that my time was up when she was still sitting with me in the examination room! I was prescribed aggressive medications that did me more harm than good. I became frightened and distrustful of the health care system. I knew that I had to reduce the level of stress in my life in order to get well again, but some of the damage already inflicted on me by inappropriate diagnosis and medication was irreversible.

In an effort to improve my physical health, I signed up for Zumba classes and instantly got hooked on this Latin-inspired dance fitness routine. The fusion of music and dancing energized me and brightened my mood. I noticed the beneficial effects that music had on my frame of mind and began to listen to my favorite kinds of pop and classical music every day. As the music played in the background, I tried to do some reading and writing. My new manuscript on the Arab Middle East had to be updated on the latest developments in the Arab revolutions. I worked on it slowly and sporadically. Every time I held it in my hands and read an earlier portion, I marveled at myself for having produced it. I was convinced that I would never be able to create another piece of work like this again.

I found another release from stress in the approaching annual Academy Awards ceremony. Many of the movies that were nominated for an Oscar were playing in my area, and I drove to theaters in Bethesda, Rockville, and Chevy Chase to see them. It was a project I engaged in every year. I was an avid moviegoer, and the Oscars night provided me with entertainment—and a form of escape. That year, I was rooting for Natalie Portman, with her impressive performance in the film *Black Swan*. I felt an affinity with her because she was born in Israel and had immigrated to the United States with her parents in her early childhood. I also loved Meryl Streep's roles in the movies

It's Complicated and *The Iron Lady*. I had always admired her for aging gracefully and resisting Botox and plastic surgery in an industry that is obsessed with youth and beauty.

I developed daily rituals: walks in the park, Zumba workout, and meditation. These rituals gave my days some structure. My mood was still unstable and I could swing from being confident and optimistic in the morning to being anxious and depressed in the evening, but at least I was more active and less isolated. I told no one in my social circle about my troubles. I followed the motto "Don't cry out loud," as expressed in the melancholy song by Peter Allen and Carole Bayer Sager.[15] The song reflected my frame of mind and I often sang its haunting lyrics to myself. Reserved and reticent, I put my best face on and acted as if everything was normal.

On March 2, the long-awaited answer from the Office of Personnel Management arrived by registered mail. I was so nervous when I opened the envelope that my fingers trembled and my heart beat fast. I took one look at the letter, and my heart sank. After two months of waiting, all that the letter said was that the information I had requested under the Freedom of Information Act was the "property" of the FBI, and the OPM was in the process of consulting with the FBI regarding the release of this information. I could write to the FBI directly, if I wished, and submit another FOIA request to them. The contact information of the Chief of Record/Information Dissemination Section of the FBI was enclosed. The letter was signed by Della Ray, a FOIA specialist.

I was frustrated. I thought that I would be able to sort things out within a few months, but the slow pace at which my FOIA request was moving made this goal unfeasible. I called Ms. Ray and asked if she intended to pursue the release of the information about my background check from the FBI, and how long this might take. She answered affirmatively but had no idea how long this might take; it could be a year or longer. She had an applicant who had been waiting for three and a half years for a FOIA response and the FBI had still not released the requested information. Cordial and sympathetic, she suggested that I check with her periodically on the progress of my request.

Two weeks later, on March 19, I submitted another FOIA request, this time directly to the FBI. I had to fill out and sign a certification of identity form, which I printed from their website. I sent my letter by certified mail. On April 2, I received a reply in which they confirmed receipt of my FOIA request and assigned me a case number that I could use to log onto their website and check the status of my request. They had a large backlog and were running four to six months behind. I was advised to wait patiently.

Spring arrived early that year and the cherry trees that lined the streets in my neighborhood were in full blossom. As I took my daily walks in the park, inhaling the fresh, fragrant air, I envied nature for its perpetual gift of renewal. Here I was, having to rise from the wreckage of my life for the second time, with no light at the end of the tunnel. I was in the winter of my life, my candle almost burnt out. I had to come to terms with what had happened and move on. It might take a year or even longer to get my FOIA response, and I could not idle my time away as I waited for news. I had to set a new goal for myself and work toward attaining it.

After remaining in limbo for many days, I decided to seek professional help. I had put it off until now because the number of sessions—three in total—that the Peace Corps offered was inadequate to expect much benefit from them. Effective therapy cannot be provided in such a short time and I was averse to medication, which always comes with side effects, doesn't go beyond symptom relief, and cannot solve the "big picture" problems. After all, taking an antidepressant pill every day wouldn't expedite the arrival of my FOIA response. I wanted to learn practical coping skills or at least to gain some insight from pouring out what was weighing on my mind to a trained listener.

I made an appointment with a therapist. Sitting in the privacy of her office, I told her my story and watched her listen to it in dismay.

"I didn't know the Peace Corps has a dark side," she said, shocked.

"Neither did I," I admitted. "The FBI thinks I'm involved in intelligence activities. I feel stigmatized."

"Has the FBI contacted you since your return?" she asked.

"No. But I feel anxious and insecure. I'm concerned that in the aftermath of September 11th, we are seeing a new wave of McCarthyism, where unsubstantiated suspicions and accusations of disloyalty are made against innocent people by the country's security agencies as a result of the war on terror. The 1940s and 1950s were the period of the Red Scare, when many people falsely accused of being communist activists or sympathizers were blacklisted or dismissed from their jobs, and their careers and lives were ruined. Today, it is the period of the Terror Scare, with similar excesses and consequences."

"Dalya, if you have done nothing wrong, you have nothing to fear."

"My trust in the system has been broken. The Peace Corps treated me callously and unfairly. First they cleared me for service, sent me overseas to Jordan, and let me complete the entire grueling pre-service training. Then they abruptly declared that I didn't qualify for service because I didn't pass the background check, forced me to resign, and unceremoniously sent me home. I have since been trying to find out what went wrong with my background check. Why am I suspected of being involved in intelligence activities? No one is willing to tell me. I feel like Joseph K. in Kafka's *The Trial*. I'm being prosecuted by a remote, inaccessible authority and have to defend myself against a charge that I can't get any information about. This is an ongoing nightmare for me."

"Let's put the issue of unfairness aside for a moment," she said. "The manner in which you were treated is appalling. But imagine for a moment that you had remained in Jordan. Ask yourself: Would you have been happy to be there now, considering your enormous vulnerabilities? How did you feel when you were in Jordan?"

"In the beginning, I didn't mind having to conceal my identity. It was like a game. I'm a scholar of Arab culture and society and being in Jordan gave me a rare opportunity to obtain a 'view from within' of contemporary Arab life. I felt like Alice in Wonderland. Then, as the weeks went by, it started to bother me. I felt like an impostor. I had to lie to my host family, to the teachers at the village girls' elementary school, and even to my fellow volunteers. I didn't like that. I felt bad about misleading my host family, who were kind and gracious to me. They had the right to decide if they wanted to host a Jewish person in their home or not. I also felt like a peeping Tom, living in their household and observing their family life without permission. All of this posed a moral dilemma for me.

"At the same time, I had to put up with racist remarks about Jews and expressions of hatred toward Israel. A local language instructor hired by the Peace Corps hated me with a passion and treated me nastily. Every person in my J15 group could talk freely about his or her background—except me. I couldn't talk about my family, my childhood and youth, my varied life experiences, or even the books that I have published, some of which are available in the best university libraries in Jordan! I had to be on my guard all the time. It was stressful and frustrating."

"What about your roommate at the Peace Corps training site?"

"We had some tension in the beginning. Her sleeping habits and mine clashed, but we worked it out and had a functional relationship. When I flew to Israel, first to visit my brother in the hospital and later for his funeral, she noticed that my bed was empty and that I was absent from classes. When I returned she asked me where I had been and if I was okay. I thought that she was genuinely concerned about me, so I shared with her that I had lost a close family member. As soon as her curiosity was satisfied, her interest in me vanished. There was no real connection between us and I don't blame her. How could I develop close ties with anyone when my survival depended on being secretive and reticent?"

"Why were you afraid to trust your covolunteers?"

"In the J13 group there was a girl who was Jewish and gay. One of her fellow volunteers accidentally gave her secret away. A huge scandal erupted and her host family wanted to expel her from their house and their village. It took a lot of effort and diplomacy on her part to explain this matter away and quell the storm. She recounted this incident to us in one of our technical sessions so as to impress on us the critical importance of protecting each other's sensitive personal information. Of course, in my case the danger to my safety was significantly greater because I was born and raised in Israel, whereas she was born and raised in the United States. My group consisted of thirty-eight members. This was a large number of people to trust my secret with. I couldn't take the risk that someone might accidentally give it away."

"Do you believe that under these circumstances you would have been happy to stay two whole years in Jordan? It sounds like you were in an impossible situation."

I pondered the question. I had experienced moments of doubt about my service when I was still in Jordan. The danger to my safety was not the only reason. I had begun to feel increasingly conflicted about what the Peace Corps had told me to do.

"I don't know if I would have been able to stick it out for two years. It was an untenable situation. Most likely, I would have asked the Peace Corps to transfer me to another country. Of the seventy-five countries in which the Peace Corps is currently active, only Jordan presents such a problem to Jewish volunteers because of its large Palestinian population. Morocco and Tunisia are far less hostile to Jews. It is beyond my comprehension why they chose Jordan of all countries to send me to. Take China, for example. The Chinese welcome Jewish volunteers. They feel an affinity with the Jews because of their longevity and ancient history and regard Jewish people as being wise and talented. Do you know that I was originally nominated for a program in the Far East?"

She raised her eyebrows questioningly. "Really? What happened?"

"To my disappointment, the program had closed. I had to wait another six months for the next program, which was intended for Jordan. When I asked my placement officer what had happened to my Far East nomination, she said that they sometimes take volunteers off a program if there are no adequate medical facilities in that country. If this is really what happened in my case, which I doubt, then it's terribly ironic. They had decided not to send me to the Far East so as to safeguard my health, and then they put me directly in harm's way in Jordan!"

The therapist looked at me pensively. "I can see that you're angry and distraught. But I also see that you're in touch with yourself. You're not afraid to look deep within."

"No, I'm not. "

"When you look within, what do you see?"

"I see all the mistakes that I made and could have avoided."

"Like what?"

"I should *not* have agreed to go to Jordan."

"Why did you?"

"The Peace Corps places a great emphasis on a volunteer's flexibility and willingness to serve wherever he or she is assigned. This is a central theme in all their brochures. I wanted to demonstrate that I was flexible and totally committed to their mission. Most importantly, I *trusted* the Peace Corps. I said to myself: They have been doing this for fifty years. They have my resume and know where I come from. If they have chosen to send me to Jordan, I must trust and respect their judgment. I was wrong and incredibly naive."

"Don't be so hard on yourself. You need to practice self-compassion, not self-blame."

"I can't ignore my own faults. Now I'm at a loss what to do. On the one hand, I want to forget and move on; on the other hand, I need closure."

"I assume that you will find closure when you get your FOIA response. In the meantime, have you tried to look for a job?"

"I tried, but it's not easy. The spring semester is already in progress and all the teaching posts are filled. If there's an opening, it will be only for the fall semester. That's a long wait from now."

"What did you do before you joined the Peace Corps?"

"I wrote books. I'm a scholar."

"Then go back to writing," she said, in all simplicity.

When I rose to leave, she handed me a prescription for medication, some kind of antidepressant pills. I declined politely. She gave me a couple of free samples anyway and encouraged me to try them. I said okay, so as not to offend her, knowing that I would flush them down the toilet as soon as I got home.

As I drove home, I reflected on the therapist's suggestion that I should go back to writing. Was I unconsciously trying to avoid this activity? Admittedly, I had a love-hate relationship with writing. When I wrote, I felt lonely and isolated. And when I didn't write, I felt a strange sense of privation, as if I had become voiceless and mute. The writing process was both tormenting and fulfilling for me. I had to be in a peaceful frame of mind to write. Any tension, conflict, or stress disrupted my creative impulse. Sometimes I would get stuck, too, or fail to find the right word to say something, and I would obsess about it for days. But when I held a complete manuscript in my hands, it was as if I was holding a new baby in my arms—a precious gift worth all the sweat and labor.

When I arrived home I went straight to my study and turned on my laptop. I clicked the file tab, looking for a certain document that I had begun several months earlier. There it was, "Out of Jordan." Hesitantly, I started reading, my fingers resting casually on the keyboard. When I got to the last page, they slowly started moving, pressing lightly on the keys. Little by little, words were forming on the screen, then sentences, then paragraphs, and suddenly my fingers could hardly keep pace with my thoughts ...

The months passed by uneventfully, and spring gave way to summer. I had still not heard back from the FBI, though I visited their site regularly to check on the status of my FOIA request. In the meantime, I tried to lead a normal life. I was still weighed down with grief and guilt over my brother's passing and needed to come to terms with his death. It was hard to find a suitable Jewish support group for bereavement, as many of those that operated in my area only served members who had lost a spouse, a parent, or a child. When they inquired which family member I had lost and I said a sibling, they responded that they could not accommodate me. I called the Jewish Social Service Agency many times and was told repeatedly that they had no suitable group for me. Finally, one of their social workers suggested that I contact the Washington Jewish Healing Network Activities, a new organization that was run by volunteers. I called them and was relieved to hear that they offered a bereavement support group that was open to everybody, no restrictions applied.

It was therapeutic for me to sit with other bereaved people and to hear their stories. Sharing brings comfort and a new perspective on grief. In addition, the various rituals of mourning in Judaism, especially the recitation of the Kaddish, provide solace to the grieving heart. Once again, I discovered how important Judaism is for me. Curiously, I was the only participant in the group who had lost a sibling. Everyone else had lost either a parent or a spouse. They wanted to hear about my brother and listened with empathy. I told them what my brother had meant to me, how we had grown up together like Irish twins, and how hard his life had been, having to cope with tragedy after tragedy, from his own rare heart condition and leukemia to the loss of his daughter to breast cancer. He was a unique person and I felt guilt over not having done enough to save his life. My support group expressed words of compassion and commiseration. They, too, experienced various feelings of guilt about the loved ones they had lost—it is a common reaction among those who are left behind. We discussed the topics of fate and afterlife in Judaism, and this gave me the impetus to delve into Kabbalah and Jewish mysticism. I had been a secular Jew most of my life, but now I felt a strong urge to know more about my faith and draw closer to my roots. Not until I had been sent to Jordan and told to conceal my identity had I felt this urge. It made me think about the persecution of the Jews throughout the ages. The more they were persecuted for their faith, the more tenaciously they hung onto it.

On July 5, 2012, four months after I had submitted my FOIA request to the FBI, I received a telephone call from their office. A woman with a young voice named Wendy Kilpatrick informed me that the FBI had not conducted a background check on me for the Peace Corps. They had an old job application file on me, dating back to 2001, which they had turned over to the Peace Corps. Was I still interested in receiving a copy of this old file? Stunned by this unexpected message, I heard myself utter automatically, "Yes, of course."

My mind flashed back to the year 2001. That unforgettable year, infused with the spirit of patriotism that had swept the country after the September 11th terrorist attacks in the United States, I applied for a job at the FBI. I thought that the linguistic skills that I possessed would be useful for the war on terror. One of the requirements in the application process was a polygraph test. I took the test, and failed. I have an anxious disposition that is incompatible with polygraph testing. The validity of a polygraph test is controversial and its results are considered unreliable. For one thing, the tester plays a major role in the outcome of the test: he can be hostile and biased toward the testee, manipulate his or her level of anxiety, and interpret his or her responses in a nonobjective way. In addition, the testee can use tricks to influence his or her responses. This is why the results of a polygraph test are *inadmissible* in a court of law. Many notorious spies and criminals are known to have passed the polygraph test, while innocent people have failed it. Nevertheless, a failed polygraph test stigmatizes the person who takes it, and a passed polygraph test earns him or her credibility.

Wendy's message astounded me. It implied that I had been disqualified from Peace Corps service on the basis of a ten-year-old job application file. This was absurd! As soon as I regained my composure, I tried repeatedly to call her back, that very same day and the following days, but she never answered the phone. Was she avoiding me? Had she told me something that she wasn't supposed to? I now possessed a *vital* piece of information: I now knew that my old FBI job application file had been used to determine my eligibility to serve in the Peace Corps. This was a major breakthrough in the wall of silence that I had faced since my return. But this information only raised other, more troubling, questions in my mind. Why was the FBI, ten years after I had applied for a job, still keeping a file on me? I was a law-abiding citizen. I had a clean record with the police. I had never been involved in any crime or litigation. I wasn't a spy and *couldn't* be a spy: my anxious disposition, reflected in the very fact that I had failed the polygraph test, was a clear indication that I wasn't made of "good spy material." The old axiom "No good deed goes unpunished" sprang to my mind. I became all the more determined to get to the truth.

Armed with this new piece of information, I called the office of the Peace Corps director, Aaron Williams. I spoke with Karl, one of his assistants, explained the unusual circumstances under which I had been forced to resign from the Peace Corps and requested a meeting with Mr. Williams. He said that he would have to look into the matter and get back in touch with me. In the meantime, he suggested that I request the records of my application and disqualification from Denora Miller, the Peace Corps FOIA officer. On July 10, I contacted Denora Miller by email, requesting these records, pursuant to the Privacy Act of 1974. I was encouraged when she replied, asking if I preferred to receive these records by electronic mail or postal mail. I requested a hard copy to be sent to my home address. Two weeks later, when the package arrived, I opened it eagerly, expecting to find in it the long-sought answers to my questions. It was a thick file comprising all the papers of my application process, as well as some papers pertaining to my pre-service training. I read everything from beginning to end, but the records of my disqualification were missing from the file. Specifically, the report about my background check, which constituted the grounds for my disqualification, and the memo with the message that I didn't pass the background check, which the country director claimed he had received from Peace Corps Headquarters, were not there.

I emailed Denora Miller again, informing her that the file she had sent me was incomplete and lacked the information about my background check and disqualification. Another FOIA specialist named Candice Allgaier replied that the Peace Corps does not keep any information about background checks because such records are the "property" of, and are maintained by, the Office of Personnel Management (OPM); therefore, I should contact them. I wrote back that I had already contacted the OPM and submitted a FOIA request to them, only to be told that this information wasn't their "property" to give either, and be directed to approach the FBI instead. Of course, I had also contacted the FBI and submitted a FOIA request to them as well, but they had not been forthcoming in providing this information to me. The next response came from Denora Miller, who notified me that since the Peace Corps wasn't the "originating" agency of the information pertaining to my background check, they couldn't release a copy of it to me unless I had authorization from both the OPM and the FBI permitting them to give it to me! The contradictions between Candice's and Denora's letters were glaring: the former *denied* having the information that I requested; the latter *admitted* to having it but denied me access to it.

My correspondence with Denora continued into mid-August. During this time, I made several additional attempts to reach the Peace Corps director, Mr. Williams. I spoke with another assistant in his office named John Bryan, who was the only Peace Corps officer to say, after hearing my story, that I deserved to know why I was disqualified from Peace Corps service. He assured me that he would look into my case and get back in touch with me, but he never did. I called the

Peace Corps office again and spoke with yet another assistant, Connor
Sanchez, who suggested that I meet with Lien Galloway, senior advisor to the General Counsel, rather than with the Peace Corps director.
I told him that I had already spoken with her twice and that she had
refused to see me or share any information with me. Once again, he
said that he would get back in touch with me, but never did. I realized that Mr. Williams was surrounded by a group of zealous assistants who made him inaccessible and unapproachable. I would not be
able to meet with him and tell him my story. If I sent him a letter,
it would most likely be opened by one of these assistants and tossed
aside. I was faced with an impenetrable wall of bureaucracy.

Then something sensational happened. On August 21,
Mr. Williams announced that he was stepping down. His resignation
came like a bombshell. Although the agency stated that he was leaving for "personal and family considerations," it was hard to separate
his sudden departure from the sharp public criticism under which
the Peace Corps had come during his time in office. The year before,
the ABC News 20/20 investigation into the murder of Kate Puzey
in Benin, which aired on January 14, 2011, had exposed a breach
of confidentiality on the part of her supervisors, additionally revealing that the Peace Corps discouraged victims of sexual assault from
reporting crimes against them and failed to take steps to ensure their
safety. Subsequently, Mr. Williams testified before the House Foreign
Affairs Committee and pledged to change the policies and culture of
the Peace Corps. On November 21, 2011, President Obama signed
The Kate Puzey Peace Corps Volunteer Protection Act. My personal
story unfolded against the background of all these dramatic events:
on December 23, 2011, I had been sent home; from January 2012
until August 21, 2012, when Mr. Williams resigned, I tried to find
someone at Peace Corps Headquarters to listen to my story—without
success.

I began calling Della Ray at the OPM regularly to inquire about
the status of my FOIA request. She said that she had sent the FBI

a reminder to give her permission to release the information that I had requested and that she was waiting for their reply; I should call her again in a month. I called Wendy Kilpatrick at the FBI office too, expecting to get her voice mail. Instead, a woman named Leslie answered the phone, saying that she was now handling my case. She said that my FOIA request had passed the first stage of the process and was "moving along nicely." The information that I was seeking comprised about five pages and I should call her again in a few weeks. Leslie was the first person at the FBI office who was willing to speak to me and update me on the status of my FOIA request. Although neither Della nor Leslie could predict how much longer I would have to wait until the report of my background check would be released, I felt, for the first time in nine months, that I had made some progress.

While a good deal of my time and mental energy were devoted to my quest for the truth, I was also reading and writing again, which had a positive effect on my well-being. My intellectual needs always superseded my social needs. I didn't try to develop new social contacts but I did my best to cultivate the ones that I already had. A piece of good news came my way from the State University of New York Press. I had published a book titled *Arab Women Writers: An Anthology of Short Stories* with them in 2005, and was pleased to hear that West Point Academy had purchased copies of it for their cadets. I asked my publisher to remove the dedication from all future printings of my book, as it was addressed to the dishonest husband whom I had since divorced. Fortunately, it was an easy thing to do because the dedication appeared by itself on a separate page, which could be pulled out altogether, and thus rid my work from this unpleasant association.

My friend Miri was back in town and we made plans to go to our favorite Starbucks coffee shop. I drove to her house to pick her up and waited inside while she got dressed. "There's something I want you to read in the meantime," she said, handing me the *Washington Post* magazine of August 26. On the cover was the picture of an attractive woman and the headline read, "Why Was a Top Navy Adviser Stripped of Her Career?" I sat on the sofa in the living room and began to read. The feature article told the story of a Washingtonian woman named Gwenyth Todd who had been a Middle East expert for the National Security Council in the Clinton administration and then worked in the office of Defense Secretary Dick Cheney in the first Bush administration. Posted in 2007 to Bahrain as a top adviser to the U.S. Navy 5th Fleet, she thwarted plans by Bush administration hawks to provoke war with Iran and refuted CIA intelligence reports linking Shiite protesters in Bahrain to Iran. Shortly afterward, she became a persona non grata, was stripped of all clearances, and was not only out of a job but also wanted for questioning by the FBI. When all her attempts to find out what this was about failed, she went into self-exile in Australia and was now afraid to come home.

"Why did you want me to read this story?" I asked Miri after I had finished reading it.

"I noticed that this woman, just like you, had to submit a FOIA request to find out the truth. And just like you, she has been waiting for a FOIA response for a long time."

"Yes," I said. "I also see a parallel between her story and that of Valerie Plame, whose career was destroyed in punishment for her husband's criticism of the second Bush administration's case for invading Iraq."

"What do you learn from this story?"

"That even a person who was born and bred in the United States, comes from a highly distinguished family, and has served the country with distinction can become the victim of intrigue and injustice. I feel exactly like Gwenyth Todd when she says, 'This whole situation is un-American. I just want to know the facts, and then I will shut up.'"

"Are you sure that this is what you want?" Miri asked.

"Yes," I replied.

But deep down, I was starting to have doubts. The closer I got to the truth, the bigger they became. Would knowing what was in the FBI's ten-year-old job application file make me happy? Restore my peace of mind? Would I then shut up? "In much wisdom is much grief; and the greater a person's knowledge, the greater his sorrow," warns Ecclesiastes (1:18). Getting the FOIA response was of vital importance if I wanted to be reinstated as a Peace Corps volunteer. Was this my goal? Did I still trust the Peace Corps after what they had done to me? Would I put my life in their hands a second time? I don't have to decide now, I said to myself. First, let's get the FOIA response, and then we'll see.

September 16, 2012, was Mr. Williams's last day in office as director of the Peace Corps. After his departure, Carrie Hessler-Radelet, deputy director of the Peace Corps, took over as acting director. Infused with new hope, I called her office to request an appointment. An assistant named Dan Westerhoff answered the phone and asked for the reasons for my request. Once again, after hearing my explanation, he said that he would look into the matter and call me back, but he never did.

I continued to call Leslie at the FBI office at regular intervals. Each time I called, she said that my FOIA request was "moving along nicely" and suggested that I call again in a couple of weeks. On Thanksgiving Eve, she said that my FOIA request was "close to completion" and that I should call again in a couple of weeks. I felt cautiously optimistic. After all, I had heard the phrase "a couple of weeks" many times before.

November was a tense month in the Middle East. The conflict between Israel and Gaza erupted in a new cycle of violence. On November 14, the Palestinian militant group Hamas launched an intense rocket attack on southern Israel in retaliation for the killing of Ahmed al-Jabari, the head of their military operations. Israel responded with heavy airstrikes against Hamas targets in Gaza and mobilized forces on the troubled border in preparation for a possible ground invasion of the Gaza Strip. I followed the news with great concern: the threat of an all-out war was imminent. Life in southern Israel came to a standstill. I called my sister Susan in Rishon Lezion to inquire about her grandchildren who lived in Ashkelon, a city that was within the Hamas missile range. She told me that all the schools were closed in Ashkelon and that her grandchildren had come to stay with her in her apartment. I called Miri to ask how her family in Israel was doing. She expressed fear about the escalating situation, then remarked, "You're lucky, Dalya, that you're not in Jordan. Imagine that you were still there now when Israel and the Palestinians are locked in a bloody battle." This thought had not occurred to me. "Do you mean that I would have been faced with a moral dilemma?" I asked. "No," she said. "I mean that you would have been killed!" Her remark was neither unfounded nor farfetched. As the fighting raged in Gaza, there were pro-Palestinian demonstrations throughout the Arab region, but especially in Jordan, whose population is predominantly Palestinian. On November 20, the US Secretary of State, Hilary Clinton, flew to Israel in an effort to broker a ceasefire. The following day, after a week-long violent conflict that brought loss of lives and materials on both sides, a ceasefire was announced in a joint conference in Cairo with Clinton and Egypt's foreign minister, Mohamed Kamel Amr. The Middle East breathed a sigh of relief: the specter of another Arab-Israeli war was averted, at least for now.

I was extremely busy in the following weeks. The second part of my research into Arab family life, focusing on fathers and sons, was accepted for publication by a leading New York publisher. I was occupied with the preparation of my manuscript for final submission and didn't feel the time passing. While leisure allows my mind to dwell on my problems, a heavy workload suits my disposition better because it distracts my mind from unhappy thoughts. I now had a deadline to meet and everything else assumed secondary importance.

I worked hard throughout the next couple of months and was productive, but the issue of the FOIA response never left my mind. When I went for my daily walks in the park, I would contemplate the famous verse from Ecclesiastes, "The greater a person's knowledge, the greater his sorrow," and consider the merits of "blissful ignorance." Occasionally, I told myself that I should let go of my FOIA request; I should forgive and forget. Forgiveness wouldn't mean absolving the Peace Corps from responsibility for their wrongdoing, nor would it minimize or justify the wrong they had done me. But forgiveness would *liberate me*, bringing me a peace of mind that would help me go on with life. "To forgive is to set a prisoner free and discover that the prisoner was you," states a wise saying.[16] In many ways, I felt like a prisoner, condemned to indefinite waiting for a FOIA response, which may or may not come.

My new book, *Fathers and Sons in the Arab Middle East,* came out in the fall of 2013. I was delighted when IslamiCommentary and Tirn (Transcultural Islam Research Network), which are scholarship forums managed by Duke University Islamic Studies Center, published a book Q & A interview with me on the Internet. My head was buzzing with new ideas for research projects and travel plans. The issue of the FOIA response slowly receded to the back of my mind and eventually sank into oblivion.

And the wheels of time kept turning.

On May 29, 2014, two and a half years after I had submitted my FOIA request, a yellow manila envelope bearing the address of the FBI office in Virginia was delivered to my mailbox. I looked at it in disbelief. The long-awaited FOIA response had finally arrived! I wanted to open it immediately—and at the same time I was afraid to open it. What would I find in it? What good would this do me now? I felt vulnerable.

I took the FBI envelope and put it on my desk, staring at it long and hard. The image of Pandora's Box flashed across my mind.

Opening the envelope would be like opening Pandora's Box: all the nasty things that are kept locked inside would burst out and assail me. Let sleeping dogs lie. What purpose would knowing the truth serve at this point? I didn't feel I had the passion or stamina to serve in the Peace Corps any more. *Illi faat maat,* as the Arabs say, the past is dead. It was about the *journey*, not the destination. I had made the difficult journey, I had endured many trials and tribulations along the way, and I had reached the finish line. I was not allowed to cross this line. But neither was Moses, and he had led the Israelites in the Sinai desert for forty years until they had reached the Promised Land, only to be told that he wasn't destined to enter it. I thought of King Oedipus's tragedy. His obsessive search for the truth was the cause of his downfall. If he had stayed in Corinth, he would not have killed his father and would not have committed incest with his mother. As for me, knowing the truth now would not heal my wounded soul and might hurt me even more. Since the days of J. Edgar Hoover, the FBI has been keeping secret files on thousands of innocent citizens in this country, among them congressmen and presidents. In the post-September 11th reality of mass electronic surveillance of ordinary people by the NSA, I was merely a statistic. I already knew enough about their absurd allegation. They labeled me as a spy. Never mind my distinct Hebrew accent that would give me away in a jiffy. Never mind that my life was an open book. Their allegation was beyond absurd; it was simply *bizarre*. Would I now start a whole new crusade against the FBI or the NSA? I had come a long way toward rebuilding my life after the cruel blow that the Peace Corps had dealt me, and I wasn't going to slide back into the dark tunnel from which I had barely emerged …

But then again, I would never have *true* peace of mind until I got answers to those gnawing questions …

I took a deep breath and reached for the FBI envelope. My fingers trembled as I opened it and removed the bunch of papers that were inside. As I began to read, I could hear the fast pounding of my heart. The first page—a letter—said:

> *Dear Ms. Cohen:*
>
> *You were previously advised we were consulting with another Government agency concerning information located as a result of your Freedom of Information/Privacy Acts (FOIPA) request.*
>
> *This consultation is finished and the enclosed material is being released to you with deletions made pursuant to Title 5, United States Code, Sections 552/552a as noted below.*

A list of exemptions followed, along with a form explaining them. The letter was signed by Mr. David M. Hardy, Section Chief, Record/Information Dissemination Section, Records Management Division, Federal Bureau of Investigation, Washington, DC.

Enclosed with the letter were seven pages of correspondence between the FBI and the CIA concerning a counterintelligence investigation into my activities. The first memorandum, dated 2/4/2003, stated:

> *This case was initiated based on information received from FBIHQ {FBI Headquarters} that the subject's polygraph results indicated deception for the counterintelligence responses. The National Security Agency checks and CIA name trace is {sic} pending.*

I skimmed quickly through the following five pages—they were written in codes and acronyms incomprehensible to the layperson and interspersed with blank boxes indicating deletions. The last page was a summary, in plain English, of the inquiries conducted about me. Dated 11/25/2003, it was addressed to Counterintelligence by the FBI office in Baltimore. It stated simply:

A number of background record checks were conducted for COHEN with unremarkable results.

. . . . .

As Baltimore [h]as uncovered no information that would indicate that DALYA COHEN is involved in any intelligence activities, it is recommended that this case be closed.

I stared at these words in disbelief! Of all the scenarios that played out in my head, this one never occurred to me! I had become such a pessimist! Yet here it was in black and white—complete clearing of my name from any involvement in intelligence activities! I felt a deep sense of vindication. It was a moment of sheer exhilaration.

After my excitement had subsided, I pondered the whole situation. That a failed polygraph test, which is scientifically considered flawed and unreliable, is legally inadmissible in a court of law, and was merely taken as part of a job application more than a decade ago, should have such calamitous consequences was shocking to me. I had applied to the FBI out of a desire to be of help in the war on terror, responding to their nationwide call for people with linguistic skills in my field. In my wildest dreams I would never have imagined that I would become the focus of counterintelligence suspicion and investigation. The old axiom "No good deed goes unpunished" sprang to my mind once again.

The more I pondered about the whole situation, the more puzzled I became. Something didn't make sense. Given that the FBI had cleared my name in 2003, stating unequivocally that *"a number of background record checks were conducted for Cohen with unremarkable results"* and that the agency *"uncovered no information that would indicate that Dalya Cohen is involved in any intelligence activities,"* why, then, was I disqualified from Peace Corps service on the grounds that I didn't pass the background check? After all, the Peace Corps had relied on the FBI for my background check and had received the selfsame FBI file that I was now holding in my hands!

I opened the drawer that contained all my Peace Corps papers and searched for the memo that I had received from the country director on the day that I was forced to resign from the Peace Corps. There it was:

To: Dalya Cohen
From: Alex Boston, Country Director, Peace Corps Jordan
Date: December 22, 2011
Re: Consideration of Administrative Separation Memo

This memo is to inform you that I am considering administratively separating you from Peace Corps service on the grounds detailed in below:
You did not pass the National Agency Clearance background check. Section 22 of the Peace Corps Act states that to ensure enrollment of a Volunteer is consistent with the national interest, no applicant is eligible for Peace Corps Volunteer service without a background investigation. The Peace Corps requires that all applicants accepted for training have as a minimum a National Agency Check. Information revealed by the investigation may be grounds for disqualification from Peace Corps service.
I would like to inform you that you have the option to resign within 24 hours in lieu of being administratively separated.

What a glaring contradiction!

I looked at the memo, which states that I didn't pass the background check, then I looked at the FBI's report, which states that *"a number of background record checks were conducted for Cohen with unremarkable results."*

The paradox defied all comprehension.

I closed the much-awaited FOIA response and pushed it away in exasperation. Ecclesiastes is right. "In much wisdom is much grief; and the greater a person's knowledge, the greater his sorrow."

12. EPILOGUE

RECENTLY, I'VE SEEN THE MOVIE *THE BEST EXOTIC MARIGOLD HOTEL*. Based on the novel *These Foolish Things* by Deborah Moggach, this comedy-drama is about a group of elderly British retirees who decide to spend their golden years in less expensive and seemingly exotic India. Enticed by an advertisement promising a life of leisure and luxury in the newly renovated Marigold Hotel, they arrive to find a dilapidated guesthouse and a chaotic place. Although the new environment is not what they expected, it opens them up to new possibilities. Profoundly changed by their shared experiences, they discover love, friendship, and a fresh beginning. There are many memorable lines in the movie, as, for example, when Sonny, the young hotel manager, tells his disgruntled guests, "In India, we have a saying: 'Everything will be all right in the end.' So if it is not all right, it is not yet the end." Or when Evelyn, the recently widowed housewife, says, "The only real failure is the failure to try, and the measure of success is how we cope with disappointment." In my case, I wish that I could say, "If it is not all right, it is not yet the end," but I know full well that it is the end. My departure from Jordan is final and

I will never return there again. As for trying, I can certainly say that I wasn't afraid to try and that I tested the limits of my endurance. I went through a rigorous Peace Corps training program in Jordan, under extremely stressful conditions, and I didn't falter even once. Sadly, I was not allowed to enjoy the fruits of my labor. Have I coped successfully with this huge disappointment? I don't know. When the harsh memories of how, just a few days before the swearing-in ceremony, the country director called me in the middle of the night to inform me that he was sending me home, how I was forced to resign from the Peace Corps, and how the very next day I was placed on a plane and sent out of Jordan—when these memories flash across my mind, my eyes become misty and I feel a lump in my throat. I gave the Peace Corps my heart and soul. I wanted so much to be an emissary of goodwill, especially to the people of Jordan. I believed wholeheartedly that I could make a difference with my experience and knowledge. My dream was crushed by uncaring Peace Corps officers who bungled my application process, ignored the FBI's report that cleared my name of any involvement in intelligence activities, disqualified me from service, and denied me the right of appeal. Fairness and humanity were sacrificed on the altar of safeguarding the image of an agency that has been rocked by many scandals in recent years.

To the best of my knowledge, I was the first Sabra ever to arrive in Jordan as a Peace Corps volunteer. This put me in a delicate, complicated, and dangerous situation. Jews have served as Peace Corps volunteers in Jordan before, but they were all born and raised in the United States. I was *different*—I was a naturalized American citizen who was born and raised in Israel; I served in the I.D.F.; and I have relatives who live in Israel. My passport says, under the entry Place of Birth: Tel Aviv, Israel, and under the entry Date of Birth: 1948, the same year that the State of Israel was established. We celebrate our birthdays together, the State of Israel and I. Although I left Israel in 1968 and lived in the Netherlands for many years prior to my relocation to the United States, I was, and remained, a Sabra at heart. At the same time I was also a "Sephardic Jew," that is, a person whose forefathers had lived for generations in an Arab land. My parents came to Israel from Baghdad, Iraq. Like all the Jews who had lived in the Diaspora, they had adopted many customs from their cultural environment. In their new home in Israel, they spoke Arabic with each other and all their relatives. My mother loved to listen to Arabic music, and the songs of Umm Kulthum, Farid al-Atrash, and Abd al-Wahhab would send her into rapture. I grew up with a strong affinity for Arab culture and Arabic language. It was only natural that after mastering English as a foreign language—a window into the Western world—I would pursue the study of Arabic. I developed a two-track career as a teacher of English, having obtained my bachelor's and master's degrees in English from the State University of Utrecht in the Netherlands, and as a scholar of Arab culture and society, having earned my doctoral degree in Arabic from Georgetown University. As can be expected, my lengthy exposures to European and American cultures have left indelible marks on me. I became more "refined" and "sophisticated" than the typical Sabra, who, like the fruit of the cactus, is "prickly" on the outside but "sweet" on the inside. My nationality evolved: I was a native-born Israeli who became Dutch by marriage and who then became American by naturalization. When I had read Edward Said's memoir, *Out of Place,* I could relate to the confusion that he had felt from the many, largely contradictory, elements in his identity (British by first name, Arab by ethnicity, Christian by religion, Palestinian by origin, Egyptian by place of residence, American by nationality) and his sense of "always being out of place." I too feel out of place wherever I am, whether in the United States, Israel, or the Netherlands.

Although my identity is made up of several components, in Jordan I came to be defined solely by one component: my Jewishness. For the Jordanians I was the Other, the Jewish enemy from across the border. The local language instructor hired by the Peace Corps for my village group for the period of pre-service training hated me with a passion and wrote biased and disparaging remarks about me in her evaluation. She knew my last name and through it my identity and made no effort to hide her hostility. I had to put up with denigrating remarks about Jews from cab drivers, clerks, and even members of my extended host families. I don't think that Abu Ali and Umm Ali would have allowed me to stay in their home had they known that I was Jewish, not so much because of extreme religious or political sentiments as because of the pressure of public opinion. The fear of gossip and of being ostracized by the village people would have compelled them to dissociate themselves from me. Their son, Usama, on the other hand, would not have hesitated to arrest me and put me in jail. I had to assume an alias, lie about my identity, conceal it, and repress it so that my safety and efficacy as a Peace Corps volunteer would not be compromised. It was a new and unsettling experience for me. My sense of self was shaken and my integrity threatened. I've been a secular Jew for most of my life, with no particular interest in the creed of my forefathers. But when I was *denied* the freedom to express the core of my identity, to say who I was and where I came from, I suddenly discovered that I was very *attached* to my Jewish roots, and I became *more* Jewish than I had ever been. I now understand why throughout the ages when Jews were persecuted and faced with the choice of either converting to Christianity (or Islam) or else die, they chose en masse to die. Foregoing your identity is tantamount to a death sentence anyway.

I'm at peace with myself these days. You can live an entire lifetime and not experience anything exceptional, and you can amass a lifetime of exceptional experiences in just a couple of months. All that has happened to me is more than a tale; it is an *odyssey*—but I wouldn't trade it for the world. My stay in Jordan was a journey of self-discovery. I've grown and become more resilient. True, I've lost the dream that I had worked so hard to attain, but I've found something more precious in the process: my core self. I now know something about myself that I wasn't aware of before: *I am Jewish through and through.*

I love my Jewish heritage. When I sing in Ladino "Non Como Muestro Dio" ("Ein Ke-Eloheinu") at the Shabbat service, I feel connected with thousands of years of Jewish tradition. When I am called to the *bimah* for Aliyah, reciting in Hebrew the blessings that precede each Torah reading, I am filled with a sense of awe for this ancient civilization that has survived against all odds through so many centuries. I'm not a devout worshipper—strict adherence to religious laws and rituals has never appealed to me. But I'm spiritually, culturally, and ethnically thoroughly Jewish. Recently I've also begun to study Kabbalah and Jewish mysticism and to read a lot of Jewish literature, especially about Sephardic Jewry.

I don't know if the Arab-Israeli conflict is soluble. My experiences in Jordan and before that in Egypt revealed to me how deep the gulf is that separates Arabs and Israelis. Although there is a peace treaty between Israel and Egypt, as well as between Israel and Jordan, it is often described as a "cold peace." When I returned to Amman from "Disneyland"—the code name for Israel among Peace Corps volunteers in Jordan—after attending my brother's funeral, the Jordanian Passport Control officer took one look at the "offending" stamp in my passport and went mad. He refused to let me enter, yelling at me to get a new visa first, although I already had a perfectly valid one. I thought that he would calm down if I showed him the sticker on the cover of my passport, which identified me as a Peace Corps volunteer, but he only got madder. Not only was I an unwelcome Israeli, born in that "damned" city of all cities, Tel Aviv, I was also an American. I was prepared to call Samir, the Peace Corps safety and security coordinator, and let him handle the matter. When the Jordanian officer saw how stubborn and resolute I was, he relented and grudgingly stamped my passport.

Intense emotions characterize both sides. Recently, I've seen the 2012 Oscar-nominated Israeli documentary *The Gatekeepers* by Dror Moreh. It is a deeply unsettling account of Israel's famed secret service agency, Shin Bet. Six former heads of the organization speak openly about their work fighting internal and external terrorism.

One of their most disheartening conclusions is that Israeli leaders missed several opportunities to end the occupation of the West Bank and repeatedly allowed illegal settlements to be established there despite the risk of violent Palestinian reaction. The vicious cycle of terror followed by retaliation followed by more terror and then more retaliation seems almost unbreakable. I believe that people like me, who come from the humanities, can help build a bridge of mutual trust and understanding between Arabs and Israelis. It was certainly one of my aspirations when I went to Jordan, hoping that through my work as a Peace Corps volunteer I would be able to dispel some of the prevailing prejudices and stereotypes about the Other.

I've come to terms with this chapter in my life. Letting go of the past is the key to finding peace of mind and moving on. I often say to myself: "Yesterday is history, tomorrow is a mystery, and today is a gift."[17] I hope that my story would lead to some positive changes in the application process, culture, and policies of the Peace Corps. The background check should be completed *before* the volunteer is sent overseas on assignment, *not after* the volunteer has gone through the entire pre-service training program, which is the hardest part of the mission. A volunteer who has completed the entire pre-service training program should have the right of appeal, whether he or she has been "technically" sworn in or not. A volunteer *should not* be sent to serve in a country where he or she is *not welcome* and then be told to lie about his or her identity and deceive his or her host family and host community. The country director should *help and support* the volunteer, not show bad faith toward the volunteer. And Peace Corps administrators who are sticklers for rules should demonstrate a measure of sensitivity and compassion when handling a traumatized, dehydrated, and famished volunteer on the point of collapse.

I'm aware that I've changed. I'm not as trusting as I was before. I tend to question what I'm told, to be critical, perhaps even skeptical. But my desire to go out in the world, to explore new places and meet new people, hasn't diminished. If you want a reward, you have to take a chance. Despite everything that has happened to me, I'm not afraid to take a chance.

We are in late March now. I'm sitting in my study and looking out the window at the falling snow. There is a little pond that is surrounded by bare maple and poplar trees in the back of my house. Everything is covered in a white soft blanket and the view is magnificent, like a scenic postcard. Now and then deer meander between the trees. If I make the slightest noise, they hear it and stand still to stare at me, their eyes and ears wide open, before they unhurriedly move on. In the background music is playing and the melodious voice of Frank Sinatra fills the room with its magic. He is singing "That's Life," one of my favorite songs. I know the lyrics by heart and I sing along, tapping my fingers on my desk to the beat of the uplifting song.

My laptop is turned on. I review the document that chronicles my journey for the last time, gripped by a sense of awe. It was an amazing journey into *terra incognita*, both literally and figuratively. I traveled to a region of the Middle East where I had never set foot in before. I also traveled inwardly, looking deep within, into my hidden, private self. Now it's time to search for new beginnings. As I close my document, memorable lines from the poetry of the Israeli woman writer Leah Na'or spring to my mind. Softly, I begin to recite them to myself:

The end is always the beginning of something else.
For better?
For worse?
I don't know which.
Something else.

Where the road ends, a path begins.
When the night ends, the morning begins.
At the end of an hour, another rolls in.
Only when knowledge ends, does the mistake begin.

Because the end is always a new beginning.[18]

GLOSSARY

1. Hebrew, "the poor man's lamb." This phrase appears in the Biblical parable about King David, Bathsheba, and Uriah the Hittite (2 Samuel, 12: 4)
2. The name of this village and the names of members of my host family have been changed to protect their identity and privacy.
3. Cited from Richard Sine, "Why We Love Scary Movies." WebMD Feature. Available: www.webmd.com/mental-health/features/why-we-love-scary-movies?
4. Pierre Bourdieu, *The Algerians* (Boston: Beacon, 1962), p. 97. I discuss this topic at length in my book, *Mothers and Daughters in Arab Women's Literature: The Family Frontier* (Leiden: Brill, 2011), pp. 27–34.
5. This saying is attributed to Laurel Thatcher Ulrich.
6. Hebrew, "Oh red rock."
7. Arabic, "the happy Arab home."
8. Hebrew, "Everything is in the hands of God except the belief in God."

9. Arabic, "God rest his soul."

10. Jewish custom of seven days of mourning for a deceased person.

11. Jewish funeral preparation home, run by the religious authorities in Israel.

12. A group of ten Jewish males, over the age of thirteen, required for certain religious rituals, such as the recitation of the Kaddish prayer.

13. Hebrew, "compass" and "conscience."

14. The Koran refers to Jews, Christians, and Muslims as "People of the Book" (*ahl al-kitab*) because they all have received a holy book from God: Jews, the Torah; Christians, the Gospel; and Muslims, the Koran.

15. Peter Allen and Carole Bayer Sager, "Don't Cry Out Loud." Available: www.songlyrics.com. Sung by Melissa Manchester and Shirley Bassey.

16. Lewis B. Smedes, *The Art of Forgiveness* (New York: Ballantine Books, 1997).

17. An anonymous saying.

18. Leah Na'or, "Sof ze tamid hatkhala." Written in 1977; *Carousel* (Tel Aviv: Masada, 1980). This is a literal translation from Hebrew. Translated by Dalya Cohen-Mor, in collaboration with Judith Levy. Translated and printed by permission of Leah Na'or.